LEADING UP

LEADING UP

HOW TO
LEAD YOUR BOSS
SO YOU BOTH WIN

MICHAEL USEEM

CROWN
BUSINESS
NEW YORK

Published by Crown Business, New York, New York.

Member of the Crown Publishing Group.

Random House, Inc. New York, Toronto, London, Sydney, Auckland

www.randomhouse.com

CROWN BUSINESS is a trademark and the Rising Sun colophon is a registered trademark of Random House, Inc.

Printed in the United States of America

Design by Leonard W. Henderson

Library of Congress Cataloging-in-Publication Data

Useem, Michael.

Leading up : how to lead your boss so you both win/Michael Useem.—1st ed.

p. cm.

Includes bibliographical references and index.

1. Leadership. 2. Management. 3. Organizational behavior. I. Title: How to lead your boss so you both win. II. Title.

HD57.7 .U83 2001

658.4′092—dc21   2001028950

ISBN 0-8129-3310-9

10 9 8 7 6 5 4 3 2 1

First Edition

CONTENTS

Contents

LEADING UP

INTRODUCTION

L EADERSHIP HAS ALWAYS required more than a downward touch: It needs to come from below as well as from the top, and leaders today must reach up as never before. As organizations decentralize authority, they put a premium on a manager's capacity to muster support above as well as below. Command and control from on high are giving way to insight and initiative down under. Contemporary leaders aren't just bosses. They're self-starters who take charge even when they have not been given a charge.

More upward leadership is essential. We have all known a supervisor or president, a coach or minister, an officer or director who should have made a difference but did not. We privately complained, we may even have quit, but we rarely stepped forward to help them transcend their limitations and be the best boss they could be. Leading up is needed when a supervisor is micromanaging rather macrothinking. Leading up is called for when a division president offers clear directives but can't see the future, or when investors demand instant gain but need long-term growth.

To come forward when an organization or superior does not encourage it can be both tremendously rewarding and extremely risky. If the upward leadership works, we can help transform incipient disaster into shining triumph. If handled poorly, such upward courage may prove little more than reckless abandon, a career-shortening or even career-ending move. Either way, though, we will have embraced a responsibility whose absence we deplore in others.

Instead of asking if we can afford to lead up, we should be asking: How can we best do so? *Leading Up* is about learning how to do it well and about building organizations that encourage upward leadership without asking for it.

The exercise of upward leadership is made easier by present-day expectations that we learn not just from our superiors but also from all points of the compass. The "360" has widely come to designate a manager's annual task of gathering appraisals from direct reports, working peers, immediate bosses, even customers and clients. So it is with leading up: Instead of just motivating those below, we must now also muster those above; instead of just learning from those above, we must listen to those below.

In an era of widespread downsizing, fear of firing keeps many would-be upward leaders on the sidelines. Prodding the boss is risky when managers don't know if they'll have a place to land should the boss react badly. In an era of burgeoning growth, by contrast, faith in the future strengthens the position of those who would dare to lead their leaders.

In good times or bad, though, leadership is required at *all* levels of an organization. The more people you have sitting on their hands, waiting to be led, the less likely you are to avoid the pitfalls that come with contraction, and the more likely you are to squander the opportunities that are afforded by growth. A company imbued with leading up is vigilant in every direction, whatever the momentum.

Leading up is not the same as *managing* up. Working well with your boss to get the day-to-day job done is also a learned skill, and one that requires concerted effort. Indeed, companies and universities devote vast resources to training present and future managers to be better at the craft. Much of my own teaching in the Wharton School's M.B.A. program over a decade has been to foster precisely that. But our focus here is on leading, not just managing. The distinction is between *running* the office and adding *value* to it, between *discharging* our responsibilities and *exceeding* them. Leadership is a matter of bringing more to the office than we were given, of adding greater value to the company or country than it would have achieved without us.

Nor is leading up a call for undermining authority or seizing power. It is about the effective exercise of power for the greater good. Abraham Lincoln said that leadership is appealing to the "better angels of our nature." In the same spirit, leading up is a call to building on the best in everybody's nature. We all want success and triumph, and the ranks will give it to us if we are ready to appeal to their better angels.

The challenge is to help both those below us and those above us achieve what we all want accomplished. If we expect our subordinates to furnish us with unvarnished information, unbiased advice, and unswerving support at the times when it really counts, we need to have cultivated a culture that encourages and rewards them for doing so. If we want to serve our superiors whose mission we support, our responsibility is to furnish them with strategic insight, timely advice, and realistic options when their future is on the line. Either way, we will want to prepare ourselves and others for the exercise of the best in upward calling. When learning and experience aren't allowed to bubble up, we are letting a vital human resource slip through our fingers.

The failed presidential campaign of Democrat Bill Bradley offers a case in point. Many factors contributed to his defeat by Vice President Albert Gore in the spring 2000 presidential primaries, but among the causes (according to those familiar with the campaign's inner workings) were a string of preventable errors, including Bradley's reluctance to counter stinging criticism by his opponent.

Bradley's instinct had been to run his campaign above politics—less as "a 21st-century politician," said a writer for the *New York Times*, "than as an Old Testament Prophet." Even though his campaign suffered defeat after defeat in the early primaries in New Hampshire, Michigan, and elsewhere, Bradley still might have recovered his early momentum had he hit back hard. To do that, though, the candidate needed to be led to the fray, a form of leading up that no one working for him proved willing to risk.

Bradley tended to take his own counsel more than that of campaign advisors, and the advisors themselves did not always articulate what he needed to hear. A top Bradley aide summarized the problem just after Bradley withdrew from the campaign in early March following losses in California and New York: "These people were always concerned about what their relationship with Bill should be, as opposed to just doing what it takes to win. It should have been, 'I don't care what you think of me, I want to win.' " The inability of Bradley's staff to distinguish between leading up and currying favor may have contributed to the aspirant's defeat. Had they more forcefully offered what the candidate should have heard even if he did not want the advice, they may have all been better served.

The root cause of the campaign shortfall goes back to the man who created the organization. Had Bill Bradley helped those who worked for him do their best by him, he might just have made the moves to have won his party's nomination, and given the razor-close general election that followed, Bradley's place in history and history itself might have turned out very differently. Leading up is no abstraction. It has tangible consequences for better or worse.

By studying in detail the chronicles of people who faced a chance to lead up, we can better appreciate what we should do when confronted with such opportunities ourselves. *Leading Up* will extract enduring lessons from such accounts that are general enough to apply to many situations yet specific enough to have real teeth.

Leading Up opens with Civil War Confederate commanders Joseph E. Johnston and Robert E. Lee, and Union commander George B. McClellan, three stark examples of the importance of keeping your superior well informed. One did it well, two did not, and the consequences for their battlefield encounters proved momentous.

Sometimes those above you just don't yet see what must be done, and your calling is to spark their attention and move them along a course of change before it is too late. That was the great challenge that we find David Pottruck facing at Charles Schwab & Co. as his enterprise was poised on the edge of an explosive new technology. That was the ominous challenge that confronted United Nations commander Roméo A. Dallaire in Rwanda as he faced a country on the verge of an explosive wave of killing.

Building the confidence of your superiors in you is essential, and failing to preserve it can be fatal. As we will see, chief executives Thomas Wyman of CBS, Eckhard Pfeiffer of Compaq Computer, and Robert Ayling of British Airways managed to lose their directors' trust—and their jobs because of it.

Working well with several bosses can be critical as well, and U.S. Marine Corps commander Peter Pace serves as our exemplar as he adjudicates competing priorities set by no less than six immediate superiors. Asking your boss the difficult but critical questions can be equally important, as will be seen when we follow mountaineers Beck Weathers and Sandy Hill Pittman up the summit ridge of Mount Everest on a fateful climb in May 1996.

When your superiors have expressed their intent but delegated its execution to you, it is your moment to shine. To do so you will need to be farsighted and determined, as were Charlene Barshefsky, the American trade negotiator delegated the task of negotiating with China, and Domingo Cavallo, the Argentine economy minister assigned the job of ending hyperinflation. Both had to achieve what their presidents required but could not fully envision.

Leading up can also require enormous fortitude and perseverance. Sometimes we fear what the boss will say. Sometimes we question our right to say it. Yet all of us have a transcendent obligation to convey what our superior should hear. Easier said than done, of course, but for paradigmatic and informative figures, we turn to the biblical prophets Abraham, Samuel, and Moses, who displayed a temerity to intercede with the greatest authority of all.

In examining these times when some upward leaders succeeded while others fell short, it's useful at the same time to recall our own experiences. Think of the disastrous manager who controlled your fate but whose strategic thinking had faltered. What steps did you take—or should you have taken—to help that person rise to the occasion before the firm faltered, too? Or recall that great manager who instilled a willingness for subordinates to face up to authority. What actions did he or she take to encourage that candid feedback and learning from below that helped prevent the firm from stepping off a cliff?

Leading up requires great courage and determination. We might fear how our superior will respond, we might doubt our right to lead up, but we all carry a responsibility to do what we can when it will make a difference. Upward leadership is not a natural skill, but it can be mastered, and the accounts ahead offer lessons for doing so.

===

CHAPTER 1

INFORMING YOUR COMMANDER

GENERAL ROBERT E. LEE INFORMED HIS COMMANDER IN CHIEF,
BUT GENERALS JOSEPH E. JOHNSTON AND GEORGE B. MCCLELLAN
DID NOT, AND THEIR CAUSES PAID DEARLY

THE AMERICAN CIVIL War brought to the fore hundreds of
military officers whose battlefield decisions have shaped
our history. Some proved adept in commanding troops, other
proved disastrous. Some worked exceedingly well with their
superiors, others just the opposite.

Those dexterous—or disastrous—at leading up could be
found on both the Union and Confederate sides of the battlefields. In this resource, neither side dominated, and both
sides discovered that its supply often spelled the difference
between triumph and disaster. Nowhere is this more evident
than in the contrasting styles of three of the great generals of
the Civil War: George B. McClellan, Joseph E. Johnston, and
Robert E. Lee.

By spring of 1862, a year after Confederate rebels fired on
Federal troops at Fort Sumter, South Carolina, a Union army
under McClellan's command was on the offensive. With more
than 120,000 troops and enormous siege guns, McClellan

sent his force up a Virginia peninsula toward the Confederate capital of Richmond. His strategy was simple: destroy the defending army, capture the Confederate leadership, end the war.

Though attacking to restore the Union, George McClellan treated its commander in chief with thinly veiled disdain. In the general's view, Abraham Lincoln was uncouth, uncivilized, and untutored in battlefield affairs. McClellan would insulate his strategy against meddling from the president by resisting policy directives, inflating enemy threats, and withholding battlefield reports. For his part, Lincoln was less interested in personalities than results, but without orders honored, numbers trusted, or intelligence delivered, how could he render McClellan the support he requested?

Meanwhile, as McClellan launched his vast and unprecedented military campaign against Richmond, the Confederacy assigned its premier commander, Joseph E. Johnston, the imperative of defending the capital. Like McClellan, Johnston was supremely confident in his own generalship and brooked no advice from political superiors. To ensure that little advice was received, he kept the Confederacy's supreme commander, President Jefferson Davis, in the dark.

But President Davis had been a military commander in his own right. A graduate of West Point and a veteran of the Mexican War, he had served as chairman of the U.S. Senate's military affairs committee and as U.S. secretary of war. He expected his commanders to welcome his advice, but he also appreciated that he could render real counsel only if his commanders informed him of what they were facing in the field and what they were intending to do about it.

When a shell fragment felled Johnston on May 31, 1862, President Davis replaced him with his own aide, Robert E. Lee. General Lee continued his own well-established practice of informing and consulting with the president. The result was Davis's unswerving support for Lee. Lee received the men and matériel he required, and within days he had stopped the Union advance on Richmond that General McClellan had been unable to sustain and General Johnston unable to reverse.

By aggressively keeping his president in the picture, Lee acquired what he needed from his superior for both to win. McClellan and Johnston had not—and they did not. As we will see in this chapter, the disparity between the upward incapacity of generals McClellan and Johnston (on opposing sides of the war) and the upward facility of General Lee could not have been greater, nor more momentous for the course of the war. Lee's exceptional ability to work with those above gave an enormous advantage to the secessionist cause in the weeks that followed. History offers few starker contrasts of upward leadership performed so differently to such great consequence, nor few clearer examples of the difference that appreciating and informing your superior can make—for you, your superior, and your mutual cause.

SETTING THE STAGE:
EARLY BATTLES IN THE CIVIL WAR

Newly elected president Abraham Lincoln had warned in his inaugural address on March 4, 1861, that a "disruption of the Federal Union, heretofore only menaced, is now formidably attempted" but that the rush to "secession is the essence of anarchy." He appealed to the "mystic chords of memory, stretching from every battlefield and patriot grave to every living heart and hearthstone." He asked that we heed the "better angels of our nature."

Lincoln's words fell on deaf ears. South Carolina, Mississippi, and five other states had already declared their exit from the Union. On April 10, 1861, Brigadier General Pierre G. T. Beauregard, commander of provisional Confederate forces, demanded the surrender of the Federal garrison of Fort Sumter in the harbor of Charleston, South Carolina. The demand refused, he opened fire on the fortress and forced its surrender on April 13 without a casualty suffered on either side. Virginia announced its exit from the Union on April 17. The first land battle of the Civil War came six weeks later when a Union brigade surprised and routed a small Confederate force at Philippi, Virginia (now West Virginia). The human toll: 26 Rebel casualties and 4 Federal losses.

The first large-scale engagement of the Civil War erupted on July 21 when Confederate generals Johnston and Beauregard confronted and defeated Union General Irvin McDowell's Army of Northeastern Virginia in a battle along Bull Run near Manassas, Virginia, just twenty-five miles southwest of Washington, D.C. The engagement brutally dispelled any notion on either side that the secession would be quickly secured or crushed. Southern forces suffered 1,750 casualties, Northern forces 2,950.

In the wake of the Federal defeat at Manassas, President Lincoln on July 27 appointed George McClellan commander of the Army of the Potomac, the Union's largest and most potent fighting machine. His immediate job was to protect Washington from further attack by General Johnston, whose Confederate forces had dug in after the battle just twenty miles from the capital. Neither general, though, was yet primed to strike a decisive blow against the other—or even start a fight. As summer turned to fall, the opposing forces recruited, regrouped, and reviewed their options, but neither moved to battle. By the end of 1861, the two sides' combined losses would not total a fraction of those cut down in a single day's fighting at Antietam, Maryland, less than a year later.

In March of 1862, the standoff in northern Virginia came to an end. After rancorous debate in the White House and War Department, the Union settled on an aggressive strategy of grand attack, with George McClellan targeting the biggest prize of all, the Confederate capital. Since little remained secret in a conflict where both sides compiled a steady flow of information from newspaper reporters, amateur observers, and professional spies, the Confederacy withdrew Johnston's forces from its offensive position near Washington to a defensive posture around Richmond.

As the great confrontation took form, the combat fate of each side—and the eventual fate of the rebellion and the republic—depended on Johnston's and McClellan's strategic theories with respect to each other's army, on their field equipment and military discipline, on their intelligence networks, and in part on dumb luck. But it also depended in no small part on the two commanders' relations with their superiors.

In both cases, the relations were lethally impaired by the flawed behavior of the two generals themselves. Historians have judged their failings harshly. President Davis "had come to view" Joseph Johnston—his own general, whom he himself had appointed—"as the enemy," concluded Craig L. Symonds, a Johnston biographer, and Johnston must bear a "major responsibility for the failure of the Confederate war effort." On the Union side, George McClellan "was inarguably the worst commander" that the Army of the Potomac ever had, offered Stephen W. Sears, a McClellan biographer, and "the record is equally clear that it was his own decisions, rather than those of the government, that doomed his grand campaign to end the war."

Among the most dooming decisions of both McClellan and Johnston were their open displays of contempt for their superiors and their consistent denial of data to them. The fatal consequences of their overt antagonism stood in pointed contrast to what Lee would subsequently achieve with the opposite tack.

Such judgments, of course, are made in hindsight. As the Union march against Richmond neared, all that could be said for certain was that the fortunes of both sides rested on a very thin reed of trust extending between the leadership in the field and the supreme commanders at the top of each army.

FAILING TO "LEAD UP" ON THE UNION SIDE: GENERAL McCLELLAN SCORNED HIS BOSS, PRESIDENT LINCOLN

In March 1862, as Washington hatched the Peninsula Campaign to end the secession, George McClellan was serving not only as commanding general for the Union Army of the Potomac, but also as general in chief for all Northern armies. With seven months in the first role and four in the latter, the thirty-five-year-old McClellan was both the youngest and most senior general officer in Federal service.

McClellan's riveting attention to engineering efficiency and combatant welfare greatly endeared him to his troops. He made a point of mastering the names of his officers, and he frequently rode and walked among his enlisted men. During one campaign, after he shook the hand of a soldier and commended his brigade for its fight, news of the general's personal compliment spread like wildfire. McClellan believed that personifying the army in the form of the commander would foster the morale and verve needed for success on the battlefield. He often conveyed his admiration and appreciation

George B. McClellan

Abraham Lincoln

for his troops, especially the front line, and they repaid the attention. On June 19, 1861, the *New York Tribune* reported to its readers that McClellan "is personally extremely popular" and "army officers and men and everybody seem to have entire faith in him." For downward leadership, he found few equals in the Federal ranks.

In stark contrast to this respect for his troops, however, George McClellan's regard for his superiors verged on contempt. Since his West Point days, he had found occasion to quarrel with almost anybody his senior. He questioned those who determined class rankings at the U.S. Military Academy, even though he would graduate second among fifty-eight in the class of 1846. Upon graduation, McClellan shipped off to fight in the Mexican War, and there he displayed a disdain for any superior officer who had come from civilian life rather than West Point.

He soon targeted political leaders with the same scorn. As early as 1853, when McClellan surveyed the Pacific Northwest for a railroad passage under the direction of the Washington Territory governor, he wrote in his journal, "I have done my last service under civilians & politicians." He told himself that he would quit his exploration unless the governor would give him "general orders & never say one word as to the means or time of executing them."

McClellan's return to civilian life as an executive with the Illinois Central railway in 1858 only added to his growing list of dislikes. McClellan wrote that a certain attorney for the railroad—one Abraham Lincoln—"was not a man of very strong character" and "was destitute of refinement."

It would be a short-lived stint in the private sector for McClellan as the gathering winds of war brought him back into uniform on April 23, 1861. Almost from the start, he was predictably at loggerheads with the Union's general in chief, seventy-five-year-old Winfield Scott, a onetime mentor. McClellan demanded more officers and troops for the Ohio forces that had been placed in his charge, and when Scott refused—hard-pressed as he was to muster troops for all the forces being mobilized—McClellan complained to the Ohio governor that "I almost regret having entered upon my present duty." McClellan soon came to resist General Scott's orders and instructions, and by the end of September 1861, Scott confided to the secretary of war that he would court-martial McClellan for insubordination were it not for its fearful effect on Northern morale. By then, McClellan was in open rebellion against his former friend. A month later, President Lincoln relieved Scott of his command and, on November 1, named George McClellan as the Union's new general in chief.

The sentiment underlying the honor that President Lincoln had bestowed upon George McClellan was not reciprocated. Indeed, the general could not even bring himself to disguise his disrespect for his commander in chief.

Abraham Lincoln had the habit of making unannounced visits to McClellan's office, and though many would feel deeply honored by such calls, for George McClellan they were a burden. McClellan occasionally hid himself at an associate's home to "dodge" a "browsing" president, but on the evening of November 13, 1861, Lincoln called unexpectedly on McClellan's own home. The president arrived with Secretary of State William Seward and personal secretary John Hay, but McClellan's orderly told the visitors that the general was attending a wedding. They decided to wait for his return, yet when the general arrived home an hour later, he walked swiftly past the parlor in which the presidential party was waiting and proceeded upstairs. Half an hour later, Lincoln and his guests sent the aide upstairs to remind McClellan of their presence. The emissary returned to report that the general had gone to bed. John Hay later described the slight as "unparalleled insolence."

By the time George McClellan was finally ready to start the Peninsula Campaign in midspring of 1862, he had managed to alienate virtually every member of President Lincoln's cabinet, most perilously Secretary of War Edwin M. Stanton. On March 11, just two days before the campaign was to commence, President Lincoln relieved McClellan from his position as general in chief, explaining that "McClellan having personally taken the field" to spearhead the attack on Richmond would have his hands full.

LEADERSHIP STRUGGLES ON THE CONFEDERATE SIDE: GENERAL JOHNSTON RESENTED HIS BOSS, PRESIDENT DAVIS

George McClellan's opening opponent in the Peninsula Campaign would be Joseph Johnston, who had been a fellow officer and close friend before the war. (Johnston had served as an attendant at McClellan's wedding in 1860; their friendship resumed after the war, and Johnston would serve as a pallbearer at McClellan's funeral.) McClellan told a friend that in confronting Johnston on the peninsula, he would anticipate his thinking well, since they had been "intimate friends." Johnston no doubt drew on his own familiarity with McClellan's mind as he prepared to defend Richmond against the Federal assault.

A classmate of Robert E. Lee and a year behind Jefferson Davis, Joseph Johnston had graduated from the U.S. Military Academy in 1829. Johnston finished thirteenth in his forty-six-person class, eleven

General Joseph E. Johnston   *Jefferson Davis*   *General Robert E. Lee*

slots behind Lee. Seemingly inconsequential at the time, the disparity in class rank would come to have large consequences decades later
for the struggling Confederacy. Johnston's military career had shot
into overdrive in 1848 when he led a battalion up the ramparts of
Mexico's citadel of Chapultepec. By the time of the first firing on
Fort Sumter, in 1861, Johnston had risen to brigadier general in the
pre–Civil War army.

With the rapid buildup of the armies on both sides, Jefferson
Davis eagerly sought Joseph Johnston's services, appointing him
brigadier general of the Confederate Army on May 14, 1861, and
placing him in command of a Confederate army forming near
Harper's Ferry, in what was then Virginia. Johnston moved his new
force of 9,000 to Manassas just in time to ensure a Confederate victory on July 21, 1861, the first major engagement of the Civil War.

Although this victory brought greater notice to General Pierre
Beauregard, who had directed the Confederacy's front lines, than to
General Johnston, President Davis still judged that he had found an
effective fighter in Johnston as well. Unfortunately, of the 420 generals Davis ultimately was to appoint to wage the Confederate cause,
none would prove more nettlesome than Joseph E. Johnston.

Johnston came to doubt the judgment of his new superior almost
from the start, and Davis promptly returned the distrust. The fallout
began with a seemingly petty dispute. When Davis promoted four
commanders—Samuel Cooper, Albert Sidney Johnston, Robert E.
Lee, and Pierre Beauregard—to full general, they joined Johnston as
the only Confederate officers wearing three stars. But generals of the
same status were also ranked by seniority, and Davis had listed
Johnston as fourth. He had done so on the basis of their graduating
years from West Point, and in the case of two who came from the
same class—Johnston and Lee—on the basis of their standing within
the class of 1829.

Johnston didn't agree with this ranking, and on September 12,
1861, he protested to Davis. The Confederate Congress had already

asserted that seniority should be judged by an officer's ranking in the Union Army before the Civil War, and there Johnston had been ahead of Lee and two of the other three. Davis later argued that even by that criterion Johnston would actually be ranked behind Lee because Johnston had held only a staff rank in the pre–Civil War U.S. Army. But in Johnston's view, Davis's ranking constituted a rebuke and a demotion. In an 1,800-word letter to his president, Johnston complained of his "mortification," claimed that he "rightfully" held the rank of "first general," and charged Davis with tarnishing his "fair fame as a soldier and a man."

Whatever the merits of either side, Davis was incensed by Johnston's protest, which he angrily read to his entire cabinet. He viewed the letter as an impertinent complaint to a head of state and an insubordinate claim on a commander in chief. He wrote back that Johnston's "insinuations" were "as unfounded as they are unbecoming." Neither would ever forgive the other, and in the judgment of historian Craig Symonds, Johnston's dispatch of the letter "was the single worst decision of his professional career."

The feud that grew out of this petty and avoidable quarrel over class rankings proved an enduring and costly schism that divided the Confederacy's inner circle until the end. More immediately, Davis and Johnston began to view each other with ever-increasing wariness, less and less trustful of the other to do what was right.

General Johnston's Failed Working Relationship with President Davis Caused His Downfall

During the fall of 1861, President Davis urged General Johnston to reorganize his army so that regiments from the same state would be grouped within the same brigade. During the rushed first months of mobilization, a regiment from Mississippi might be arbitrarily assigned to the same brigade with those from Alabama or North

Carolina. With no fall offensive in store, Davis believed it was an opportune time to gather state regiments together under a general officer from the same state in keeping with the Confederacy's battle cry of "states' rights." Johnston did not see any urgency or even real need for such a reorganization, however, and he feared in any case that it would weaken his command at a time when a dangerous Yankee army still confronted him near Washington.

Without consultation, President Davis added to General Johnston's woes by authorizing sixty-day furloughs for Johnston's men as a reenlistment incentive. Johnston complained to Davis that his actions "not only impaired discipline, but deprived me of the influence of the army, without which there can be little hope of success." Several witnesses overheard Johnston indiscreetly muse that Davis must have been installed in the presidency by the Yankees to "perplex and annoy" Southern commanders.

Davis and Johnston also diverged on matters more momentous. The population of the industrializing North stood at 22 million, while that of the still agricultural South totaled 9 million, of which a third remained in slavery. The Confederacy would be hard-pressed to defend all of its states' territories against a far superior Union force, and Johnston took the view that it was wiser to concentrate in essential areas and abandon the periphery. If Richmond fell, it mattered little if northern Virginia or coastal Carolina remained in Rebel hands. While that made sound military sense, it was nonetheless unwise politically, since none of the secessionist governors saw their own territory as anything less than essential.

Other military leaders, including Robert E. Lee, shared Joseph Johnston's philosophy, and later in the war Jefferson Davis came to adopt it as well. But in early 1862, as the Confederacy mobilized to meet the Union's anticipated attack against Richmond, Davis was not yet of that opinion. Insensitive to Davis's reading of his political realities, Johnston was so sure of his own view that he continually declared it to be obvious. To Davis, his defiant subordinate was as insolent as he was unpersuasive.

Johnston dished up his defiance in small ways as well as large. When Lee assigned an officer to Johnston's staff on behalf of the president, Johnston took umbrage that the order had not come from Davis himself. Lee had ample authority from Davis to effect the transfer, but Johnston refused to recognize it. Instead, Johnston wrote to the president's adjutant general, who officially spoke for the president, that he could "admit the power of no officer of the Army to annul" his own selection of another officer for the staff position, since "being myself the ranking General of the Confederate Army." After reading the letter, Davis wrote one word at the bottom: "Insubordinate."

With the Union Army's decision to attack the rebel capital, President Davis appreciated that he had no choice but to concentrate all available forces around Richmond, but precisely when that aggregation should start was still another source of dispute. The Confederate cabinet met at length on February 19, 1862, to review the timing, and Davis and Johnston emerged from the meeting with opposing memories of what had been concluded. Johnston's own army of 36,000 had remained at Centreville near Washington since the Battle of Manassas the prior July, but the cabinet now agreed that it should be pulled back for Richmond's defense. By Johnston's recollection of the cabinet's decision, he was to withdraw "as soon as practicable," but Davis remembered differently: The withdrawal was to wait until forced by events. With no further instructions or discussions, Johnston abruptly ordered the evacuation on March 5, and fearful of security leaks, he did not inform Richmond until his army had crossed the natural barrier of the Rappahannock River eight days later. President Davis was shocked to learn of such a major movement after the fact. He complained to Johnston of being "much in the dark" as to the purpose of the "precipitate retreat": "Having heard of no cause for such a sudden movement, I was at a loss to believe it."

Johnston's failure to inform his superior led to a result precisely the opposite from what his keep-them-in-the-dark practice was intended to achieve. Instead of creating greater latitude for the exercise of his field judgment, it only tightened headquarters' control over command decisions that could not be fully trusted. President Davis no longer trusted Johnston, so he undercut Johnston by giving de facto authority to Lee.

The day after Johnston informed Davis of the Southern withdrawal from northern Virginia, President Davis granted General Lee overall authority for all armies of the Confederacy, including several in Virginia that Johnston thought he still controlled. Lee began issuing orders to the armies still nominally under Johnston's command. When letters from their commanders addressed to Johnston passed through Richmond, Lee opened and responded to them without consulting or even informing Johnston of their existence. Johnston had failed at the most basic task of keeping his boss in the loop, and now he was paying the price.

Lesson in Leading Up

Disdain and contempt for your superior—whether a country president or a company manager—will be returned in kind, thus shortening your leash and limiting your assets. Petty quarrels with your boss will similarly damage your name and invite greater oversight and fewer resources.

THE PENINSULA CAMPAIGN: JOHNSTON AND McCLELLAN IGNORE THEIR BOSSES

The leadership struggles between both Confederate and Union generals and their respective presidents came to a head during the Peninsula Campaign. On March 13, 1862, Union general McClellan began moving his army of 121,500 men down the Potomac River and Chesapeake Bay in a vast armada of nearly 400 steamers and schooners. On April 2, McClellan himself arrived at Fort Monroe, the main landing point on the peninsula. A vital Union enclave on the tip of a Virginia peninsula between the York and James Rivers flowing southeast from Richmond, Fort Monroe stood only seventy miles from the office of Jefferson Davis and the Confederacy's nerve center.

McClellan ordered the advance to begin the next day against an already entrenched Confederate line only a dozen miles northwest up the peninsula. That position had been established by Joseph Johnston under protest. Jefferson Davis had concluded that the first line of defense should be there, sixty miles southwest of Richmond, but Johnston argued for falling back closer to the capital, a more impregnable position. Davis overruled him, and Johnston reluctantly fortified the forward position.

Anchored at Yorktown and extending southwest across the peninsula, the line was still lightly defended as McClellan's juggernaut approached, but the 13,000 Confederate troops had fanned out along the ramparts to create an impression of far greater strength. It worked. McClellan halted his advance and transformed his plan from frontal assault to protracted siege. Frustrated by the ensuing delay, Lincoln wrote McClellan on April 9 that "it is indispensable to *you* that you strike a blow" and that "*you must act.*" McClellan refused. He confided to his wife in a letter that if Lincoln wanted a breakthrough now, "He had better come & do it himself."

On the other side of the battle, Johnston was also ignoring his boss: On May 3, Johnston abruptly ordered the withdrawal of troops from the Yorktown line to stronger positions up the peninsula before McClellan's force could lob more than a few shells on the line. McClellan was confounded by Johnston's abrupt decision to abandon the Yorktown line before any fight, but it led to a stronger Confederate defense near the capital. The only problem with this decision was that Johnston had not informed the president of his precipitous withdrawal until a day before it happened. "Your announce-ment," Davis wired back, "takes us by surprise." Johnston fired back that he "can do nothing here" and by "delay we may insure the loss of Richmond too."

A Union soldier wandering through the abandoned Confederate camp came across a charcoal message written on a tent wall: "He that fights and runs away, will live to fight another day. May 3." The mes-sage was prescient: Had Johnston remained a day more, his troops would have been bombarded by twenty-eight additional heavy artillery pieces that McClellan had readied, which might have so pinned down Johnston's troops that withdrawal would have come only at great cost.

Meanwhile, McClellan continued to ignore his own boss. President Lincoln was so alarmed by McClellan's tepid tactics and sluggish pace (both before and after the Yorktown evacuation) that he came to Fort Monroe on May 6 to learn what he could and pres-sure where he might. War Secretary Stanton and Treasury Secretary Salmon P. Chase accompanied the president, but none would gain anything from McClellan or even see him during the visit! McClellan sent word that his presence with his advancing army was too impor-tant to permit a meeting with his boss. Although Lincoln spent four days on the peninsula, he never managed to convene with the com-mander to whom he had entrusted the Union's future.

In the weeks that followed, McClellan finally succeeded in push-ing Johnston's lines back to the gates of Richmond. By the end of May 1862, the Union front was within six miles of the Confederate capital, its steeples visible in the distance. With his back against the wall, Johnston finally turned from defensive retreat to offensive response on May 31 in what came to be known as the Battle of Seven Pines, though once again his own president was almost the last to know. Davis learned of his general's do-or-die counterattack only when he heard its opening gunfire.

So curious and uninformed was the Confederate president (like

Lincoln on the Union side) that he ventured forward to see for himself. When Davis rode into Johnston's headquarters in midafternoon on May 31, Johnston knew that he would have to explain the offensive and the disposition of his troops—just at a moment when he wasn't certain where his troops were located and feared his offensive might already be faltering. In a manner very similar to that in which his opponent McClellan had ignored Lincoln, Johnston pretended not to see President Davis's arrival and hurried off toward the battlefront. Davis laid eyes on Johnston, though, and he probably drew conclusions akin to Lincoln's when McClellan intentionally took no notice of his visit.

Robert E. Lee Takes Command of the Confederate Army

It was not Johnston's insubordination that caused President Davis to replace his command by appointing Robert E. Lee. Instead, it was a bullet wound. On the afternoon of May 31, 1862, Johnston rode far forward to oversee the unfolding events at the Battle of Seven Pines. His decision to lead perilously close to the battle lines was not uncommon among Civil War generals. Given the primitive communication systems, commanders often obtained little real-time data at the rear, so Johnston climbed a knoll that had a commanding view but that was also well within range of Union firepower. As bullets whizzed by, a staff officer instinctively ducked, but Johnston smiled and warned the young colonel that "there is no use in dodging. When you hear them, they have passed." One did not pass, however, hitting Johnston in the shoulder, and a moment later he was blown off his horse by a fragment from a shell that exploded in front him.

Johnston's staff carried him to a sheltered spot, and when the wounded general regained consciousness he saw Jefferson Davis standing over him, gravely concerned. In great pain from the shrapnel that tore his chest and thigh, Johnston was carried later that

evening to Richmond, where he would need six months to recuper-
ate. At the moment, though, the Confederate Army was leaderless.

To fill the void, Davis on the spot elevated Johnston's second in
command, Major General Gustavus W. Smith, as its new chief. Smith's
tenure was extremely short-lived, however: he retained this post for
less than a day. When the president and his aide, Robert E. Lee, met
with Smith at 8:30 that evening, Smith seemed at an utter loss for what
next to do with the Army of Northern Virginia. Though a blustery
West Point graduate, Smith earlier that day had been unnerved by the
responsibilities of leading his own division into battle. When pressed
by Davis to describe his immediate plans for an entire army, Smith
asked Davis what the president knew about the day's battle and confessed that he "could not determine" without further information
"what was best to be done." The next morning, Smith's forces
achieved little on the battlefield, and Smith appeared on the verge of
a nervous breakdown. When Lee rode up to Smith's headquarters at
2:00 P.M., he found Davis relieving Smith of his command.

In his place, Davis appointed Lee, who promptly dispatched his
cavalry commander, twenty-nine-year-old Major General J. E. B.
Stuart, to explore the right flank of McClellan's army. Meeting little
resistance, Jeb Stuart and his 1,200 riders circled all the way around
McClellan's army, returning on June 15 and making "Stuart's Ride
Around McClellan" one of the legendary events of the war. Lee
opened a full counteroffensive on June 25 in what became known as
the Seven Days' Battles, a series of encounters that ended with a
bloody struggle. In the weeks that followed, Lee was unable to score
a decisive defeat of McClellan, but winning was not the issue. It was
enough to have irreversibly put the Union Army on the defensive.

In the weeks that followed, more deeply mired on the peninsula
and disinclined to either advance or retreat, McClellan began
demanding 20,000 reinforcements, then 50,000, and at one point
even 55,000. President Lincoln had become convinced that
McClellan was incapable of reversing his fortunes whatever his num-

bers, and on August 3 he ordered McClellan to terminate the Peninsula Campaign and come back to Washington. McClellan removed his last troops from the peninsula on August 26, and none would return. The 160 days of the campaign would stand as the largest sustained conflict of the entire war, engaging a quarter million troops. By the end, the casualty rolls totaled 30,450 Confederate and 25,370 Union soldiers. The Union campaign failed to produce the Confederate Waterloo it had envisioned—a failure that would lead to three more years of bloody conflict.

McClellan's Peninsula Campaign offers a powerful reminder that great events can sometimes be driven and determined by commanding personalities. It also reminds us that fatal flaws can result in lethal outcomes. Johnston himself recognized the critical turn in the Confederacy's fortunes when he called the bullet that hit him the best shot "ever fired for the Southern Confederacy." It was less Lee's strategic brilliance that Johnston complimented than Lee's exceptional capacity to work with the powers that be. Because Lee had "the confidence of this government," Johnston explained, Lee would achieve the success on the battlefield that Johnston could not.

Lesson in Leading Up

Building your superiors' confidence in you requires giving them your confidence. Once you and they have established it both ways, your organization may have an unbeatable competitive advantage, whatever the battlefield.

JOHNSTON'S WITHHOLDING INFORMATION ALIENATED PRESIDENT DAVIS

During his brief command of the Army of Northern Virginia from the fall of 1861 through the following spring, Joseph Johnston had adopted a strategy of divulging as little information as possible to his superior. To Johnston it made perfect military sense. "I did not consult the president," he wrote, "because it seemed to me that to do so would be to transfer my responsibilities to his shoulders." By deliberately withholding information from Davis, Johnston also hoped to prevent the president from breathing down his neck: "I could not consult him without adopting the course he might advise, so that to ask his advice would have been, in my opinion, to ask him to command for me." Johnston's posture was to execute and then report. Any forewarning of his intentions only invited second-guessing.

Some chiefs prefer Johnston's modus operandi. Because they want results but do not necessarily know how best to get them, they look for great managers to run their operating divisions. Then they extend their managers a long leash for making decisions and maintain a short leash on getting results. Jefferson Davis, however, was hardly that kind of boss. He had devoted his professional life to military affairs, and he had distinguished himself as a frontline officer.

Upon graduating from the U.S. Military Academy in 1828, Davis served in uniform for seven years. Following a stint in the U.S. Congress, he reentered active service in 1846, leading his troops with distinction in the Mexican War. There, after Davis suffered a battle injury, his major general (and future president) Zachary Taylor officially complimented the young officer for courage under fire. "The Mississippi riflemen, under Colonel Davis," Taylor wrote to the secretary of war, "were highly conspicuous for their gallantry and steadiness, and sustained throughout the engagement the reputation of veteran troops. Brought into action against an immensely superior force, they maintained themselves for a long time unsupported and with heavy loss, and held an important part of the field until reinforced. Colonel Davis, though severely wounded, remained in the saddle until the close of the action. His distinguished coolness and gallantry at the head of his regiment on this day entitle him to the particular notice of the government."

On combat matters Davis was far more than just a battlefield veteran. Few political leaders on either side were more experienced in military practices and national policies than he. In 1847, President James Polk had offered Davis an appointment as brigadier general, but Davis chose instead to enter the U.S. Senate, where he served as chair of its Committee on Military Affairs. He joined President Franklin Pierce's cabinet in 1853 as secretary of war, a position he held until he reentered the Senate in 1857, again serving as chairman of the military affairs committee.

For President Davis, the added title of commander in chief was far more than ceremonial: This was a head of state well versed in military affairs and battlefield strategy. Yet Johnston would not allow any of his superior's prior military experience to inform his own.

Johnston was also unprepared to tell Davis of his own military experience as it unfolded, a grievous insult, since Davis obsessed over military trivia. He often called his cabinet into several sessions a week, some running five hours or more, and much of that time was devoted to battlefield matters. The Confederate Navy secretary observed that Davis had an "uncontrollable tendency" to digress from grand strategy to military minutiae. Whether appropriate or not, Johnston refused to bring forward the details for which Davis so hungered.

Not all bosses require that you provide an upward flow of detail, but those who do will hold it against you if you don't. Reading their requirements is an essential quality of upward leadership for which Johnston proved a near perfect *anti*exemplar. Johnston's contrarian attitude gave his superior—who wanted field intelligence and knew from experience how to use it—ample cause to doubt his subordinate, constrain his resources, and limit his options. If leading up helps you and your boss both win, Johnston's antileadership helped him and Davis both lose.

Lesson in Leading Up

Withholding vital information from above is sure to make your superior's job far more difficult and damage his or her trust in you, making your own job far more difficult as well.

MCCLELLAN LOSES WHAT WAS LEFT OF LINCOLN'S RESPECT AND TRUST

With the conclusion of the Peninsula Campaign, the standings of both George McClellan and Joseph Johnston had reached all-time lows. Neither had acquitted himself well during the campaign, and neither could properly claim any genuine victory. Worse was to follow.

For McClellan, signs of his waning status were already evident before the Peninsula Campaign had concluded. On July 11, 1862, Lincoln appointed Henry W. Halleck as his new general in chief, handing him the role that had been taken from McClellan on March 11. Lincoln had met with McClellan on the peninsula just three days earlier, but even though McClellan's army was by far the largest and most important entity under Halleck's new purview, the president neither consulted with nor informed McClellan of the pending appointment.

With Halleck's accession, George McClellan privately griped that he would rather resign than report to "a man whom I know from experience to be my inferior." But McClellan expected in any case to be relieved momentarily by the president. When his dismissal did not materialize immediately, he wrote his wife on July 27 that President Lincoln's "cowardice alone prevents it." McClellan added that he could now "never regard him with other feelings than those of contempt—for his mind, heart & morality."

Cowardice, though, wasn't Lincoln's problem: a talent shortage was. The president asked Ambrose Burnside (whose North Carolina–

based troops had recently joined McClellan's army as its Ninth Corps) to replace McClellan. Burnside demurred, insisting that McClellan was still the right officer to lead, and Lincoln could think of no other candidate ready for the Union's most critical command.

Spared dismissal, McClellan finally sailed from the peninsula for Washington on August 23, but upon arrival, he found himself frozen out of the War Department's inner circles and much of his army reassigned to the defense of Washington, which once again was being directly threatened, this time by Robert E. Lee's Army of Northern Virginia. On August 28, another great battle erupted at Manassas, just miles from the White House. The new crisis—13,830 Union troops fell during the three-day battle against the Confederacy's 8,350—temporarily revived George McClellan's standing by placing him once again in the thick of the action.

As Lee moved his Army of Northern Virginia northwest into Maryland, McClellan—anxiously urged on by Lincoln—quickly reassembled the Army of the Potomac and, on September 5, set off in hot pursuit. Fate soon presented McClellan with a unique opportunity to redeem his name. Not only did he face a smaller enemy—Lee was bringing 51,800 men into battle against McClellan's 75,300—but by a remarkable windfall McClellan had also learned of Lee's battle plans. On September 13, a corporal in McClellan's Twelfth Corps found an envelope in a meadow that contained three cigars wrapped in an order with Lee's operational plan. Four days later, the two armies met along Antietam Creek near Sharpsburg, Maryland. It would become the most deadly single day of the entire war—casualties exceeded 26,000 men—yet in the end it would do nothing to redeem the Union general's tattered reputation.

McClellan again failed to destroy a smaller force; he also refused to pursue Lee's retreating army in the days that followed. Appalled by McClellan's reserve, Lincoln visited his field headquarters on October 1 and warned against such overcautiousness. The following day, the president stood with a friend overlooking the Union's still-inert army and asked if the friend knew what lay before them. The friend replied that it was obviously the Army of the Potomac. "So it is called, but that is a mistake," Lincoln replied. "It is only McClellan's bodyguard."

Several days after departing McClellan's encampment, the president ordered his general to "cross the Potomac and give battle to the enemy or drive him south." Lincoln told McClellan that he "must move now." For the next thirty days, however, McClellan refused to budge. During this prolonged immobility, Confederate cavalry commander Jeb Stuart and 1,800 troopers once again rode all the way around McClellan's army. When McClellan tried to explain that this newest disgrace was the result of an exhausted Union cavalry, Lincoln retorted, "Will you pardon me for asking what the horses of your army have done since the battle of Antietam that fatigue anything?"

Finally, on October 26, McClellan began crossing the Potomac with his more than 100,000 troops. But it was too late to catch Lee or save his own command. On November 5 Lincoln instructed Henry Halleck to replace McClellan with Ambrose Burnside. McClellan would never again command.

Abraham Lincoln meeting George McClellan near
Sharpsburg, Maryland, October 4, 1862.

Numbers Count: The Importance of Reporting Accurately to Your Boss

Modest miscalculations of competitors' strength are expected from anybody studying fast-changing fields of action. Consistent errors, by contrast, are warning signs of an unreliable mind. Whether the errors are deliberate or illusory, they lethally erode whatever trust an otherwise effective manager has managed to create in those above. George McClellan cost himself and his country dearly with repeated overestimates of his opponent's strength and underestimates of his own.

Early doubts emerged in the White House immediately after Joseph Johnston completed his evacuation of Centreville on March 9, 1862. McClellan had been insisting that the Confederate encampment threatening Washington harbored no fewer than 100,000 armed men. But Union officers inspecting the abandoned facilities found that they could have housed fewer than half that number.

After departing for the peninsula, McClellan reported to the War Department on April 1 that he had left ample troops behind in Washington to defend the nation's capital while he attacked that of the enemy. He had stationed 18,000 men in the fortifications around Washington, he said, and positioned another 55,000 as a mobile covering force for them.

Yet when President Lincoln and War Secretary Stanton studied the numbers, they discovered that McClellan had counted one brigade and four regiments twice, attributed 3,000 more soldiers to one garrison than it held, and included 3,500 raw recruits still in Pennsylvania. Moreover, two-thirds of the covering troops were stationed eighty miles away in the Shenandoah Valley, unable to cover much at all. Therefore, instead of positioning 73,000 troops to protect the capital, Lincoln and Stanton concluded that McClellan had left them fewer than 27,000. The president, a senator reported, was "justly indignant."

Still, given the overwhelming concentration of enemy forces around Richmond, McClellan contended that he needed every soldier available. He wired Washington from the peninsula on April 7 that he now "had the whole force of the enemy on my hands" and placed it at 100,000 men. To help the president appreciate the long odds he faced, he reported his own force at 85,000.

Washington had no way of knowing at the time that McClellan was reporting an enemy figure twice its true number, but it did know that McClellan's own force was far larger than he was allowing. By the War Department's calculus, the Army of the Potomac numbered 108,000, not 85,000.

Lincoln asked McClellan two days later to explain the "curious mystery" of the missing men, and only then did he learn of McClellan's private math. For reporting purposes, the general counted only his enlisted personnel ready for frontline duty. Officers, noncombatants, and any enlisted men not ready for combat were simply left out of the count. To estimate the latter for lack of precise figures, McClellan arbitrarily cut his enlisted numbers by one-sixth. By contrast, in estimating the other side, he counted everybody in gray. In officially reporting both totals, McClellan chose to reveal the implicit algorithm under neither.

Without reliable numbers from the field, Abraham Lincoln predictably withheld the men and matériel that George McClellan claimed he required for the simple reason that the president could never be sure what was really needed. Just as McClellan was preparing to lay siege to the Confederate troops at Yorktown, Washington informed its field commander that his First Corps under Irvin McDowell, scheduled for momentary arrival on the peninsula, was being withheld. The War Department explained to McClellan that this was because the president now viewed "the force" he "left in front of Washington insufficient to insure its safety." Though much of his own making, McClellan was stunned by the reversal. "It is the most infamous thing that history has recorded," he wrote privately. "The idea of depriving a General of 35,000 troops when actually under fire!"

McClellan's radical misperception of battlefield reality led to grave errors of his own. Just before Joseph Johnston abandoned Yorktown on May 3, 1862, Johnston was overestimating McClellan's strength by 20%, but McClellan was overestimating Johnston's strength by more than 110%! Johnston wisely abandoned Yorktown at a moment when McClellan—had he appreciated his relative strength—might have inflicted a mortal blow.

As McClellan inched his juggernaut up the peninsula, he repeatedly warned Washington of his understaffing against Richmond's superior manpower. "If I am not reinforced," he wrote the war secretary on May 10, "it is probable that I will be obliged to fight nearly double my numbers." Four days later he complained to Lincoln that he faced 150,000 Rebels with just 80,000 soldiers of his own. The War Department still depended on McClellan for the opposition figures, but once again, it certainly knew its own, and by its reckoning, McClellan now had 128,000 men at his disposal, more than half again higher than what he was allowing.

On the evening of June 25, the day Robert E. Lee launched his counteroffensive, McClellan telegrammed war secretary Stanton that "I regret my great inferiority in numbers." Confederate forces had now swollen to 200,000, he said. But if his inferior army was "destroyed by over-whelming numbers," he was personally "ready to die with it & share its fate."

Yet in fact, Lee's Army of Northern Virginia had been able to muster only 85,000 men—the largest single force the Confederacy ever assembled during the war's four years and hardly the behemoth that McClellan projected. At that moment, the Army of the Potomac totaled 104,300. The ratio of Union to Confederate forces thus stood at 1.23 to 1. In McClellan's reports to his superiors he placed it at 0.4 to 1.

Several days later, as McClellan reeled from Lee's aggressive action near Gaines's Mills, he made the fateful decision to begin a general retreat toward the James River. On the evening of June 27, he dispatched a cable to War Secretary Stanton, explaining his historic reversal. "I have lost this battle because my force was too small," he asserted. He had deployed all of his reserves to naught, he claimed, even though 64,000 Federal troops under his command had sat idly by that day. McClellan added a final charge: "If I save this Army now I tell you plainly that I owe no thanks to you or any other persons in Washington—you have done your best to sacrifice this Army."

George McClellan received no response to his charge of official treachery from either Stanton or Lincoln. They never saw it, because the colonel responsible for telegraph traffic at the War Department was so shocked by McClellan's message that he recopied the dispatch with the offending sentence omitted and only then gave it to Stanton.

Old habits, even self-defeating ones, die hard. During the Second Battle of Manassas, Virginia, at the end of August, McClellan wired Washington that Robert E. Lee was advancing toward Arlington and planning to attack Washington with 120,000 troops. Several days later, pursuing Lee's army into Maryland, he again saw 120,000 men—"a gigantic rebel army"—ahead of him. On September 13, McClellan warned Halleck that he expected a "severe general engagement," and ten days after the September 17 engagement at Antietam, McClellan reported to Washington that in "the last battles the enemy was undoubtedly greatly superior to us in numbers."

In fact, McClellan had fought at Antietam with 75,000 troops, with another 20,000 ready for service. Lee had held him at bay with a mere 38,000 men.

Lesson in Leading Up

Strategy requires an accurate comparative appraisal of your competitor's strengths and your own. Skewed assessments are more likely to fool you in the long run than anyone else, and they are sure to undermine your superior's confidence in you and responsiveness to you.

ROBERT E. LEE ACHIEVED WHAT GENERALS JOHNSTON AND McCLELLAN COULD NOT

What placed Robert E. Lee at the head of the Army of Northern Virginia and what gave his army the resources he required was his open and frank relationship with his president, a relationship that both Johnston and McClellan needed but failed to cultivate with their respective bosses.

After his elevation to army command by Davis on June 1, 1862, Lee formulated a plan of attack and immediately informed Davis of it. Lee wrote Davis on June 5 to detail his military intentions and field conditions, explaining that "our position requires that you should know everything."

From his months of mediating between Johnston and Davis, Lee knew of the president's need to know precisely what his field commanders were doing and planning in the field. "I will keep you informed of everything of importance that transpires," he wrote Davis on August 14. These soothing words were in implicit contrast to what Johnston had offered. "When you do not hear from me," Lee continued, "you may feel sure that I do not think it necessary to trouble you." Lee added that he was ready to receive the president's guidance as well: "I shall feel obliged to you for any directions you may think proper now." During the next seventeen days, Lee wrote another fifteen messages to the president. Davis responded with words that Johnston and McClellan would have savored: "Show me with the necessary precision how I could best promote the success of your operations."

In taking time to characterize and explain his plans in advance, Lee acquired the unwavering support of his commander in chief. Jefferson Davis had sometimes delayed or blocked the command appointments that Johnston sought, but he invariably approved those Lee now recommended, telling him, "I give you the material to be used at your discretion." Johnston had repeatedly called for the concentration of all Confederate manpower in the defense of Richmond, but Davis had equivocated. When Lee now asked for Stonewall Jackson and the 5,000 men he commanded in the Shenandoah Valley, Davis readily delivered them. Indicative of how important such reinforcements were to any Southern counteroffensive, Lee timed his attack to coincide with the arrival of Jackson's force, a vital part of Lee's successful drive against McClellan.

Ever hungry for information, Jefferson Davis and his staff rode to Lee's headquarters on the outskirts of Richmond as the attack unfolded on June 26. They even followed Lee as he went forward at one point to witness his own troops in action. When artillery shells landed near the entourage, Lee asked Davis about his staff: "Who is all this army and what is it doing here?" Davis replied: "It is not my army, General." Lee then responded: "It is certainly not my army, Mr. President, and this is no place for it," whereupon Davis promptly withdrew. Recall that Johnston, in a similar situation with Davis, had insulted Davis by pretending not to see him in order to avoid managing a battle with his superior gazing over his shoulder. Lee deftly achieved the same with no damage to his president's pride or their relationship.

During the counterattack, General Lee was confident of unfettered support from his president. Meanwhile, his opponent was despairing of any further backing from his boss, President Lincoln. McClellan believed that the secretary of war was by then hoping to see him defeated, and that Lincoln had "fallen into the hands of my enemies." McClellan's disregard for his superiors and his disreputable numbers from the field had in fact created just those enemies he now feared at home.

Because Lee had a supportive superior and an opponent hamstrung by the lack of one, he repulsed a Union army threatening to end the war on its terms, achieving what McClellan feared most and what Johnston had most wanted. With the resources and support that came with a far more effective relationship with his president, Lee was able to do what McClellan and Johnston could not.

Robert E. Lee went on to command the Army of Northern Virginia for nearly three more years. In the seven battles with the largest combined losses during the Civil War—Antietam, Chancellorsville, Chickamauga, Gettysburg, Second Manassas, Spotsylvania, and the Wilderness—Union forces were led by no fewer than six different commanders. In contrast, General Lee alone served as the Confederate commander for six of those seven battles, a command-level stability that would have been impossible had Lee been less deft at leading from below.

Lesson in Leading Up

The vital bond between commander and commander in chief, between manager and executive, is an enduring and enriched relationship. For that, an open flow of information and an open display of respect are essential. Without long-term rapport and mutual exchange, you will receive little more from above.

CONCLUSIONS

George McClellan had waged the most deadly single day of fighting of the entire Civil War at the age of thirty-five. Antietam would be his last battle, but his failure to destroy the Confederacy's greatest army there or earlier on the peninsula would resonate on and on. The war that most had thought would be over in months continued for nearly three more years.

Many factors contributed to McClellan's military limitations, not the least of which was a proclivity to prepare for a fight but then to avoid it. In the fall of 1862, as McClellan showed no signs of moving against any Confederate stronghold, Ohio senator Benjamin Wade spoke for many in complaining that "the general is determined his troops shall all be veterans before he permits them to come under fire." Yet whatever McClellan's combat shortcomings, he fatally added to them by showing so little respect for his superiors and sharing so little information with them. In return, President Lincoln and his cabinet gave McClellan far less than he wanted because his intolerable behavior had shattered their initial confidence in him.

Fretful of failing and fearful of blame at a moment when his own actions had made the administration less tolerant of either, McClellan came to see twenty soldiers behind enemy lines for every ten actually present. During the Peninsula Campaign and at Antietam, he thought he was outgunned two to one when in fact the ratio was just the opposite. McClellan's consistent inflation of enemy numbers and deflation of his own further eroded the president's faith that earlier had been placed so completely in him.

Similarly, and although his errors were distinctive, Joseph Johnston caused himself comparable problems with his own commander in chief. His intemperate letters to Jefferson Davis, his impolitic statements about Davis, and his withholding of information from Davis led to the president's conviction that Johnston was not a commander to be trusted, much less wholeheartedly supported. Not surprisingly, Davis both tightened his leash on the general and lessened his support of him, impairing Johnston during his Richmond defense.

In contrast, Robert E. Lee had mastered the art of leading up, and when called to replace Johnston in the middle of the Richmond defense, he turned the tide against the Union. In the summary of Civil War historian Douglas Southall Freeman, General Lee was able to do so in part because he "understood the President thoroughly, and he employed his knowledge to remove misunderstandings and to assure cooperation." With that as an unassailable foundation, Lee achieved what neither Joseph E. Johnston nor George B. McClellan ever could, not only on the peninsula but also at Antietam and beyond.

Blinded by personal prejudice and trapped by overwhelming egos, McClellan and Johnston ultimately did a disservice not just to their own reputations but also to the separate nations that they had pledged their honor to serve. Neither petty nor vain, Lee held to four guiding principles that are as pertinent to corporate warfare today as they were to the war between the states:

1. Keep your superiors well informed of what you have done, what you are doing, and what you plan to do.
2. Regardless of how you feel about your superiors, display a respect for their positions.
3. Avoid petty quarrels with your superiors in which you may be right but from which your reputation will suffer.
4. Estimate your competitive advantage as precisely as possible, not only to avoid the twin dangers of overconfidence and overcautiousness, but also to sustain your superiors' confidence in your capacity for precise analysis.

These are not necessarily natural skills, but they can be learned and mastered. Frequently forcing yourself to inform those above you about what is happening below you will ensure they are knowledgeable about what they are ultimately responsible for. At all times requiring yourself to show a proper respect for those on high to whom you owe it will assure that its absence does not get in the way of far more important matters. Consistently avoiding avoidable disputes with superiors will keep your relationship with them free of the routine irritants that can otherwise cloud judgments and misdirect resources. Always offering precise and unvarnished facts to your superiors will guarantee that you all can calculate with the facts instead of having to take action without them. Above all, a frequent, dependable, and respectful upward conveyance of good information will ensure that you and your boss can both make the best of trying circumstances and ultimately achieve what you both want.

CHAPTER 2

CONVINCING A COMPANY TO TURN INSIDE OUT

DAVID POTTRUCK OF CHARLES SCHWAB & CO. KNEW HIS COMPANY
HAD TO GO DIGITAL, BUT TO GET IT THERE, HE WOULD NEED
TO CONVINCE HIS SUPERIORS TO TRANSFORM AN INDUSTRY LEADER

LEARNING TO LEAD is a lifelong endeavor. As we will see in
this chapter, its upward component can be greatly facili-
tated by a willingness to learn over the years from past mistakes and superiors who are willing to suggest how it's done.

Effective mastery of leading up can also be essential for
moving up, and in this chapter we follow a manager whose
rapid ascent up the company hierarchy confirms that a personal determination to improve one's upward skills can indeed
make them far better. Some individuals begin with a head start,
but everybody can perfect their ability for upward service.

The central figure is David S. Pottruck, whose early education in the art of leading took him to the upper reaches of
corporate management. He became the number two executive for Charles Schwab & Co., Inc., one of the nation's largest
brokerage firms. It was in that role that he came in 1997 to
face the most critical decision of his career: whether he

should he convince his chief executive and company directors to endorse a move of client trading fully onto the Internet. It would be expensive, it would be risky, but it would also bring profound advantages if successful.

Meeting the Internet challenge at Schwab required keen insight and a reasoned capacity to risk much when others doubted the proposed path. In this chapter, we will see that success also depended on a boss ready to be persuaded and a board ready to be moved. But that readiness was not a given. Rather, it was the product of steps that David Pottruck had earlier taken to establish a relationship of confidence with those above. His capacity to transform the Internet threat into a business opportunity, and to do so on a dime before the window closed, depended on groundwork he had been painstakingly—and at times painfully—building for years. We will see as well the importance of working with, rather than bucking, your superiors, getting the facts lined up before seeking to persuade your superiors of a risky venture, and staying the course once they back the venture but it meets resistance along the way.

Though this chapter focuses on Pottruck, keep in mind that executive teams have become far more important in driving company performance than in the past, and Schwab especially placed a premium on teamwork at the top. Many of Pottruck's actions could only be taken because of a culture and camaraderie that founder Charles R. Schwab, Pottruck, and others had long cultivated among the senior management ranks. Yet we concentrate on Pottruck because upward leadership can often best be appreciated by listening to the thinking and watching the moves of single individuals who are called upon to exercise it. In mastering his own upward leadership, he learned from major mistakes along the way, and our account draws on an unusually candid self-assessment that Pottruck has himself provided.

FACING THE INTERNET DECISION

To appreciate the moment of decision that Pottruck would face and the upward leadership he would need, we must go back to the company's founding some two decades earlier. When the U.S. Securities and Exchange Commission terminated fixed brokerage rates in 1975, Charles Schwab seized the opportunity to launch a no-frills alternative to traditional brokerage houses. Named for its founder, Charles Schwab & Co. offered less but charged less. Determined that his company should prove "the most useful and ethical provider of financial services in the world," Charles Schwab paid his brokers a fixed salary rather than a sales commission, ensuring they would focus on client service rather than on generating trades.

Two decades later, Charles Schwab's revolutionary formula had bred a legendary success. Schwab's revenues in 1990 stood at $387 million. By 1995, they had soared to nearly $1.42 billion, and by 1997 to $2.29 billion. Earnings had multiplied more than tenfold over the same seven years, from $17 million to $270 million. Through its thousands of customer service representatives, Schwab bought and sold shares for a million clients, and in the astounding bull market of the 1990s, everyone seemed to benefit.

The rise of the Internet, however, threatened to undo all that, undermining a rich web of relationships painstakingly assembled over years. The Net furnished free and fast access to company information that had long been the province of the brokerage representatives, and it opened a way to acquire stock at a fraction of the time and cost required to dial a broker. To David Pottruck, who had become chief operating officer in 1992, the logical consequences of this onslaught of easy e-brokering seemed obvious: If clients could decide what stock to acquire and execute the trade entirely on their own, never talking to a customer service representative, what value would Schwab representatives still add?

Some clients were already making it clear that they desired nothing else. They had embraced the e-age, and for them, Schwab had built an e-service, charging a mere $29 per trade. Other customers, though, still wanted real dialogue with real people, and it was from them that the serious money came, as much as $80 per transaction. But how long would the company's loyal clients continue to pay $80 when they knew other clients were trading for just $29? Conversely, would the traditional customers remain with the business if Schwab decided to drop the full-service option that had attracted them in the first place? Bare-bones e-trading at a rock-bottom price, or full-service brokerage services at a price that was increasingly uncompetitive? These are the dilemmas that can turn executives prematurely gray.

One solution would be to bundle full-service and online trading into one offering and thereby provide all customers with the combination that many increasingly wanted. But here Pottruck confronted one of the constant laws of the client universe: Customers applaud downward savings and abhor upward pricing. They would eagerly embrace both full and electronic services if they could pay as if they were at the e-end. But doing so would come at a very high price to the company's prosperity, and there could be no going back. Pottruck did the math, and it added up to a colossal loss. Yet if Schwab didn't come down to something near $29 per trade, it faced a massive exodus of Web-savvy customers who knew that pure online superdiscounters like E*Trade and Ameritrade would do it for even less.

POTTRUCK JOINED SCHWAB TO CREATE A REVOLUTION IN THE WAY PEOPLE INVEST

David Pottruck had never planned to reach the upper ranks of one of the world's largest brokerage firms. After earning a college degree in psychology and an M.B.A with a concentration in health care, he joined the U.S. Department of Health, Education, and Welfare in

David Pottruck and Charles Schwab

1972. His father had been a factory worker, his mother a nurse, his household Democratic, and he believed that if he were to become a change maker, the natural venue for making serious waves was public service. Although a Republican was in the White House, the Nixon years were activist ones, and Washington was already looking to reinvent our national health system. HEW assigned Pottruck to work on prepaid health plans and professional service organizations—forerunners of what would later converge in health maintenance organizations. But the glacial pace of change dismayed the would-be transformer. Oh God, he thought, this is not for me. This is too slow! Private enterprise looked far faster.

Given the mutual antipathy between the public and private sectors, Pottruck found few natural pathways across the great divide. He was forced to build his own bridge, and he did so by capitalizing on his government experience: After two years with HEW, Pottruck talked his way into the accounting firm of Arthur Young as a specialist in government affairs. Two years later he abandoned his public persona completely, jumping to Citibank as a division comptroller.

The hiring executive figured that Pottruck's Wharton M.B.A. must have trained him in balance sheets and cash flows, and Pottruck eagerly accepted the financially demanding post to broaden his fiscal experience, since he had arrived with practically none.

The newcomer learned fast, and he learned something else: The best way to master what you are clueless about is to take company responsibility for it. Knowing nothing about promotion and selling, Pottruck moved on to become director of marketing for Citibank's home mortgages and lines of credit. Then, with no technological background either, he readily took the reins of a technology group to preside over fifty full-time programmers. Rather than being held back by his areas of ignorance, Pottruck exploited them to complete his education and drive himself forward.

To other fast-trackers at Citibank, the jobs Pottruck sought looked like backwaters, but for him, they were his own path to the fast track. "I discovered that the glamorous jobs that everybody wanted would always go to the person who had the most qualified résumé," he recalled, "which means you work your way up very incrementally. But if you look for the jobs that are not so glamorous that people don't seem to want, those can be leaps because they don't know where to find the person and they need someone yesterday."

By age thirty, Pottruck knew he had to know still more about finance, technology, planning, sales, marketing, and operations. The reason was plain enough: He needed to master the complete repertoire of general management if he was going to reach his personal goal of running a business by age forty. But that in itself was just an avenue for the forefront action that he really craved. "I liked the thought of being a leader," he recalled. "I like creating, and I like having some degrees of freedom and then being held accountable for my results."

David Pottruck also saw that the financial sands were shifting: Commercial banks and brokerage firms would soon be either competing or merging. To Pottruck, the lesson was clear: He had better master brokerage before it mastered him.

His eye still on the final prize, Pottruck secured a position at one of the great stock-selling machines of the era—the Shearson division of American Express—and plunged into promoting retirement funds for it. At Shearson, Pottruck was the fish who finally found water. Soon, he was selling mortgages, mutual funds, restricted stocks, certificates of deposit, and anything else that seemed financial and that customers wanted. Within a year, Shearson had him running all of its marketing and advertising. He had just turned thirty-five.

Fast-trackers ingratiate, but their eagerness can also irritate. "My peers were not very fond of me," Pottruck candidly recalled. "They were troubled by a guy that flew up that fast. They just saw me as very ambitious." And, he conceded, "I *was* very ambitious."

Pushed by collegial resentment and pulled by a headhunter, in 1984 Pottruck looked at the lead marketing position for the then less well-known upstart brokerage and banking firm, Charles Schwab & Co. Compared to Citibank and American Express, Schwab was small potatoes: At the time, client assets were a mere $5 billion, the company employed only 800, and on revenue of $100 million, it had managed to extract a minuscule profit of $1 million.

What's more, Schwab was based in San Francisco, far from the financial ground zero of New York City. But Pottruck found the company culture irresistible. "We're on a mission to save people from full-commission brokers ripping them off," explained the human resources executive who pitched the job. "We're here to help them achieve their financial goals and dreams, and if you want to be part of that, great!" It was music to the ears of a man who had always ached for a mission, first in the slow-moving public service, now in the fast-acting private sector. "Everybody talked about customers," remembered Pottruck, but here was a company that really served them. "I loved it. It was joining a revolution. Schwab *was* a revolution." He eagerly enlisted in the cause as its executive vice president for marketing.

Lesson in Leading Up

Learning all the ropes and finding the right venue are essential to the exercise of upward leadership, and you are the only one who can direct the learning and do the finding.

MASTERING LEADERSHIP THE HARD WAY: LEARNING THE LESSONS FROM FAILURE

Larry Stupski was president of Schwab when David Pottruck arrived, and in him Pottruck found both a tough competitor and a personal mentor. Stupski's ideas on what the company should do—where to locate a call center or how to position a product—frequently clashed with Pottruck's. But Stupski was also a counselor who quickly saw the need to rewire this newly hired marketing executive whose style so often got in the way of his own potential for success.

Pottruck came with an outsize presence—he had been a heavy-weight wrestler and football linebacker in college—and a powerful personality. He tackled challenges with confidence and doggedness, he recalled, and expressed opinions with unquestionable firmness. Pottruck acted, then asked, and his management style could be over-whelming if not outright intimidating. Marketing is the art of persuasion, and he was the company's premier practitioner for the world outside. On the inside, however, his bulldozing often won the battle but lost the war, imposing decisions but alienating those who had to live with them.

For General George Patton, such a leadership style had proven effective, but Schwab's employees had signed up to fight a battle for business, not internal warfare. Just three years Pottruck's elder, Larry Stupski could see the damage, and he said so at performance appraisal time. "You're too persuasive," he informed Pottruck. "Your colleagues don't trust you." "Why?" a stunned Pottruck asked.

"Because you're so persuasive," Stupski answered. "Aren't I supposed to be persuasive?" Stupski: "Well, yes and no. When you come in to present an idea, you present all the reasons why that idea should happen and none of the reasons why it shouldn't happen. You never present both sides. You sell. You come in and you say, 'Here's what we have to do, it's life and death, and here's why we have to do it.' There's no room for any dialogue, Dave. That's completely disrespectful. You have an agenda and you give no one a chance to own the decision with you, and there's no way to argue with you because they don't have enough facts to argue, and you're such a powerful guy that it's overwhelming." Stupski concluded, Pottruck recalled, with blunt words: "It's not fun for anyone to work with a guy like that."

The message registered. Yes, Pottruck realized, he's absolutely right. And the lesson was learned. "He taught me to be more thoughtful and less impetuous," Pottruck said. "He taught me the importance of planning, even when I knew instinctively what I wanted to do and there was no doubt I was going to do it." Stupski forced Pottruck to ask the right questions before his potent personality imposed a solution: "Are we on course or off course? Are we getting where we want to go? What's the impact?" At first, Pottruck rankled at the coaching and the self-discipline. "I rebelled. I hated it. I wanted to move and I wanted to move now." But in time he came to recognize the value of "bringing everybody on board and getting everybody lined up."

What mentoring couldn't solve, though, was the competition between the two men—or their profound difference in styles. Pottruck was a producer, and by 1989, his stellar results had rocketed him up the Schwab chart until only one person stood between him and his goal of achieving unfettered leadership of a company by age forty. That person was Larry Stupski.

Stupski had helped Pottruck polish some of his roughest edges, but as president of Schwab's operating company, Pottruck was still instinctive and impulsive, he recalled. As president of Schwab's parent company, Stupski was more cautious and controlling. Caught in a venue that couldn't contain both of them, the two fell to fighting over policy after policy until the personality clash brought CEO Charles Schwab himself into the fray. Schwab demoted Pottruck, stripping him of his "chief operating" title for the brokerage business. Stupski was already chief operating officer for the parent, and having two COOs only confused the outside world.

Pottruck recalled that he seethed over the humiliating downgrade, and he hit back by challenging Stupski at every turn, most visibly at the company's top management meetings. Weekly gatherings of the management committee included the chief financial officer, chief administrative officer, and other top executives. What Stupski proposed, Pottruck tended to oppose. As the two bosses repeatedly squabbled, their associates sat mutely aside, wondering with whom they should align themselves. Predictably, Pottruck remembered, the majority sided most often with the more senior of the two, and Pottruck increasingly found himself the odd person out.

"You guys are not in touch with the revenue side," he would respond as his colleagues lined up behind Stupski's proposals. "I'm the one voice on the revenue side." True enough, in that the brokerage business was Schwab's biggest producer, but Pottruck still had much to learn about nuance, he remembered, and his was not the premier voice in executive circles in any event. The more he pushed, the more Stupski and his supporters resisted.

Because he had once run the budgeting process for a division of Citicorp, Pottruck pressed Stupski and the chief financial officer to devise a new budgeting process for Schwab. The current system, he argued, was broken, but his proposed solution only accelerated the turf war. Stupski wanted to fashion the budget centrally around revenue growth, using key ratios to control expenses; Pottruck preferred a more bottoms-up approach, allowing each cost center to come up with its own request for the coming year. The two chiefs openly battled at a top management meeting, an awkward and embarrassing moment for Stupski, the CFO, and Pottruck. The budget process ended up a mess.

Why, Pottruck came to ask himself, was he once again alienating those around himself, his boss and mentor foremost? Demoralized and contemplating resignation, he arranged a private dinner with Stupski to see what might lie ahead. "This is not much fun," Stupski began bluntly. With the incessant conflict, he added, "I'm not enjoying going to work anymore." Pottruck confided that he felt much the same way. Stupski then delivered an even blunter message: "This company is not big enough for the two of us, Dave. One of us is probably going to have to leave." Since Stupski was his superior and nowhere near retirement, Pottruck knew who Stupski had in mind.

Boston-based Fidelity Investments, a Schwab arch rival, had long sought to wean Pottruck away, and now he was receptive. Fidelity prepared to make a written offer that the company believed was irresistible. Pottruck and Fidelity had reached the point of negotiating the cost of moving his former wife to Boston with him when Charles Schwab suddenly entered the picture. He called both Pottruck and Stupski into his office and told them that he had heard they were battling. "I need both of you," he said, "and I need both of you to work together. Larry, I want you to let Dave run his part of the company, and Dave, I want you to recognize that Larry runs the firm. I am holding both of you responsible for making sure your teamwork is effective. I need you both to be successful."

Pottruck knew he loved working at Schwab, and it dawned on him that if Stupski was willing to work with him, which he said he was, Pottruck had to be willing to work with Stupski, which he had not been. Determined to transcend his own self-defeating conduct, he recalled, Pottruck soon marched into his boss's office with a new message.

"Look," Pottruck began, "I realize that I have argued with you in public, so our meetings end up being a two-way dialogue with seven onlookers. It simply polarizes our team. So I'd like to make the following deal with you. I won't ever, ever argue with you. I might ask a question, but I will never argue with you and try to persuade a different point of view in our meetings. But I would like the opportunity to discuss these kinds of issues with you privately. My acquiescence or lack of debate shouldn't be viewed necessarily always as agreement because I will quickly let you know when I don't agree. But we have to have one person running the company, and you're the one person, not me."

All open conflict would end, Pottruck declared. "I will hold my tongue and I will wait until we meet one-on-one; then I will tell you what my issues are. But in public I will always support you." Pottruck sealed the deal with an offer of what was to follow: "My job is to make you the most successful executive I can. I'm here to make you look good." Stupski cautiously smoked the peace pipe. The two of them agreed to move beyond the past, and Pottruck terminated the Fidelity flirtation.

In the months that followed, Pottruck discovered to his surprise that Stupski valued his ideas and proposals. Until then, Stupski had admired his subordinate's intellectual capacity but hardly his personal demeanor, and in reacting to the latter Stupski tended to resist whatever came from his rival. Now, with Pottruck questioning his boss only in private, his opposing ideas came as constructive criticism rather than as defiance of authority. Under this new framework, he recalled, the long-simmering issue of reforming the budget process was instantly solved. Stupski told Pottruck to work it out with the chief financial officer, and within weeks they had a plan. When the CFO announced his new scheme at the next management committee, saying, "Here's what I think we should do," the top executives immediately embraced it.

Pottruck appreciated that he had undergone a profound transformation. "I was really a pain in the ass to get along with," he recollected. "I thought I had all the answers and it made people not like working with me"—his superiors first among them. But neither Larry

Stupski nor Charles Schwab gave up on him, and he learned from them how to work with them.

Lesson in Leading Up

Battling your boss is a losing proposition—especially if it becomes a public spectacle. Learning to question your boss behind closed doors, by contrast, will get your ideas into the room and keep power struggles out of it. Private criticism coupled with public support will ensure that your voice is heard, your superior finally gets it, and the company is better for it.

TAKING OVER THE HELM AND STEERING TOWARD A NEW BUSINESS MODEL

In 1992, Larry Stupski suffered a heart attack. Fortunately, he recovered to good health, but he decided to retire, and that paved the way for Pottruck to become president of the parent company. The upward move came close to fulfilling Pottruck's goal of running a business, but he was sorry to lose the newfound mentoring relationship that he had established with Stupski, whom he had come to greatly admire and respect.

Now second in command to Charles Schwab himself, Pottruck served as the corporation's chief operating officer, and as a sign of his new stature, he was asked to join the governing board. Chairman and chief executive Charles Schwab still handled many of the firm's relations with customers and its directors, but Pottruck became the inside power. He was not CEO, he was over forty, but he was as tangibly close to his professional goal as he could possibly be without actually reaching it. Like so many aspiring managers who had arrived, Pottruck could savor the achievement. But unlike so many managers in eras past, the timing would permit little opportunity for enjoying the office.

The Internet age was arriving, and it came with a speed and vengeance that few had anticipated and none could ignore. In 1993, Schwab introduced StreetSmart, a Windows-based, modem-connected method for trading electronically. Meanwhile, others were opening the Web itself to electronic commerce. Jim Clark created Netscape in 1994, Jeff Bezos launched Amazon.com the same year, and Pierre Omidyar founded eBay in 1995. By 1995, only one in twenty of Schwab's customers had migrated to StreetSmart, yet David Pottruck believed that the online channel would become far more important, given the rise of the Web and the birth of a new generation of discount firms that saw cyberspace as a means for even deeper discounts. To get the company into the game, Schwab created a separate division, e.Schwab, to fashion an online system that would charge no more than $39.95 per trade, about half of what the company charged its full-service customers at the time.

The company launched e.Schwab in January 1996, offering customers the chance to buy or sell up to 1,000 shares of any stock for the new discounted price, though the lower price came with diminished service. Customers could not place more than a single call for advice per month, nor could they walk into a Schwab branch office to discuss their personal holdings or financial future. They could e-mail questions, but more than one real discussion a month was ruled out. Despite its personal limitations, e.Schwab proved an instant success. Company forecasts had been that 25,000 customers would sign up by the end of the year; in fact, that number had registered by the end of the second week.

But there was no time to sit back and savor victory. In February, just a month after e.Schwab's start, upstart E*Trade announced Internet trading at $14.95 for up to 5,000 shares. The competitive fray was becoming a frenzy, and Pottruck knew he had to take a rapid-fire set of countermeasures. In March, Schwab introduced Web-based Internet trading at $39.95; in May, it extended its Internet channel to all full-service customers, giving them a 10% discount off their standard trading expense of $80; in July, it cut the e.Schwab rate to $29.95 per trade; and in December, it increased the full-service discount from 10 to 20%, bringing the standard transaction rate down to $64.

Schwab's swift moves appeared to bring resounding success. By the end of 1997, its online accounts totaled 1.2 million, up from 300,000 two years earlier, and the assets in those accounts reached $81 billion, up from $23 billion. Moreover, customers who migrated from full-service to e.Schwab typically doubled their trading activity, nearly making up the difference between the old $64 trade price and the new one of $29.95.

From a start-up just two decades earlier, Schwab had become a premier player in the brokerage industry: It had attracted over $350 billion in customer accounts and had placed more than 12,000 people on its payroll. Not surprisingly, the capital market applauded. By the end of December 1997, Schwab's total market capitalization had reached $11 billion, double its value of just a year earlier. And it had become number one in online accounts, outpacing by far its nearest rivals, DLJ Direct and E*Trade.

But that very success worried David Pottruck, and it was a worry that he knew he would soon have to take up with his boss and his

Number of Accounts Among Online Brokerage Firms, December 1997

Brokerage Company	Number of Accounts
Charles Schwab	1,200,000
DLJ Direct	390,000
E*Trade	260,000
Waterhouse Securities	162,000
Ameritrade	147,000
Datek Securities	55,000

board. The bull run was drawing legions of new investors into the market, and the Web was giving them the tools for informed and inexpensive trading. So attractive were the commercial prospects that new online competitors were coming into existence almost weekly. Fifteen companies offered Internet trading at the start of 1997, but by the end of the year sixty did. Schwab still ruled the roost, but for how long Pottruck could not be sure, especially as the Internet frenzy drove prices lower and lower. In June, established competitor DLJ Direct cut its trading commissions to $20, and in October newcomer Ameritrade announced a fee of $8.

While Schwab was threatened from below by the superdiscounters, the blue-chip behemoth above still displayed scant interest in the Internet. Merrill Lynch had 14,000 brokers and 600 analysts deployed in 1997 to service its vast clientele. The typical Merrill client was fifty-two years of age and had placed $200,000 under management; the average E*Trade customer was only thirty-nine and had invested a mere $25,000. The customer universe appeared to be dividing between those who never used the Web and those who wanted nothing but the Web, and Merrill treasured the former and disregarded the latter. The Merrill vice chairman responsible for retail brokerage services, John L. (Launny) Steffens, summed up the perceptions of many in the business: "The do-it-yourself model of investing, centered on Internet trading, should be regarded as a serious threat to Americans' financial lives."

Words of warning, but that was not what David Pottruck was hearing from his own customer service people. From them he was learning that while the Internet was transforming Americans' financial lives, most investors wanted the new without jettisoning the old. Yes, there was a divide, but it had been created by the providers, not the consumers. Internet clients repeated time and again the same complaint: "I love what you do, but why do you prevent me from going into your branch office and getting service from a person?" Full-service clients had their complaints as well, and their grumbling reached Pottruck, too: "I love the multichanneled offering. I can go into the branch, I can call you on the phone, I can trade online, but why do I have to pay so much more money than at e.Schwab or all of the other online brokerage firms?" Each side was complaining about the privileges of the other: We like the price, why don't we get the service? We like the service, why don't we get the price?

To bridge the gap, customers were retaining their full-service accounts but moving most of their assets into e.Schwab accounts. That way, they could maintain access to Schwab customer service representatives but pay far less for most of their trading.

To some, the consumer world seemed split between pre-dot-com and only-dot-com, but to Pottruck it looked as if that was largely an artifact of what the business world was offering them. Schwab had a well-established tradition of putting customers first, and it was evident that their first wishes were not being met. If so, Pottruck appreciated that he would have to invent a solution, and it would have to be one that both Charles Schwab and the company's directors would find compelling.

David Pottruck reached the conclusion in the spring of 1997 that the two-tiered system had to go, even though he was personally responsible for building much of it. In its place he would create a single full-service offering with Internet trading. The pricing would be key. Since Schwab believed it offered better service and more products than its online competitors like DLJ Direct and E*Trade, he could charge more per trade. But he could not charge too much more, since the Net was imposing a price discipline on retail brokerage like never before. Pottruck tentatively concluded that the only viable price point in the market would have to be $29.95 per trade.

Pottruck turned to his boss, Charles Schwab, for guidance. Schwab was already on board with the concept of the Internet itself. He had early appreciated the power of the Web, and it was he who had pushed the company in 1995 to move onto it. The founder and chief executive was known to have an exceptional feel for market trends and a great sense for customer pulse, and as Pottruck explained his thinking, Schwab immediately affirmed his interest in the proposed move. But he also posed hard questions that had to be answered before making any such move: How much would it cost, how would it affect the organization, and how soon could benefits be expected? Charles Schwab was willing to take large risks and place big bets when the odds were known, and he pressed Pottruck to nail them down now.

Pottruck instructed his staff to detail the impact of slashing the full-service commission of $80 and providing full service to everybody at $29.95 per trade, including the 1.2 million e.Schwab customers. The strategists came back with a shocking conclusion. If the firm allowed the more than 3 million full-service account holders currently paying $80 per trade—or $64 if they went online to do it—to migrate to $29.95, it would depress the company's revenue in 1998 by $125 million and its earning by $100 million, more than a fifth of its projected pretax profits. Wall Street would jeer because it loved consistency and predictability, and it would sink Schwab's share price with a vengeance. That, in turn, could destroy morale since many employees held huge numbers of shares, collectively owning about 40% of the firm's stock. Moreover, the expected crimp in cash flow would make it difficult to promote the new service at a moment when competitors were aggressively ramping up their marketing. It could, Pottruck said, be a "devastating" constraint at a time when Fidelity, E*Trade, and others were spending massively on their online offerings.

What's more, the proposed course of action—a single, full-service offering with an Internet channel at $29.95 per trade—would appear to be irreversible once it was instituted. Downward pricing pressures would make it virtually impossible to restore the $80 rate. Even to Pottruck, it was not clear if Schwab could retain its low-end customers against the siren call of the still cheaper Internet competitors, but it would have no choice but to do so. The economies of an immense customer base were essential if the company was to sell its services profitably at a commission rate of $29.95. Unlike its low-end competitors who offered nothing but online trading, Schwab still had to feed and care for a vast information and advisory apparatus.

David Pottruck knew it was a near bet-the-company decision, and he appreciated that his superiors would have to buy into it. He understood the compelling arguments he was hearing against a single-tier model, but he also knew that Web technologies were changing the market so fast that any delay in the decision could be tantamount to no change. The risks of going to the single discounted rate with full service were enormous; but so too were the risks of not doing so. It's never going to be cheaper to take the hit than now, he thought. Is there any reason why postponing this shift is going to make life easier? He finally concluded that the company simply had to make the move: It would offer full-service brokerage with a $29.95 online trading commission.

In Pottruck's view, anybody could run the company for steady growth. Where he could add real value was to engineer a breakthrough before competitors could even imagine it, and for this he had to be ready to bear the momentary pain for a far more enduring gain. "Our choice was to slowly erode our position or to make this bold move and hope that the positive effects would kick in reasonably quickly." He had avoided the error of shooting from the hip but also the equally pernicious error of analysis paralysis.

Pottruck was sure of the new service, but less sure if its financial returns would come fast enough to avert a death spiral. He had little doubt that this was perhaps the most important decision of his entire career, and one that would require vigorous CEO and board support. Yet despite the mammoth stakes, he knew he was best positioned to make the call.

Lesson in Leading Up

Risk taking is a defining element of any leadership, and calculated management of it is essential. To succeed as a risk taker on behalf of those
above you, decisions need to be arrived at both quickly and accurately,
and despite the grave uncertainties and large stakes that may be
involved, if they are yours to take, it is essential for you to make them
rather than kick them upstairs.

PERSUADING THE BOSS AND THE BOARD TO REINVENT THE BUSINESS

With the decision firm in his mind, David Pottruck set out next to
bring everybody along, including the governing board. He began
with the management committee. "Okay, does anyone in this room
think that what we're doing now with these two different services,
e.Schwab and Charles Schwab, will be successful for the next ten
years?" No. "Do you think this structure is easily understandable to
customers?" No. "Is it in the customer's best interest, and do you
think it will be able to withstand change in the next ten years?" No
again, and he knew that he'd cleared the first hurdle.

Pottruck then turned to his superior, whose name was in the
logo and whose immense fortune was on the line. Pottruck detailed
to Charles Schwab the financial implications of a single, full-service
model at $29.95 per trade, and cautioned of the downside. "I'm con-
vinced that this is the right thing to do, but I've got to warn you that
the benefits will not be immediate—they will accrue over time. In
the short term, the pricing impact will be immediate and it will go
straight to the bottom line. It's going to get ugly here fast. In fact,
1998 as a whole may be a pretty painful year."

Charles Schwab asked for more of the rationale, and Pottruck
elaborated: "You do this because you're going to have less attrition,

more consolidation of accounts, more power in the marketplace." Moreover, "it's easy to measure the revenue given up by lowering price. But there's an undeniable benefit of lowering price in the sense that when you improve the value to the consumer, good things happen. They do more business with you. They're happier. They tell their friends. They consolidate relationships under one roof. It becomes more efficient." And finally, "At the end of the day you do this because you think it's also going to make you more money." He ended with a straightforward plea to his boss: "I need your support and the board's support on this."

Following several weeks of frequent discussion, Charles Schwab endorsed the detailed plan that he had earlier approved in principle. "It's the right thing to do," he told Pottruck. "We'll take whatever pain comes." Charles Schwab had always insisted on putting customer service first, and Pottruck had made that his main principle; Charles Schwab had consistently stressed careful analysis, and Pottruck had worked the numbers; Charles Schwab had delegated much to those he trusted, and Pottruck had already earned his confidence.

The private pain could be enormous, and nowhere more so than at the very top. Charles Schwab himself owned 21% of the company, more than $2 billion, and a plummeting stock price would cost him dearly. A drop of 18%, for instance, would remove some $400 million from his family assets, and it could well be more. If the road proved rocky, the boss would pay.

The next stop for David Pottruck was the company directors, without whose wholehearted approval it would be foolhardy to proceed. Here, too, Larry Stupski had provided invaluable coaching. He had advised Pottruck to become personally acquainted with the board, whose members included such heavyweights as Donald G. Fisher, CEO of The Gap, and Anthony M. Frank, former postmaster general and CEO of First Nationwide Bank.

In his earlier meetings with the governing board, Pottruck had fallen into his familiar mode. His cases were persuasive, he recalled, but the lasting impression was one of an executive selling. Listen and don't push so hard, he remembered Stupski urging, and Pottruck forced himself to say less, hear better, and explain more. He came to appreciate that the board wanted a balanced, calm, and wise executive.

Pottruck first brought the plan to a regular board meeting in September 1997. "Do we want to remain a leader or do we want to harvest the company?" he asked. The answer, he went on, was unavoidable. "If we want to remain a leader, we have no choice." Some directors wondered why any choice was required, since the year was already proving to be the best in company history. After-tax profits were approaching $270 million, and Pottruck was now proposing to cut it by a third or more. "Why do we have to do this?" questioned one. Others wondered if alternatives had been thoroughly studied. Still others asked if the downside could be weathered. Pottruck's confident response: "It will be fine, but it will take some time," possibly a year and a half or more.

Meeting little real resistance from a sobered but accepting board, Pottruck reassured the directors that his employees were up to the task. "Our company is magnificent under crisis," he reminded the directors. As revenues and profits were squeezed, employees would rise to the occasion. "They will respond brilliantly; they always have," he suggested, "and we know we can count on them to do so now."

Pottruck turned the boardroom discussion to implementation. After reporting the expected $100 million earnings shortfall, he asked, "Do you have any suggestions about how we mitigate the impact, or advice on how we pull this off?" He brought his directors into not only a review of the plan but also how to make it work, and few upward steps were more important than this for building confidence and commitment above.

The board's main concern was to get it right with the Street.

Explain privately to the major stockholders and key analysts why the new service and pricing made sense, they urged; give investors the compelling rationale that no press release could ever convey. The board meeting that had begun at 8:30 A.M. ended by noon, and the die was cast. The directors closed ranks around what would be the company's most fateful decision of the era.

Selling the plan internally was Pottruck's next test, no small challenge, since management bonuses were driven by revenue growth and profit margins, and the forecasts for both under his plan were fearsome. Pottruck had already decided that there could be no bonus adjustments, which meant that for most of his managers the new model would result in a bleak year, especially for top executives, whose compensation was leveraged around company performance. For some, the personal loss in annual bonus could run as much as $500,000 or more. A sinking share price would also put thousands of stock options under water, transforming substantial personal wealth into worthless paper assets. Without energetic support within the company, though, Pottruck knew his one-tier plan would be dead in the water.

Pottruck organized an event for the top 130 executives at Schwab. The goal was to convert their growing anxieties into affirmative energies, hoping for a ripple effect through the firm's 12,000 employees. He appreciated that in an enterprise as large as his, events that powerfully symbolized and persuasively communicated his message would be essential for spreading the gospel. If he could electrify the top tier, then they could carry it forth.

At the gathering in October 1997, Pottruck explained what they were going to have to do, why they would need to do it, and how it would best be done. He candidly described the losses that should be anticipated. He then bused the executives to the San Francisco end of the Golden Gate Bridge, one of the most appealing vistas in the world. He knew that he had to do more than talk the case for a new beginning; he would have to illustrate it, and there were few more dramatic metaphors for achieving what looked unachievable than the building of the Golden Gate Bridge.

An historian explained how the construction of the bridge demanded fresh technology and big vision: The new bridge would require the tallest towers, longest cables, and largest underwater foundations ever constructed. Its foundations would have to be laid in the often violent currents of the ocean below, long considered an impossible feat. Almost as daunting, it would have to be funded at a time when the Great Depression was upon the land. But the advocates had it right, the historian concluded. Despite pitched opposition from the ferry companies and doubts about both financing and technology, they pressed ahead, and when the bridge opened in 1937, more than two decades after its conception, it transformed the Bay area.

Now, it was Pottruck's turn to deliver the metaphor: If Schwab could engineer its own new offering despite the swirling and sometimes opposing currents, he said, it would achieve what many thought could never be done but what consumers ultimately deserved. To do so, it would have to harness little-tested technologies to serve customers and drive down costs. "To be successful," Pottruck contended, "we have to reinvent our company around the Internet" and "embrace the Internet in the core of everything we do." As trading prices plummeted, Schwab's costs would have to as well, and since the Internet was forcing the first, it would have to achieve the latter, too.

Led by Pottruck, the 130 executives walked the bridge, "crossing the chasm" of the two-mile-wide Golden Gate Strait as a prelude to crossing the Internet gulf ahead. Symbols count, especially when anxieties are high, and Pottruck knew he had to powerfully represent the idea of leaving the old model behind in favor of the new. "This was not a new product or a new website," Pottruck explained. "This was the beginning of the reinvention of our company."

David Pottruck had identified his cause, researched the cause, and then persuasively presented the cause to the powers that be. For

Crossing the Chasm

that he required the facts and a foundation of confidence that he had long been building with the boss and board. Charles Schwab and the directors gave the cause their vigorous support, and now it was up to him to galvanize the forces that would make it happen.

Lesson in Leading Up

The first step in winning the support of the boss and board is to make sure your plan is thoroughly analyzed and fully developed. The second is to communicate carefully why the proposed course of action is necessary for the organization and how it can be accomplished with the minimum upheaval to process and employees.

TRANSFORMING THE BUSINESS MODEL INTO A NEW REALITY

With executive approval for the new business model in hand, David Pottruck set out to make it happen. He worried that the threat of a thunderous migration of customers to the impersonal world of online trading would demoralize his brokers, but he made a case for the opposite: His intention was to brand the company around "clicks and mortar," creating a win-win combination of the best technology and the best people. "We're not an online brokerage firm," he would say, but rather a "new model of a full-service firm." He underscored the message with money: Service representatives would be compensated by the assets they brought to the company and customer migration to the Net, not customer trading. The branches had never been busier, he asserted, and they will become even more so. Work quality will only improve as the Internet eliminates tedious tasks and frees up time to service clients.

On January 15, 1998, Schwab announced it was offering all customers Internet trading for $29.95 per trade for up to 1,000 shares (and 3¢ per share for more). Equally, it was extending all services to all customers—branch walk-ins, telephone consultation, personal advice. Instead of dedicated brokers, Schwab customers would have a team of investment specialists for counsel on investment ideas, large trades, or variable annuities, as well as access to a vast array of Web-based information, ranging from earnings forecasts and analysts' reports to insider trades and expert commentary. Customers, however, would not receive recommendations for buying or selling a particular issue, a defining service of the traditional full-service brokerages.

Schwab trained all of its 4,000 branch and telephone consultants to use and explain the new Web services. It added customer migration to the Internet to their incentive pay. To underscore its message, the company removed public counters from branch offices and installed desks in their place.

The team approach also meant that customers, especially high-volume ones, had many sentries looking for market glitches, not just one. One active customer tells of being called by a Schwab team representative on a day when the value of an option in which he had taken a large position would plummet from $15 to $2 by closing time.

Alerted, the client was able to sell early in the day at $12, averting a loss of at least $75,000. "It's like having eight pairs of eyes working for me," he offered.

In launching the single-tier service, David Pottruck knew he needed a swift ramping up of trading volume to make up for the diminished revenue on each transaction. He also realized that if he vigorously promoted the new service, he risked focusing too much attention on the trading price of $29.95. Schwab had always stood for fine service as well as good price. An aggressive marketing campaign that stressed the eye-popping low price might win new clients at the cost of permanently tarnishing the hard-won service brand. Moreover, the superdiscounters were already offering trades at still lower prices, albeit without much service, and a riveting focus on price could cause unwanted comparisons.

Hampered by such marketing constraints, Pottruck soon saw that he would have to stretch time still further so that the new service could be ramped up in stages: first for the most active traders, then for others in wave after wave.

FROM SLOWDOWN TO ACCELERATION

Pottruck had always been a sound sleeper, but now his nights proved wakeful. Through January and February he worried about whether the long-term volume increase would come fast enough to avert the short-term loss in morale. "The question was, how fast would those benefits happen and how far down would the stock price go?" A prolonged decline in an era of prosperity could create an irreversible human exodus. If the stock price goes down, are employees going to bail? he anxiously wondered, and if employees bail, where are we going to find the talent we need to grow the company? It was a time, he said, when "dot-com competitors are trying to pick off our employ-

ees, the stocks are down, the options are under water." He worried
that he might simply be giving away revenue, profit, and share price.
With vigorous support from the chairman and the board, he never
feared for his job, but he did fear for his reputation. Pottruck didn't
want to be remembered as the guy who "ran the Schwab ship into the
coral reef." The next several months, he knew, would tell the story.
But what would the story be?

The first quarter's final results were hardly encouraging. Schwab
was indeed cannibalizing its full-service, high-priced accounts. The
expected migration was under way—not massively at first, but
enough to seriously depress revenues. During the final quarter of
1997, Schwab received an average of $63 per client trade; during the
first three months of 1998, that figure had dropped to $57. Quarterly
revenues had been growing at 6.5% per quarter in 1997; now they
declined 3%. Pretax income had been rising by 8% per quarter in
1997; now it dropped by 16%. Wall Street did not like the trends it
saw: Schwab's existing customers were taking the bait, but they were
not trading significantly more now that they had the Internet at their
fingertips. On the day Schwab announced first-quarter earnings,
investors drilled its share price down by 9%. Shortly before Pottruck
had introduced the new service, Schwab's stock had hit $41 per
share; by the end of June, it had sunk to $28, a 32% decline at the
same time Merrill Lynch had enjoyed a 29% increase.

Yet David Pottruck's and Charles Schwab's expectation that the
world was moving to the Web proved remarkably prescient. During
the first five months of 1998, the floodgates opened. Fresh clients
started half a million new accounts and placed $40 billion in them.
By the end of the year, the number of Schwab customers with online
accounts hit 2.2 million, up from 1.2 million a year earlier. Account
assets reached $174 billion, up from $81 billion twelve months
before. The number of daily trades had increased by nearly half, aver-
aging 115,300 per day during the final quarter of 1998. The average
commission rate continued to fall—dropping to $53 per trade—but

surging volume was finally making up for declining price. Attrition of existing clients was way down, acquisition of new clients way up.

Fortunately, the company had the staffing to accommodate the deluge. Despite Pottruck's gravest anxieties, no key people abandoned ship, even as their own fortunes sagged and many of their options proved worthless. Schwab finished the year with a 20% growth in revenue and 29% rise in net income. It had not even taken a year for the model to work. The turning point came within nine months, and analysts and investors loved the comeback. During the last quarter of 1998, Schwab stock more than doubled, handing the company one of the great symbolic prizes of the era. At a moment when Merrill Lynch still had three times the assets under management and a brand almost synonymous with Wall Street, Schwab edged it out in total value. Merrill's market cap stood at $25.4 billion, Schwab's at $25.5 billion.

Far from jeopardizing the company's future, David Pottruck had caught one of the biggest consumer waves of all time. In 1997, investors made 18% of their trades online, but in 1998 the proportion rose to 28%, and a year later to 42%. Being there at the beginning gave Schwab an asset base and customer reputation in online trading equal to none. The anticipated savings from electronic trading came to pass as well, with the firm estimating that its increased reliance on the Internet had cut annual operating costs by $100 million.

Other momentous changes were still to come, a reminder that evolution is continuous in an always evolving economy. Schwab acquired U.S. Trust Corporation for $2.7 billion, a foray into asset planning and management for the wealthy (the net worth of its clients averaged $7 million), and spent $488 million to buy CyberCorp, an online brokerage that offers specialized screening tools to active traders. But Schwab remained the premier online broker, far outpacing its nearest rivals. By early 1999, it held a third of the Internet trading market, equal to the share of the next three competitors combined.

THE FRUITS OF LEADING UP

David Pottruck's strategic foresight and preemptive action earned him what he had long wanted: In early 1998, Charles Schwab asked Pottruck to serve with him as co-chief executive. Pottruck had failed to reach the corporate apex by age forty, but he was still under fifty, and this pinnacle offered him wealth and power that few firms could match. Several months later, Intel CEO Andy Grove invited David Pottruck to join his governing board, one of the citadels of American technology. Pottruck, Grove said, brought "experience at the cutting edge of electronic commerce." In early 1999, a *Fortune* writer opined that "right now, Pottruck has Schwab eating everybody's lunch." At the end of the year, mutual-fund tracker Morningstar named Pottruck and Charles Schwab as CEOs of the year, and the *Industry Standard* named him the most effective financial-services executive.

By the end of 2000, Pottruck copresided over a company where more than 25,000 people went to work every day. Schwab operated more than 360 branch offices across the country and offered customers a choice of 1,900 mutual funds. Clients had placed $900 billion in 7.5 million accounts, and more than half of them were online. On one day alone in January 2000, Schwab drew 96 million site visitors who executed more than 14 million transactions.

When Schwab went public in 1987, it was valued at $450 million; in 2000 it was worth $36 billion. Once again, the end-of-the-year honors came pouring in. *Information Week* named Pottruck and Schwab's CIO Dawn Lepore "Chiefs of the Year," and *Business Week* selected Pottruck and Charles Schwab for its annual list of the top twenty-five managers.

Even Merrill Lynch was forced to pay homage. Launny Steffens, the manager of Merrill's retail brokerage operation, was still deriding the Internet in mid-1998, but by early 1999 he was conceding that "online trading in and of itself is not bad," adding that in fact, "it is a refreshing wind in our industry and one we welcome and embrace."

By the end of the year, Merrill, too, had introduced online trading at a rate of $29.95 for up to 1,000 shares, provided the customer maintained an account balance of $20,000, though it did not include personal access to a broker. In late 2000, Merrill even acquired the domain name of "merillynchschwab.com." Created by a cyber-squatter, Merrill lawyers seized it for "safekeeping."

Morgan Stanley Dean Witter (later renamed Morgan Stanley), the other towering full-service brokerage, joined ranks in 1999, introducing online trading at the same $29.95 rate to hit directly back at Schwab. In two short years, Schwab's pioneering combination of electronic technology and personal services had become the dominant model. Instead of a discount upstart nipping at the heels of the great names of Wall Street, Schwab's clicks-and-mortar method had out-foxed the Street, reversing the pecking order. Superior value was now less in telling customers where to invest and more in coaching and enabling them to make fast and smart choices of their own, and where superior value went, market value followed. "We're not going to become another Merrill Lynch or Dean Witter," David Pottruck had vowed when he launched his one-tier plan, but at least in one sense, the Street made a liar of him.

Schwab "is no longer David, but now Goliath," offered Steve Galbraith, a stock analyst at Sanford C. Bernstein. It had "moved from predator to prey." Used to being the brash upstart, Pottruck suddenly found himself with a back to cover and a whole new set of challenges to cope with. "You don't want to slap the face of a giant," Pottruck warned, and Merrill Lynch is "a giant of our industry." The "the last thing I wanted to do was kick sand in their face. I wanted to just fly under the radar screen as much as we could. Well, when we passed their market cap, this got everyone's attention, and the days of flying under their radar screen were over." Ironically, it also induced some employees to depart. During the terrifying early months of 1998, Pottruck had feared that declining income and worthless options would drive his best people out the door. He never anticipated that come the halcyon days of 1999, some of them would opt for early retirement after Schwab's soaring stock had made them millionaires.

David Pottruck transformed the company, and he could not have done so without the vigorous backing of those to whom he reported. Their backing was earned, not given, and for that he drew upon his years of learning to lead up, not just down. To make the case, he built a factually based and persuasively argued model, one with high risks but also high payoffs if successful. In the early months of implementation, it appeared that the risks were heading in the wrong direction, but by the end of the year the rewards had become spectacular. Pottruck's perseverance proved critical: if he had not taken the case to his boss, to his board, and to his employees, and if he had not pressed ahead when the first quarter's results proved daunting, one of the preeminent transformations of the Internet era might never have occurred.

Lesson in Leading Up

Persistence often pays, but it requires an extra willingness to stay a rocky path when you have persuaded those above and below you to embrace the course.

LOOKING THE LEADER

David Pottruck brought a hulking frame, a broken nose, and a lilting voice to Schwab, hardly what a Hollywood casting director might have sought for a corporate executive. The point was driven home when Pottruck's daughter brought a friend home. When the friend said that his mother and Pottruck had been high school classmates, the Schwab co-CEO called to renew an old acquaintance. His former classmate said she had seen his name in the newspaper, and she asked about his "father-in-law," who ran the firm. Pottruck answered that he was actually not related to Charles Schwab, but his old acquaintance wasn't giving up. "So you're divorced, right?" she asked. Pottruck replied that Charles Schwab was not even his *former* father-in-law. "Well then," she said, "how *did* you get that job?"

The exchange was a useful reminder that in performance-driven companies what matters most is how you think and what you do, not who you know or the image you present to the world. For David Pottruck, it had been a long road to wisdom. Throughout his relentless charge up the middle ranks, he recalled, he had neither looked like the leader nor, too often, acted like a leader. But even though he learned leading up the hard way, one knock on the ego after another, he had more than caught on. "You have to be able to move the group without overwhelming the group," he now advised, and that of course included not just subordinates and coequals but also the chairman and the board.

Had Pottruck not mastered the skills of upward leadership along the way, he would most likely have left the firm for an uncertain future elsewhere. Despite the starting deficits, he did learn to lead with the president and then with the CEO and board, and his mastery of the art of leading up has served him well. "I used to be a John Wayne leader," said Pottruck. "I wanted to be the first guy up the hill." Now Pottruck deems himself "leading from the middle," ensuring that those below and above are all working "to take the hill together." David Pottruck's account is a reminder that the capacities for working with those above must be learned, and they can often best be learned when your individual determination to work more effectively with your superiors is complemented by your superior's willingness to work with you. Upward leadership is both learned and taught, and had Charles Schwab and Larry Stupski not coached Pottruck in the ways of leading, he might never have served them as well as he did, nor would the company have served its customers and shareholders as well as it did.

CHAPTER 3

BEGGING YOUR BOSS TO UNTIE YOUR HANDS

U.N. COMMANDER ROMÉO DALLAIRE WARNED OF THE COMING GENOCIDE IN RWANDA, BUT NOBODY LISTENED

STATE-SPONSORED GENOCIDE in Cambodia, Germany, and Rwanda are among the great catastrophes of the twentieth century. Thousands of public officials and their agents sent hundreds of thousands of citizens to their death, often in the most barbaric fashions imaginable. Their killing machines rolled through cities and across countrysides in merciless elimination of entire communities.

In the case of Rwanda, one man had stood in the way, seeing what was coming before it occurred, begging for assistance before it was too late. He beseeched his superiors to give him troops, arms, and a mandate to prevent the killing. Once it began, he repeatedly pleaded for assistance to stop it before it engulfed the country. He was in a position to prevent one of the defining disasters of our age, and later to stop it before it ran its full course, yet nobody above him listened to his pleas. Had his superiors heeded his calls, had he caught their attention, they might have prevented the decimation of a nation.

Rarely does upward leadership have as much potential for making a difference as in Rwanda in 1994. Seldom has one person's failed effort to convince his superiors of a pending disaster had such terrible consequences. Rarely has the failure of those above to accept an upward effort from below had more catastrophic results.

A single date in the Rwandan conflict captured much of what might have been done by the way of upward leadership. On January 11, 1994, less than three months after arriving in Rwanda as force commander of the United Nations peacekeeping operation, forty-seven-year-old Canadian brigadier general Roméo A. Dallaire cabled his superiors at U.N. headquarters in New York.

Labeled "most immediate," Dallaire's message was addressed to Major General Maurice Baril, a fellow Canadian and friend who was serving as military advisor to Boutros Boutros-Ghali, the secretary-general of the U.N. In it, Dallaire explained that he had made contact with a Rwandan informant involved at the highest level in training Hutu militias, paramilitary groups apparently organized with the blessings of the Hutu-dominated government of President Juvénal Habyarimana.

The subject of the meeting, Dallaire explained in the cable, had been the Tutsis, Rwanda's beleaguered ethnic minority, and the news was deeply chilling. Dallaire reported that his informant had "been ordered to register all Tutsi in Kigali. He suspects it is for their extermination. [The] example he gave was that in twenty minutes his personnel could kill up to 1,000 Tutsi." The dire news didn't stop there, Dallaire continued. The same informant had told him that the Hutu-extremist militias had a plan to force the withdrawal of Belgian troops, who made up a significant part of the U.N. peacekeeping force. Belgian soldiers would be provoked to use force, and then would be killed, prompting Belgium to withdraw the rest of its soldiers. Finally, Dallaire said that the informant could lead him to an important arms cache—if the U.N. agreed to protect the informant and his family.

Dallaire recommended that the informant be given protection and evacuated. Furthermore, he planned to have his U.N. forces raid the arms dump within the next thirty-six hours, pending approval from headquarters. His cable was, in short, a call to action, ending with the simple French phrases: "*Peux ce que veux. Allons-y*," roughly "Where there is a will there's a way. Let's get to it." Tragically for all, at the top of the U.N. there was a way but no will. Nor was Dallaire able to instill that will from below.

The reply from U.N. headquarters told Dallaire, in essence, to sit on the information. Less than three months later, the world would watch in horror as events unfolded almost precisely as Dallaire had detailed in his cable. On April 6, Rwanda's president, Juvénal Habyarimana, was mysteriously assassinated. The next day, Hutu extremists tortured and executed ten Belgian peacekeepers, prompting a Belgian withdrawal and further weakening an already limited U.N. force.

The Hutu extremists then expanded the killing far beyond the scale predicted: In just 100 days, an estimated 800,000 Rwandans, both Tutsis and moderate Hutus, were murdered. Although their technology was rudimentary—machetes were the main device—the killers achieved an extermination rate five times greater than at Nazi concentration camps. By June, more than four-fifths of the Tutsi population residing in Rwanda had been massacred.

Roméo Dallaire had anticipated and forewarned against the human catastrophe that swept Rwanda. With more support from the United Nations, and more troops from its member nations, he might have averted an African holocaust that ranks as one of the great calamities of the era. For Dallaire and his U.N. superiors, the haunting question in the years since has been whether he could have more forcefully delivered his message to New York and whether New York could have been better prepared to hear what he said. If ever there was a time to heed your subordinates, it was on January 11, 1994. As this chapter suggests, had Dallaire's efforts at upward leadership succeeded, had his dire prophecy been heard, Rwandan history might have lurched down a very different path, and 800,000 of its people today might instead be going to school, tending their herds, or simply savoring a sunset.

CYCLES OF VIOLENCE AND THE RISE OF HUTU POWER

The world into which Roméo Dallaire and his troops of the United Nations Assistance Mission for Rwanda (UNAMIR) were sent in late 1993 by the U.N. Security Council was a human cauldron with roots stretching back to Belgium and the colonial era.

Roméo Dallaire

Rwanda had long been the home of Hutus, which make up 90% of the population, and Tutsis, a 10% minority. Although both populations were commonly termed "ethnic" groups, they spoke the same language, lived in the same villages, and married one another.

After replacing Germany as Rwanda's colonial master following World War I, Belgium chose to rule through the proven method of dividing and conquering. Drawing on the pseudoscientific theories of social Darwinism, Belgian colonials asserted that Tutsis were of superior racial stock, since they tended to be taller and lighter skinned; they deemed Hutus more "primitive." By 1934, Belgium was requiring that every Rwandan carry an ethnic identity card, converting a faint distinction into a defining boundary, and Belgium then transformed that distinction into caste. When Hutu peasants were forced to perform work for the colonial administration, Tutsis supervised them.

Communal violence was in the making, but a recorded outbreak did not come until Rwanda's first democratic election in 1959. When a group of Tutsi activists attacked and severely beat a Hutu political leader, Hutus responded with violence, and more than 300 people, most of them Tutsis, were killed. The first elected government of Rwanda quickly became a Hutu dictatorship, and when a group of Tutsi rebels invaded Rwanda in 1963, the government authorized Hutu "self-defense" units to clear out the "counterrevolutionaries," which meant not only the rebels but also many Tutsi villagers. Ultimately, the so-called self-defense units would kill some 10,000 Tutsis and send hundreds of thousands more into exile, deepening a rift that would eventually explode in 1994.

Each side organized in the years that followed to impose its own solution. Exiled Tutsis in Uganda established the Rwandan Patriotic Front (RPF). Their resolution: Overthrow the Hutu dictatorship of president Juvénal Habyarimana, who had ruled since 1973; repatriate the Tutsi refugees; and establish a nonethnic democracy. Hutu leaders, by contrast, turned to ethnic extremism, officially regarding

Tutsis as foreigners and tracing all of the country's ills, from abject poverty to civil strife, to Tutsi émigrés. Their approach: Cleanse Rwanda of all Tutsis.

At the center of the Hutu extremists in the early 1990s was no less than the president's wife, Agathe Habyarimana. She and her associates, "Le Clan de Madame," established a nominally independent newspaper, *Kangura*—"Wake It Up"—to champion "Hutu Power." Its "Hutu Ten Commandments," published in 1990, promoted the concept of ethnic supremacy. All Tutsis were dishonest and unworthy of business dealings, declared one commandment. Hutus must control all aspects of Rwandan society, asserted another. The eighth commandment was particularly relevant to the events that would follow: "Hutus must stop having mercy on Tutsis." To implement the decree, Hutu extremists with government backing began organizing groups of young men into militias, sometimes drawing on local soccer clubs. Trained, disciplined, and armed, the militias came to be known as "Interahamwe," for "those who attack together."

The ruling party's vice president, Leon Mugesera, carried the ideology to its extreme. In a November 1992 speech that was widely disseminated, he called on Hutus to force all Tutsis out of Rwanda. If they did not leave quickly, Mugesera demanded, Hutus should "destroy" them. Why, he asked, were Hutus waiting to eliminate these "cockroaches"?

With this ideology in place and an informal network of militant groups organized in collaboration with a disciplined civil service, the Hutu extremists effectively established the rudiments of an apparatus for state-directed genocide. To field-test and refine it, they carried their anti-Tutsi and antidemocratic doctrine of Hutu Power across the countryside during the early 1990s. In "consciousness-raising meetings," local officials would instruct Hutu peasants that they had a community service to perform: They must "clear the bush," rooting out all who support the Tutsi rebels. Radio stations and newspaper articles urged them on, and militia units, often assisted by the police and army, would spearhead the attacks. The instigation worked: Organized Tutsi massacres erupted in October 1990, January and February 1991, March and August 1992, January and March 1993, and February 1994.

DALLAIRE REPORTED FOREWARNINGS OF GENOCIDE TO THE UNITED NATIONS

The United Nations's 1948 convention on genocide called upon all signatories to do whatever was required to prevent it, but in 1993 the U.N. was preoccupied with brokering a settlement between the warring Rwandan Patriotic Front and the government of Rwanda, and its efforts were finally paying off. Meeting in the city of Arusha in the neighboring country of Tanzania, the two parties reached an accord in August 1993, agreeing to form a transitional government leading to new elections, to merge the rebel and government armies into a single force, and to open the borders to the estimated 1 million Tutsi refugees who had fled the country. The U.N. agreed to send an international force to supervise the agreement.

The Arusha accords called for a U.N. force that would "neutralize" armed militias, protect returning refugees, and guarantee security. The U.N. Security Council, however, reduced the mission's mandate to one of supervision, limiting the peacekeepers to monitoring the cease-fire, assisting mine clearance, tracking refugee repatriation, and facilitating humanitarian relief.

Before the U.N. dispatched its peacekeepers to Rwanda, it required a reconnaissance mission for assessing the situation. The colonial legacy meant that the mission would have to be led by a French speaker but not a Belgian national. Nor would a French national be appropriate, since France had been arming the Habyarimana government against the Rwandan Patriotic Front. U.N.

secretary-general Boutros Boutros-Ghali turned to bilingual brigadier general Roméo Dallaire of Canada to lead the mission in August 1993.

Dallaire returned from his reconnaissance with a proposal for 4,500 military personnel, but Boutros-Ghali reduced the force to 2,500, and the Security Council finally approved 2,548. Boutros-Ghali appointed Dallaire to command the peacekeeping mission, and as a parallel measure, he appointed Jacques-Roger Booh Booh, a former foreign minister of Cameroon, to serve as the U.N.'s political representative in Rwanda.

A disciplined commander and outgoing personality, Roméo Dallaire quickly inserted himself into the rich cultural and social life of the Rwandan capital of Kigali, getting to know the nation's political leaders and taking the measure of its ethnic divisions, but his mission was hamstrung by his superiors from the start, and not just by the radical force reduction imposed on him. Dallaire had requested $200 million to run the twenty-one-month operation, but the U.N. cut it to $54 million. He had asked for a full battalion of Belgian soldiers to serve as a rapid reaction force, but he received just half a complement. Nearly a thousand soldiers arrived from Bangladesh— 40% of his assigned troop strength—but they proved undertrained, underequipped, and underled. Twenty-two armored personnel carriers had been promised, but only eight arrived, and of those, just five proved roadworthy. His military mission was without a legal advisor, humanitarian expert, or human rights officer. Dallaire had planned to act fast but was delayed by paperwork: He often devoted nearly three-quarters of his workday to unraveling logistical nightmares. Instead of protecting the peace, he said, "I spent most of my time fighting the heavy mechanical U.N. system with all its stupidity." Troops arrived without transport or weapons, vehicles arrived without operating manuals, and even flashlights arrived without batteries. "Seeing to the most immediate needs," he said, "stopped us from seeing what was reserved for us in the future."

Dallaire asked U.N. headquarters in New York for power to intervene if his forces witnessed "ethnically or politically motivated criminal acts," but his superiors never replied. Though Hutu activists were secretly plotting such acts, his superiors prohibited him from collecting military intelligence about the planning. Dallaire would later say: "We were blind and deaf in the field."

Even without an intelligence apparatus, it was clear soon after Dallaire's arrival in Kigali on October 23, 1993, that a crisis was in the making. More than 60 people died in political violence in November and December. Across Rwanda's border to the south, a Tutsi junta had assassinated Burundi's first democratically elected president, a Hutu named Melchior Ndadaye, adding grist to apocalyptic warnings within Rwanda about its own "Tutsi threat." More than 50,000 were killed in Burundi, and 300,000 refugees flooded across the border into southern Rwanda. From a group purporting to be senior army officers, Dallaire received an unsigned letter on December 3 warning of a "Machiavellian plan" by President Habyarimana to undermine the Arusha accords by massacring Tutsis and assassinating politicians.

But for Dallaire, the most chilling portents came from a well-placed informant. A former presidential security guard and now a senior trainer of the Hutu militias, the informant described genocidal intentions and a murderous scheme to force the withdrawal of the 440 Belgian troops in the UNAMIR forces. The informant, whose code name was Jean-Pierre, disclosed that he and others had trained 1,700 Interahamwe (the Hutu extremist militias) in three-week programs at Rwandan army camps on the use of explosives and weapons. Now these men, he said, had been divided into teams of forty and scattered around Kigali. The informant coldly estimated they were prepared to kill at the rate of 1,000 Tutsis every twenty minutes, and he himself had been part of an effort under way for the past three months to register all Tutsis living in Kigali.

"Jean-Pierre" also predicted that at the next attempt to install the transitional government, already delayed several times by President

Habyarimana, opposition politicians would be assassinated as they entered Parliament, and if Belgian peacekeepers reacted, they too would be killed to provoke their withdrawal. He had originally been training his militias to fight the Rwandan Patriotic Front, but now that his movement was turning on Tutsi civilians, "Jean-Pierre" wanted out, and he asked Dallaire for protection for himself and his family.

On January 11, 1994, Dallaire sent the startling information to his superiors in a cable entitled "Request for Protection for Informant" and reported that he planned to seize the arms caches—hundreds of AK-47s stashed throughout the city—that "Jean-Pierre" had disclosed. Dallaire's news, though, had far from the desired effect. Iqbal Riza was serving as assistant secretary-general under Kofi Annan, undersecretary-general for the U.N.'s Department of Peacekeeping Operations, and his immediate reaction on reading the cable was "Not another Somalia!"

Just four months earlier, on October 3, 1993, U.S. Army Rangers had set out on a ninety-minute mission to capture a warlord in Mogadishu, the Somalian capital. Instead, they became entrapped in a firefight that lasted seventeen hours and left them with eighty-four wounded and eighteen dead. This action, in turn, had been provoked

Iqbal Riza

by an earlier U.N. effort to inspect weapons that had led to the death of twenty-three Pakistani peacekeepers—the same sort of weapons seizure that Dallaire was proposing now. The American-led U.N. force of 28,000 had been sent "to establish a secure environment for humanitarian relief operations in Somalia," but it had blundered into far more than it had bargained for. A subsequent appraisal of the mission by a special commission of the U.N. had drawn a critical policy lesson: The "U.N. should refrain from undertaking further peace enforcement actions within the internal conflicts of States." The gradual widening of a peacekeeping mission—"mandate creep"—had lured the U.N. into the Somalia disaster, and it should not be allowed to happen again. Now, the so-called Somalia effect was casting its shadow over Rwanda, even as all the elements of genocide were reaching critical mass.

Responding to Dallaire on Annan's behalf, Riza not only denied the request for an arms raid and but also tightened New York's control: "No reconnaissance or other action, including response to request for protection, should be taken by UNAMIR until clear guidance is received from Headquarters," he cabled. Peace, not force, he reminded Dallaire, was the U.N.'s mandate: The "overriding consideration is the need to avoid entering into a course of action that might lead to the use of force and unanticipated repercussions." The U.N.'s self-defined role was not to prevent ethnic violence; it was to assist the government in preventing it.

Later that same day, Dallaire reported back he had met with the prime minister-designate who affirmed "total, repeat total, confidence in the veracity and true ambitions of the informant." Kofi Annan replied quickly—still on January 11, 1994—that Dallaire was not to provide protection to the informant, and he instructed Dallaire to inform President Habyarimana of what the informant had disclosed and to insist that arms caches and arms training be shut down immediately since they violated the Arusha accords.

Dallaire followed his superior's directive, and President Habyarimana reassured the U.N. commander that he knew nothing of the

Kofi Annan

militia activities and pledged that he would look into them. More important than what Dallaire had said, though, was what he had left unsaid: Even though the U.N. mission knew of the militia's plan—and even though the armed militia itself was a clear violation of the Arusha accords—New York had apparently decided to take no enforcement action other than jawboning. Annan's cable to Dallaire had said as much: The "overriding consideration is the need to avoid entering into a course of action that might lead to the use of force and unanticipated repercussions." For Kigali's Hutu extremists, Dallaire's January 11 cable to his superiors and his subsequent visit to President Habyarimana amounted to a call to action: not to disband or to turn back, but to hasten their distribution of arms.

In early February, Jacques-Roger Booh Booh, the special representative of the U.N. for Rwanda, warned Kofi Annan that President Habyarimana had never followed up on Dallaire's information about the Hutu militias and that security was worsening. "We are receiving more and more reliable and confirmed information that the armed militias of the parties are stockpiling and may possibly be preparing to distribute arms to their supporters," he wrote. Moreover, the country was rocked by "increasingly violent demonstrations, nightly grenade attacks, assassination attempts, [and] political and ethnic killings." Given the growing risk of "outright attacks on UNAMIR installations and personnel," the cable to New York again asked that Dallaire be authorized to raid the arms caches, now not only to protect the peace process but also to ensure the mission's own safety.

Kigali was fast becoming a vast market for weapons of a primitive but highly effective nature. The main distributor of agricultural hand tools in East Africa, Chillington Tool Company, reported more machetes sold in February 1994 than the entire year before. Kofi Annan, however, reiterated that an arms roundup was the province of the Rwandan government and not the U.N. force.

At the same time, the United Nations was pressing hard for the two parties to implement the terms of the Arusha agreement—the purpose for which the U.N. had come to Rwanda in the first place. President Habyarimana had repeatedly delayed the key provision— the formation of a power-sharing transition government—even though Secretary-General Boutros-Ghali warned him time and again that he must implement the accords. The president was, in fact, boxed in: His extremist supporters saw any power-sharing government as political suicide, since the Tutsis would again dominate, just as they had in colonial days, and then retaliate for years of massacre. Still, under intense international pressure, Habyarimana set February 22 as the start of the transitional government.

On February 17, less than a week before the new government was to be launched, Dallaire informed New York that he had learned of a plot to kill opposition politicians. Although protecting moderate politicians was not explicit in the U.N. mandate, Dallaire deemed their safety essential for the peace process, and he posted U.N. guards at the homes of Prime Minister Agathe Uwilingiyimana, a moderate Hutu politician; the prime minister-designate for the transitional government, Faustin Twagiramungu; and the president of the Constitutional Court, Joseph Kavaruganda.

February 21 and 22 saw the assassination of two Hutu politicians from opposite ends of the spectrum. Rioting erupted, leaving thirty-five dead in Kigali and the outlying city of Butare.

Extremist media stoked the fiames. One February headline declared, "The Tutsi Race Could Be Extinguished." *Kangura* was forecasting warfare within a month, asking rhetorically "Who Will Survive the March War?" and even predicting that President Habyarimana himself would be assassinated by other Hutus. The broadcast voice of the Hutu militants established in mid-1993—Radio Mille Collines ("radio of a thousand hills")—repeatedly played Simon Bikindi's "I Hate These Hutus," a pop song about the treachery of moderate Hutus who failed to embrace Hutu supremacy. "I hate these Hutus," he sang, "these de-Hutuized Hutus."

On February 23, Dallaire told headquarters that information on weapons caches and death lists was now circulating widely in Kigali. "Time does seem to be running out for political discussions, as any spark on the security side could have catastrophic consequences," he wrote. On the same day, the U.N. representative in Rwanda for refugees warned New York of "a bloodbath of unparalleled proportions" unless stability was soon restored.

On March 22, Dallaire's troop strength had finally reached 2,539 from twenty-four countries, built around a core of 440 Belgians, 843 Ghanaians, and 942 Bangladeshis. Soon thereafter, in the first days of April, Radio Mille Collines told listeners that "something very big" was going to happen in the next few days.

The Importance of Redundancy and Credibility for Upward Communication

Roméo Dallaire appreciated that something very big was indeed coming. He was at ground zero of the militant Hutu preparation for mass murder. He had been informed of arms caches and death lists, he had heard hate broadcasts and witnessed Tutsi terror, and he believed that his own worst fears about the future were more than likely to be realized. He understood better than his superiors at the United Nations, probably better than anybody in the world, what was about to explode, where the killing would start, and how it would unfold. He was uniquely positioned to inform his superiors at the U.N. what they should know and how they should respond. Yet all of his efforts to do just that had fallen so far on deaf ears.

It is useful to ask what other forms of communication might have helped Dallaire deliver a compelling message to his superiors. His cables had not worked and had even backfired, as Kofi Annan and Iqbal Riza in response had limited his latitude, not expanded his mandate. Might he have repeated his warnings in recurrent cables, asked his own government to appeal, lobbied key ambassadors in Kigali, and worked with international reporters? He had tried all of these avenues, but none proved productive. Might he have returned to New York to deliver the message personally—or threatened to resign? We cannot be sure if these or any other measures would have worked, yet if the circumstance is extraordinary and your superiors are still not appreciating it, resorting to every feasible form of communication may be obligatory. Dallaire himself would have never resigned, but the costs of failing to deliver a message up the organization are sometimes too high not to try all other avenues.

Lesson in Leading Up

If your superiors need to appreciate a grave threat to the institution but are simply not getting it, you may find it essential to transcend the normal channels of communication to drive home a message that they must come to appreciate.

Interpreting Dallaire's explosive January 11 cable also would have been easier if authorities in New York had been more familiar with the Canadian's manner and his style of expression. Without a professional intelligence apparatus like the U.S. Central Intelligence Agency, the U.N. had no choice except to rely upon its field commanders, yet in this case it had not developed the means for properly discerning what its representative in the field was saying. Boutros-Ghali had never met Dallaire, and the secretary-general's operation had not even developed a capacity for managing sensitive information from Dallaire. Dallaire had taken to using the telephone rather than writing, since the contents of his early cables to headquarters had sometimes found their way into the press and beyond.

"We made all that information available daily and the international community kept watching," Dallaire would later complain, but information without context makes its effective use in policy formulation difficult. If during the months leading up to April 6, 1994, Dallaire had established a clearer understanding of how he communicated and how he used words, his message of alarm might have gotten through to his superiors. Consumed with the aftermath of Somalia and a burgeoning crisis in Bosnia, the superiors made little effort to discern the message themselves.

Dallaire would have been better served, too, if the communication channel between Kigali and the U.N. offices in New York had been less muddled. He sent his January 11 cable only to Maurice Baril, the Canadian general serving as military advisor at U.N. headquarters in New York. Given the explosive information—plans were afoot to exterminate the Tutsis and massacre Belgian soldiers—the challenge was to ensure that its contents registered with everybody at the top. Secretary-General Boutros-Ghali later reported that he did not read the cable until many days later, nor did the U.N. Security Council ever see it. In explaining why the cable did not receive attention from the top, Iqbal Riza would subsequently explain: "We get hyperbole in many reports" and the threat of violence against Tutsis "was nothing new."

The quality of the information coming from Dallaire may have been at issue. Dallaire himself had been concerned about the possi-

bility of having received disinformation from the well-placed informant, and U.N. officers in New York may have shared the same concern. But Dallaire quickly reconfirmed the credibility of the source
in a conversation with the prime minister-designate, who served as
his intermediary with the informant, and Dallaire conveyed that
reconfirmation to his U.N. bosses. Moreover, when Dallaire sent a
Senegalese peacekeeper with the informant to confirm the arms
caches, the informant showed him a store of 137 Kalashnikov assault
rifles in the headquarters of one of the extremist parties close to the
president, as well as other stockpiles scattered across Kigali.

Though Maurice Baril, the military advisor to the secretary-
general, knew Dallaire well from their years together in the Canadian Army, other ranking U.N. officials knew Dallaire less well, and
they may have presumed that he was prone to overstatement. How
else to explain Iqbal Riza's rationale for downplaying the January 11
message?

While U.N. officers in New York certainly can be faulted for their
inaction on what proved credible and unexaggerated information—
and a later U.N. assessment is savage on this point, terming this headquarters oversight "incomprehensible"—Dallaire's challenge was to
somehow overcome headquarters' skepticism and misunderstand-
ing, as well as its distraction in managing seventeen other missions
with 89,000 peacekeepers in the field at the time. He tried repeating
the message, sending it to the secretary-general, conveying it indi-
rectly to the White House, intensifying the tone, delivering it in person, conveying it through third parties and media reports. Even the
huge risk of flying Boutros Boutros-Ghali, Kofi Annan, and Iqbal Riza
into Kigali to see the ground for themselves might well have been
worth the peril. All were steps that might have helped more effectively deliver what in retrospect proved to be a potentially history-
altering message.

Members of the Security Council requested information directly
from Dallaire, but Riza and Boutros-Ghali made neither it nor him

available to council members. Had Dallaire appreciated this disconnect at the top, a risky but understandable course would have been
to appeal to the council members directly, perhaps through the
Canadian government and its ambassador at the U.N., possibly
through other national ambassadors in Kigali, or perhaps even in
person. Doing so would have violated U.N. protocol and threatened
his career, but those costs would have paled against the benefits had
his entreaties succeeded.

Lesson in Leading Up

For achieving an organization's mission, communicating evolving conditions upward is essential, especially when they threaten what an organization stands for. The more credible the messenger, the more powerful
the message, and the more redundant its delivery, the more likely the
word is to get through. Close familiarity with the messenger's style and
manner also can help superiors distinguish false information from the
true understandings they need.

ASSASSINATION OF THE RWANDAN PRESIDENT TRIGGERS THE ANTICIPATED GENOCIDE

For six months, Roméo Dallaire had recurrently warned his superiors of the arming of Hutu militias, the circulating death lists, the plotting against the U.N. His efforts to persuade those above of the need
to intervene before it was too late had not worked, and now a deadly
event would make it too late to prevent a killing spree that would
engulf the nation. On the eve of April 6, even Dallaire's most night-
marish predictions became far worse realities.

President Habyarimana and Burundi president Cyprien Ntarya-
mira were returning together from a regional summit hosted in Dar
es Salaam by the Tanzanian president. There, under pressure from

his neighbors, the Rwandan president had recommitted himself to implementation of the Arusha accords. But at 8:23 P.M., as his private jet was about to land at the Kigali airport, it was hit by two antiaircraft missiles. The jet crashed into the garden of the presidential palace, killing all on board. Though it was not known who had fired the missiles (nor have the perpetrators ever been identified), within hours the Hutu extremists had initiated their premeditated program of Tutsi extermination.

The militant Hutu radio station Mille Collines immediately blamed Habyarimana's death on a rebel attack and urged listeners to take revenge. Within forty-five minutes of the crash, the Hutu Interahamwe militia groups as well as Hutu army units and the presidential guard erected roadblocks throughout Kigali. When Roméo Dallaire learned of the president's death at 9:00 P.M., his first reaction was, "This is going to be a catastrophe." By 9:30 he had his force on red alert, and at 10:10 he called U.N. assistant secretary-General Iqbal Riza to brief him on the unfolding events.

Later that evening, Dallaire and his commander for Kigali, Colonel Luc Marchal of Belgium, joined a meeting of Rwandan military officers convened as a "crisis committee." Théoneste Bagosora, a retired colonel who served as chief administrator for the Rwandan Ministry of Defense, asserted control of the gathering and argued that this group would have to run the decapitated government. Dallaire knew Bagosora to be part of the Hutu president's wife's group, Le Clan de Madame, and he urged instead that Prime Minister Agathe Uwilingiyimana should be the proper national successor, and that she should immediately address the nation by radio. Bagosora refused a broadcast or even to accept the prime minister's legitimate claim, while insisting that he was not staging a coup.

After the meeting, Dallaire instructed Colonel Marchal to take control of Radio Rwanda, secure the site of the plane crash, and bolster his guards around the prime minister's home and prepare to escort her to the national radio station. But Kigali had already slipped too far into chaos. U.N. forces sent to Radio Rwanda were stopped by roadblocks. Soldiers sent to the plane crash were taken into militia custody at the airport. Those sent to the prime minister's home required three hours to navigate what normally would have taken fifteen minutes, through a capital city quickly becoming a cauldron of hate and revenge. By now, the militant Hutu Radio Mille Collines was telling listeners that the president's airplane had been brought down by the Rwandan Patriotic Front and U.N. forces.

The ten Belgian commandos dispatched by Luc Marchal successfully cordoned off the prime minister's home by 6:00 A.M. on April 7. But at 6:44 A.M., Belgian unit commander Lieutenant Thierry Lotin radioed his senior officer, Lieutenant Colonel Joe Dewez, to say that they were being fired upon, and at 6:55 Lotin reported that they were surrounded by twenty Rwandan soldiers demanding their arms. Dewez ordered Lotin not to surrender, but after Lotin reported that four of the Belgian soldiers had already been disarmed, Dewez ordered the rest to follow suit if necessary. They did, and the Rwandan troops forced the disarmed Belgian soldiers onto a minibus for a short drive to what they claimed would be U.N. quarters. Instead they were driven to Camp Kigali—an army base with more than a thousand soldiers. As the Belgians were ushered in with their hands in the air, an army intelligence officer told soldiers at the camp entrance that these were the Belgians who had brought down the president's airplane. Borrowing a Motorola radio from a Togolese military observer, Lotin told Dewez at 9:06 A.M., "They are going to lynch us."

Sensing that the U.N. troops could no longer protect her, Prime Minister Agathe Uwilingiyimana fled over the wall of her garden into a neighboring compound that housed a United Nations volunteer program, and she sent her husband and five children—the youngest age three—to hide in a separate building nearby.

Dallaire called Riza at U.N. headquarters in New York again at 9:20 A.M. to say that he might have to use force to protect the prime minister, but Riza told Dallaire that his troops could fire only if fired upon and could not be used to protect a third party. Soon after

10:00 A.M. the issue became moot: Rwandan soldiers entered the U.N. compound and dragged Prime Minister Uwilingiyimana out of her hiding place. A member of the national police shot her point-blank in the head. She was left half-naked, and her husband was assassinated as well. A U.N. employee miraculously spirited the five children away to a hiding place from which they would secretly board a French convoy out of the country on May 1.

This time, Dallaire cabled New York: "Give me the means and I can do more." But his superiors had consistently refused to give him any more, or even allow him to do more with what he already had, and no more assistance would be forthcoming now than after any of his prior appeals. Dallaire had repeatedly contended that state-backed genocide was coming, and now that his direst warnings were being confirmed by the harshest of realities, he would still receive no new resources. Even with the murder of the prime minister and the Belgian soldiers, his superiors remained utterly unresponsive.

Lesson in Leading Up

When a subordinate's fearful forecast becomes terrible fact, it is surely past time to heed the warning and seek a solution, but it is never too late to act on appeals from those below when your actions can still make the difference. Upward leadership requires a two-way street: your subordinates must render their best counsel, and you must seek to appreciate and then make good use of it.

DALLAIRE REACHES A MOMENT
OF DECISION

Learning only that his captured troops had been taken to Camp Kigali, Dallaire headed to another gathering of the top military officers and public officials scheduled for late morning. On his way to the meeting, he was delayed by numerous roadblocks before presidential guards finally ordered him out of his jeep. Escorted on foot by Rwandan soldiers, he walked to the home of the prime minister. It was by then deserted, but a passing Rwandan army officer offered to drive Dallaire to his meeting. Dallaire asked him to drive past Camp Kigali on the way, and peering in as they passed, he "caught a brief glimpse of what I thought were a couple of soldiers in Belgian uniforms on the ground at the Camp." Dallaire asked the Rwandan officer to stop, but the officer said that the men inside were out of control and sped on by. "I did not know whether they were dead or injured," Dallaire recalled, but "I remember the shock of realizing that we had now taken casualties."

That moment of shock also became Roméo Dallaire's moment of decision. "A commander must be able to make certain decisions in a nanosecond," he said. "This was one of those moments. Before we arrived at the school for the meeting, another thirty seconds' drive away, I had decided on my course of action."

Dallaire's immediate course of action included attending the planned meeting and not mounting an armed attempt to rescue any surviving Belgian soldiers, an effort he deemed suicidal. Nearly half his force consisted of a Bangladeshi contingent that had essentially stopped taking orders, barricading itself in a sports stadium and even refusing entry to other U.N. soldiers who sought refuge from an attacking mob. It was not clear if Dallaire had effective command at that moment over any forces, but whatever he did command would be far outgunned by the soldiers massing at the army base. Beyond the day's crisis, Dallaire's resolve for the short run was to prevent a resumption of fighting by the Rwandan Patriotic Front, and for the longer run to do what must be done with the resources available, whatever the instructions from New York.

At a subsequent meeting with Colonel Bagosora, now the de facto head of the Rwandan military junta, Dallaire demanded that he himself be allowed to enter the camp to find the Belgians, but

Bagosora explained it would be unsafe. The soldiers, he said, were rioting because the Belgians had fired on Rwandan soldiers and because of rumors that they were also responsible for the death of President Habyarimana. Bagosora promised Dallaire that he would secure the release of the Belgian troops.

As militias opened their arms caches and spread across the streets of Kigali, Roméo Dallaire and his Kigali commander, Luc Marchal, received dozens of calls from terrified residents seeking protection. Tutsi leader Landoald Ndasingwa reached Marchal by phone, and as he began to beg for help, Marchal could hear the sound of gunfire and a grenade. Ndasingwa told him that fifteen presidential guards were about to attack his home. Then he said, "It's too late" and the phone line went dead. Ndasingwa and his Canadian wife, mother, and two children were later found executed on their living room floor. Despite the presence of U.N. guards at his home, Constitutional Court president Joseph Kavaruganda would not survive the day either. Prime Minister-Designate Faustin Twagiramungu, also with U.N. protection, survived because an American businessman hid him in a broom closet next door, though he was soon thereafter rescued by U.N. troops.

Evidence later suggested that some of the Belgian soldiers held captive at Camp Kigali, though severely beaten, had remained alive until the afternoon, even seizing weapons and fighting back for as long as six hours. But at 10:30 P.M., Dallaire found the bodies of the Belgian peacekeepers stacked on the grounds of the courtyard of a Kigali hospital, murdered and apparently mutilated afterward, some with genitals severed. Later that evening, back at his own office, he feared that his headquarters, defended by only thirty lightly armed peacekeepers, would soon be assaulted, but no attack materialized.

The failure of Dallaire's forces to save any of those it had pledged to protect told the killers that their gamble on U.N. headquarters passivity had so far been correct. The next day, April 8, Dallaire dispatched an urgent cable to New York, pleading for support for what he believed had to be done if the impression of passivity was to be reversed: "The appearance of a very well planned, organized, deliberate and conducted campaign of terror initiated principally by the presidential guard since the morning after the death of the head of state has completely reoriented the situation in Kigali." He went on: "The particularly barbarous murder of the 10 captured Belgian soldiers emphasizes this situation. Is the mandate of UNAMIR still valid?" Dallaire asked for a quick response, since his food, water, and fuel were already in short supply, and his ammunition stocks and medical supplies would prove meager, too, if the situation were to worsen and his mandate was to be broadened.

Little more aid of any kind would come from U.N. headquarters, but Dallaire had already decided that he would remain true to his mission and do the best he could with what he had on the ground. While cynicism or anger over the absence of top-down support might lead some to despair, withdraw, or resign, Dallaire chose the opposite course. He would have to make do with what he had and focus on saving as many lives as he could. Instead of battling his superiors or accepting their passivity, he rose to the occasion, appreciating what his superiors would want and what the organization should achieve, even if the superiors had proven incapable of seeing it that way. Dallaire did what any boss should want: He wrote his own good script when he was receiving none from above.

Lesson in Leading Up

Even if your superiors reject your appeals or offer little guidance, you must make your own decisions for achieving the organization's mission. The decisions must transcend the personal resentments that might otherwise get in the way of an unswerving focus on the ultimate aims of the enterprise. If your decisions serve the mission, they will ultimately serve your superiors as well, however shortsighted their perspectives may be at present.

Staying the Course When Chaos Abounds

While Roméo Dallaire waited in vain for more backing from New York, Colonel Théoneste Bagosora had established an interim government on April 9, and it immediately expanded the systematic killing from the streets of Kigali to the fields of Rwanda. By the end of April 11, the fifth day since President Habyarimana's assassination, at least 20,000 Tutsis and moderate Hutus had been killed.

Both military officers and civil servants carried the gruesome task beyond the city limits. Government officials called village peasants together and told them the time had come to eliminate the Tutsis. One of the most densely settled regions of Africa, the terrain offered virtually no place for victims to hide. Some 50,000 militia fanned out across the country, and search parties methodically tracked down almost all who tried to hide, checking closets, ceilings, privies, cars, forests, swamps, islands, and bush. Dead bodies piled high from massacres in churches and schools were methodically prodded to make sure no survivors lay hiding below.

Radio Mille Collines exhorted listeners to join the modern pogrom: "You must go back there and finish them off." It continued: "The graves are not yet full. Who is going to do the good work and help us fill them completely?" Completeness became an essential part of the strategy. If all Tutsis were destroyed, there would be no survivors who could later bear witness. For the same reason, whoever was discovered sheltering Tutsis was killed as well.

Because Tutsis and Hutus had long lived side by side in villages and countryside, the killing spree meant that neighbors killed neighbors, teachers killed students, doctors killed patients, priests killed penitents. Some victims were told to kill their own children in order to save themselves. Others watched as family members were burned alive or hacked to death; pregnant women were disemboweled in front of their husbands. Body parts were severed, often before the victims received the coup de grâce. Most of the killing was carried out house to house, face-to-face, primitive weapons in hand, with none of the detachment permitted by gas chambers or bombsights.

As Colonel Bagosora and others in the interim government began accusing Dallaire of being partial to the Rwandan Patriotic Front, Dallaire learned that he himself was being named as a target of assassination plots. Despite grave risk to himself, Dallaire remained determined to stay on the ground and somehow reverse the momentum. He concluded that with sufficient force he could close the incendiary radio stations, open the roadblocks, and confiscate the arms. On April 12, he asked New York to dispatch a rapid reaction force of 5,000 well-equipped and well-trained troops to take the offensive. He also directly but unsuccessfully appealed for the Belgium, French, Italian, and American forces that had been sent to Kigali to evacuate their citizens to stay on after the rescue.

But U.N. headquarters officials were leaning toward just the opposite course of action. Mistakenly believing Rwanda had erupted in civil war rather than ethnic cleansing, Belgium and other governments called for the U.N. not to halt the slaughter but to arrange a cease-fire between government forces and rebel armies or, failing that, to withdraw its peacekeeping force altogether. On April 13, Kofi Annan expressed hoped for a cease-fire, and on April 15 the president of the Security Council, New Zealand's Colin Keating, asserted that "the immediate priority in Rwanda is the establishment of a cease-fire between the government forces and the RPF."

The next day, reeling from the barbarous murder of its soldiers, Belgium unilaterally announced that it was withdrawing all of its soldiers, the U.N.'s best troops in Rwanda. Dallaire said it was "a terrible blow to the mission," and as he watched their last plane depart at 11:30 A.M. on April 19, his feelings were bitter: "I thought that almost exactly fifty years to the day my father and my father-in-law had been fighting in Belgium to free the country from fascism, and there I was, abandoned by Belgian soldiers. So profoundly did I despise them for it."

With two weeks of mayhem and no "cease-fire" in sight, U.N. headquarters asked Dallaire about the advisability of withdrawing all of his forces. He responded on April 19 with unequivocal opposition: "A wholesale withdrawal of UNAMIR would most certainly be interpreted as leaving the scene if not even deserting the sinking ship." He added that a withdrawal "will definitely have an adverse effect on the morale of the civilian population, especially the refugees, who will feel that we are deserting them."

On April 21, the U.N. Security Council went a long way toward embracing the desertion option, slashing the authorized Rwandan force to 270. Fearing he would be without such essential personnel as truck drivers, Dallaire fought to maintain a force of 456, the extra number composed of soldiers who had volunteered to remain when Dallaire gave them a choice. They had seen what he had seen: "My force was standing knee-deep in mutilated bodies, surrounded by the guttural moans of dying people, looking into the eyes of children bleeding to death with their wounds burning in the sun and being invaded by maggots and flies. I found myself walking through villages where the only sign of life was a goat, or a chicken, or a songbird, as all the people were dead, their bodies being eaten by voracious packs of wild dogs." Secretary-General Boutros-Ghali chose to ignore Dallaire's resistance, explaining it away as the product of insufficient airlift capacity.

Dallaire's superiors at the U.N. persisted in defining the violence as civil rather than genocidal. On April 20, Secretary-General Boutros-Ghali offered an explanation for events that was at almost complete variance from what Dallaire had been telling headquarters: "Reliable reports strongly indicate that the killings were started by unruly members of the Presidential Guard, then spread quickly throughout the city. Despite the best efforts of UNAMIR," Boutros-Ghali said, the Rwandan Patriotic Front "broke out and started to engage government troops." Then, "authority collapsed, the provisional government disintegrated and some of its members were killed in the violence."

With no further backing from above, Dallaire mobilized what resources he could on his own. Having failed to convey the case to his own superiors, he sought assistance from whatever sources would heed his appeals. If he was proving unsuccessful in leading up, at least he would try leading out.

Dallaire pleaded with his own national government, and Canada responded with twelve military officers and two transport planes to deliver emergency supplies and to secretly evacuate Rwandan refugees. He collaborated with the few relief agencies still on the ground, including Médecins Sans Frontières (Doctors Without Borders) and the International Red Cross. And he even appealed to the world through a flock of some 200 Western journalists who had converged on the region. "I fed them, I transported them, I guaranteed them a story a day, and it would get out by hook or by crook," he recalled. He arranged for groups of 60 reporters on a rotating basis to fly from Nairobi for short stays in Kigali, and he even transported them around the perilous countryside in U.N. vehicles. "Unless the international community acts," he told the world through a Reuters correspondent, "it may find it is unable to defend itself against accusations of doing nothing to stop genocide."

Dallaire kept a disciplined schedule for himself and insisted that others do the same. "The only way that I found to be able to handle the stress was to work people till they dropped," he explained. He met with his top people twice a day, and he exemplified what he expected of others. An aid worker who arrived in late May found Dallaire to be "clear, firm, strong, and uncompromising." Dallaire's faith helped, too. "I had met the devil," he said, "and I thus knew there was a God."

Roméo Dallaire remained steadfast through the extraordinary times. Drawing on self-discipline and personal faith, he had stayed focused on doing the best with what he had. Even as the rug was being pulled out from under by his U.N. superiors, he never lost sight of what was required and what he must do.

Lesson in Leading Up

When the risk is greatest to yourself and your organization, your only choice may be no choice at all. Steadfastly pursuing your mission in the face of personal danger and even organizational ignorance is sometimes both the sole course to be followed and the greatest service you can render.

BEARING WITNESS FROM CARNAGE TO CONCLUSION

In the days that followed, the enormity of the unfolding events in Rwanda began to register on the world beyond. With an estimated 200,000 already killed, Boutros-Ghali finally recommended that the U.N. forces act not as a mediating force between warring factions but as a humanitarian power preventing still greater slaughter. Boutros-Ghali asked the U.N. Security Council to reconsider the force reduction, and on April 30 the council acknowledged the massacre of civilians and called for an expansion of forces. Finally, on May 17, the council voted to send 5,500 new troops to Rwanda and to impose an arms embargo.

On May 31—fifty-four days after the campaign of killing had commenced—Boutros-Ghali issued a report saying that as many as half a million had already perished. He admitted that Dallaire had forewarned him of the genocide that had come to pass, and that he and others had fallen short: "We have failed in our response to the agony of Rwanda and thus have acquiesced in the continued loss of human life."

Dallaire had never acquiesced, but those at headquarters certainly had. The complete disconnect between the front line in Kigali and the executive suite in New York was a reminder that getting an unwanted message up to the top can be one of the most challenging but also one of the most important actions for the upward leader.

Even though he was now aware of the enormity of the catastrophe, Boutros-Ghali still failed to recruit even a fraction of the force that the U.N. Security Council had authorized him two weeks earlier to recruit for Dallaire. Most member nations resisted his call for volunteers; several West African countries readily offered their soldiers, but no First World countries offered the necessary transport to fly them into Rwanda. It was not until July 25 that Boutros-Ghali was able to send Dallaire any more troops, and then only 550.

France intervened on its own on June 23. For Dallaire, this was a decidedly mixed blessing at best. The arrival of a large and disciplined military force would end the killing in some areas, but it was widely perceived that the French had invaded to prop up the Hutu regime, and that perception mistakenly turned some moderates against the U.N. forces.

By now, however, the Rwandan Patriotic Front was successfully sweeping through the countryside, its forward wake pushing both the killers and more that a million refugees into neighboring Zaire. Militia units, presidential guards, and public officials mixed with hundreds of thousands of fleeing peasants who feared reprisal at the hands of the triumphant rebels.

Dallaire proposed a humanitarian repatriation plan and also requested permission from U.N. headquarters for hot pursuit into the cross-border refugee camps. "There was an opportunity to get into those camps and get those bastards," he said, but his U.N. superiors once more applied the brakes because Dallaire's plan would again have gone beyond the narrowly defined peacekeeping mandate. In response, Dallaire prophesied the next disaster if he could not root the militias out of their Zaire camps: an eventual overthrow of Zaire's longtime dictator Mobutu Sese Seko and a struggle for power in Zaire—later named Democratic Republic of Congo when Mobutu was forced out—into whose vortex surrounding nations would inevitably be pulled. Sadly, he couldn't have been more right.

By July 18, 1994, the holocaust had run its course as the Rwandan Patriotic Front gained control of the entire country except for a small area still under France's control. But though the savagery was ended, devastation abounded. Of Rwanda's 7 million inhabitants, 800,000 were dead, 2 million had fled, and another 2 million were displaced. The capital had been reduced from a population of 300,000 to 50,000. Of the children who survived, 90% had witnessed bloodshed, mostly of family and friends. The country was decimated, literally: a tenth of its population had been destroyed. Remarkably, such whole-sale death had been achieved mostly by some of the simplest manu-factured weapons on earth.

Few moderate Hutus and Tutsis were still left to kill in Rwanda, but at least the state-sponsored genocide had ended, and the interim government of Théoneste Bagosora was gone. Many of its principals had fled the company, though some, including Colonel Bagosora, would later be captured and tried for genocide.

Because Kigali's bloodbath had been enough to panic virtually every foreign national into fleeing Rwanda, Roméo Dallaire was one of the few Westerners to have borne witness. "I was standing in my office," he told of one incident, "standing by the window, and I had a screen and there were houses across the street from the compound. To this day," he continued, "I'm never sure if what I heard was the wind coming through the screen or the cries and moans of women and children who were being slaughtered." Several days later, "because the smell and stench was so bad in the area, I sent a team across to those houses." What the team found, no more than a hundred yards from Dallaire's headquarters, were more than eighty-nine corpses. That was the number before they stopped counting.

The Traumatic Aftermath of Leading Up but Falling Short

By August 1994, with the genocide over, Roméo Dallaire badly needed out. He began wandering alone in the streets of Kigali, knowing that many there still wished him dead. "I was trying to get myself killed," he later admitted. "I wanted to be ambushed." He had lost his sense of mission and felt that he was even becoming a danger to the mission. One day when dogs attacked several goats that had been tethered at his headquarters, in a fit of rage he rushed at the dogs with a pistol and killed them all. His nearby staff blinked in disbelief at what they had just seen their commander do, and he knew his time was up.

Exiting via Nairobi, Dallaire met his family in Amsterdam, and together they walked the European battlefields where Canadian troops including his father and father-in-law had once battled Nazis. On September 3, 1994, he took up the post of deputy commander of the Canadian Army and threw himself into his new assignment.

Dallaire's actions on April 7 and beyond were viewed by many as heroic. When terrified Tutsis and moderate Hutus in Kigali had telephoned the U.N. for rescue, Dallaire's troops retrieved at great risk as many as they could for deposit at safe havens such as Kigali's foreign embassies. Undermanned and woefully undersupported, Dallaire did what he could with what little he had to work with. Arguably, it was only his iron determination to keep a force in place in Rwanda that kept his superiors at the U.N. from abandoning the killing fields completely, a desertion of duty and moral responsibility from which the international body might never have recovered.

Canada awarded Dallaire its highest honor, the Meritorious Service Cross, and the United States bestowed its Legion of Merit. Canada promoted him to major general in 1994 and later to lieutenant general.

For Roméo Dallaire, however, time would take its toll, not heal his wounds. By 1997 he found himself taking personal responsibility for too much of the colossal human disaster he had witnessed at such close range three years earlier. Dallaire was haunted by whether he could have intervened before it proved disastrously too late. The "mission failed," he said, "and I consider myself intimately involved with that responsibility." That failure proved very consequential: "I'm fully responsible for the ten Belgian soldiers dying, for others dying, for several of my soldiers being injured and falling sick because we ran out of medical supplies, for fifty-six Red Cross people being killed, for two million people becoming displaced and refugees, and for about a million Rwandans being killed."

Dallaire worked hard but could rarely sleep. "I couldn't go into a bedroom and lie down," he confessed. "The sound of silence was deafening." The smell of fresh fruit in a market brought tears. Stacked wood along highways brought back images of human corpses stacked by the road. In the winter of 1997, he intentionally drove his speeding car into a highway median wall, but it miraculously bounced free and his suicide attempt failed.

Dallaire was medically released from military service on April 18, 2000. In June, one day after turning fifty-four years old, he was found inebriated and unconscious on a park bench. In a subsequent letter to a radio program about his stupor, he explained: "The anger, the rage, the hurt, and the cold loneliness that separate you from your family, friends, and society are so powerful that the option of destroying yourself is both real and attractive."

Lesson in Leading Up

When the stakes are high, the personal cost of attempting upward leadership but falling short can be traumatic, and coping with the consequent stress is one of the burdens that comes with the calling.

IF MORE SOLDIERS HAD BEEN SUPPLIED

To destroy 800,000 people in a little over three months—a rate of 8,000 deaths a day for 100 days—required such a mammoth killing machine that the slaughter might have been well beyond anybody's means to contain once it had begun. But smaller steps before the explosion might have prevented its ignition. Could Dallaire's forces, for instance, have forced the incendiary Hutu Radio Mille Collines off the air? Might it have confiscated the arms caches being stockpiled around Kigali? Should Dallaire have pressed more forcefully for the formation of a transitional government?

Once the killing erupted in Kigali, could Dallaire's troops have prevented its spread into the countryside? Might he have brought the butchery to a swifter end so that 400,000 or 200,000 perished, not 800,000—a disaster still, but of lesser scope?

Few individuals are ever positioned to create national triumphs or prevent national disasters. Only organizations and institutions can move personnel and resources on a truly national scale. Sometimes, though, individuals do find themselves at one of those crossroads of history where they are granted extraordinary power to help determine whether good or evil will triumph. It is at such moments that they can direct or redirect missions, allocate or reallocate resources, create or deflect world attention on a scale that can define the future.

Dallaire and his bosses at the United Nations may well have faced precisely such a moment. "The facts are not in question," concluded an assessment by the Organization of African Unity. "A small number of major actors could directly have prevented, halted, or reduced the slaughter."

The bigger force and broader mandate that might have made Roméo Dallaire one of those "actors" weren't his to provide—that was up to his superiors. But given the horror that ensued, it is imperative to consider what could have made the difference. What would have been required for Dallaire to have moved Iqbal Riza, Kofi Annan, Boutros Boutros-Ghali, and the entire U.N. Security Council to have provided him with the resources that could have spelled the difference for nearly a million victims and millions more whose lives were forever changed?

Roméo Dallaire had headed the 1993 U.N. reconnaissance mission to determine what was needed before his full military force was dispatched to Rwanda, and he later acknowledged that the capacities of his mission were insufficient for appreciating the depth of the unresolved hostilities between the belligerents. The hatred that would erupt so disastrously was below the surface but there for the seeing if sufficiently examined. Just weeks before Dallaire's own mission arrived, a separate U.N. mission on human rights in Rwanda published a report warning at length of genocide. Dallaire never saw the report. In January 1994, the U.S. Central Intelligence Agency had notified the U.S. State Department that the Arusha agreement was likely to fail, violence would flair, and in its wake half a million could die, but that assessment was never made available to him either. Dallaire was starting from scratch.

Even without access to external evaluations, had Dallaire acquired stronger staffing, more resources, and better intelligence, his reconnaissance team might have better comprehended the murderous atmosphere and potential for collapse of the Arusha accords. With a better understanding of what Rwanda was hurtling toward, Dallaire might have pressed more persuasively for a larger military force and more contingency planning for the peacekeeping mission itself. But Dallaire would have no such capacity for intelligence gathering, since his U.N. superiors had rejected his request for such a capability. As a result, he was far more sanguine about his mission in its opening days than circumstances should have ever allowed. "There was absolutely no perception that there was anything but the very positive vibrations that were coming out of Rwanda from both sides," he would later say.

Without alarmist information and a compelling rationale coming from Dallaire in his first days in the field, Riza, Annan, and Boutros-Ghali did not have a sufficient case for pulling out all the stops from the start. And without a perception that it was a moment for decisive action, Secretary-General Boutros-Ghali had been unable to persuade the U.N. Security Council to honor Dallaire's original request for 4,500 military personnel, granting him instead only a little over half that.

Lesson in Leading Up

Due diligence is everything. Without detailed intelligence on the conditions the organization faces, senior people will be unable to make fast, accurate decisions in response to requests from below.

Within a month of his arrival in Kigali, Dallaire had sent a document to the U.N.'s Department of Peacekeeping Operations outlining his rules of engagement. Alarmed by the depth of hostilities that he saw by then, he stated: "There may also be ethnically or politically motivated criminal acts committed during this mandate which will morally and legally require UNAMIR to use all available means to halt them. Examples are executions, attacks on displaced person or refugees." Anticipating the future, Dallaire made a case for preserving the peace by inhibiting crime, and he asked for latitude for use of "all available means" to stop it.

Dallaire's U.N. superiors never replied to this submission, and he reasonably assumed that the rules of engagement had been approved, at least on an interim basis. In this instance, however, silence did not imply genuine acceptance. As events unfolded, the U.N. consistently blocked his application of any available means when politically motivated criminal acts did sweep the country. Through such acts, his superiors whittled down his original mandate to a far narrower interpretation.

In his January 11 exchanges with U.N. headquarters in New York, Dallaire had reported that he planned to seize the arms caches that could have been created only for criminal purpose. When Kofi Annan vetoed the proposed action, an action that Dallaire believed was well within the original mandate, he was dumbfounded. Instead of taking the U.N.'s earlier silence as de facto acceptance, Dallaire might have pressed his superiors for explicit approval or an expanded mandate. Even if it had still been withheld, he would have known precisely where he stood as chaos descended on Kigali and plans had to be made on the run.

Lesson in Leading Up

Clarifying your superiors' understanding of your situation and their intent for it is a first step for knowing what further measures are required to address the challenges in front of you and build support for them.

Later events suggest that a larger force could have made a difference, both before and after April 7. Sizable forces that moved against the Hutu militia were able to terminate the genocide. When the Rwandan Patriotic Front finally marched across the country, it stopped the killing as areas came under its control. When France moved in, the presence of its troops also ended the massacres. The critical difference was in the scale of the forces: Both the RPF and French troops far outnumbered what Dallaire had at his disposal.

In reviewing the events, Dallaire himself concluded that had the U.N. provided more troops with better equipment and better training, or even just given him the go-ahead early on to counter the militia activities, the worst of the genocide would have been averted. In a 1999 report critical of its own actions leading up to and during the Rwandan holocaust, the U.N. concluded much the same. Its failure, said the assessment, "can be summarized as a lack of resources and a lack of will to take on the commitment which would have been necessary to prevent or to stop the genocide." In the absence of that will, concluded an analysis by the Organization of African Unity, came a cataclysm that was preventable. "All that was required was a reasonable-sized international military force with a strong mandate to enforce the Arusha agreements."

An independent inquiry organized by the Carnegie Commission on Preventing Deadly Conflict, Georgetown University, and the U.S. Army reached the conclusion that a reasonable size in this instance need not have been more than several thousand. "A modern force of 5,000 troops," concluded one white paper, "sent to Rwanda sometime between April 7 and April 21, 1994, could have significantly altered the outcome of the conflict." Such a force would have "stemmed the violence in and around the capital, prevented its spread to the countryside, and created conditions conducive to the cessation of the civil war." Dallaire was of a well-founded opinion that a force of just that magnitude would have made the difference. Just prior to the Rwandan assignment, he had commanded a Canadian brigade of 5,200 troops for two years, and he knew what control a disciplined force of that size can bring to bear.

Lesson in Leading Up

Large-scale developments often defy individual intervention, but not always, and when you see an opportunity to make the difference though your superiors still don't, your mission is to turn them around.

LEADING UP CAN REQUIRE REDEFINING REALITY

The U.N. peacekeepers had arrived to keep the peace. If the Rwandan government and Rwandan Patriotic Front failed to honor the articles of the accords, Dallaire was in Kigali to remind them of their obligations. Or so the theory went. The reality on the ground, though, was far different, especially after the mass killings began on April 7. Nonetheless, U.N. officers in New York persisted, even as the bodies mounted, in defining the problem as an agreement breakdown, not a human decimation.

Secretary-General Boutros-Ghali did not publicly use the term "genocide" until May 4, and then only on the U.S. television program *Nightline*. It was not until May 25 that he used the term in an official press conference, and only on May 31 that he put the word on paper in a report to the Security Council. Moreover, in meetings at the U.N. with representatives of Rwanda, including its ambassador, who was then serving on the U.N. Security Council, Boutros-Ghali continued to criticize the failure of the cease-fire, saying little or nothing about what by then had become an unambiguous policy of genocide.

Roméo Dallaire's challenge in those weeks was to alter the way his superiors saw his reality as soon as it was becoming evident that an enduring conflict was moving toward its final resolution. Since his bosses saw none of the carnage, heard none of the agony, knew none of the victims, it was up to Dallaire to deliver the message that an evil empire had replaced a benign world in Rwanda. For this he used startling language even in his earliest cables. In reporting the massacres of fifty-five people in November 1993, he told his bosses at U.N. headquarters on January 6 that the "manner in which they were conducted in their execution, in their coordination, in their cover-up, and in their political motives leads us to firmly believe that the perpetrators of these evil deeds were well organized, well informed, well motivated, and prepared to conduct premeditated murder. We have no reason to believe that such occurrences could not and will not be repeated again in any part of this country where arms are prolific and political and ethnic tensions are prevalent."

At U.N. headquarters in New York, though, the old reality remained the only reality, even as the analog for what was happening in Rwanda shifted from the intractable civil conflicts in Angola,

Colombia, or Somalia to the directed population annihilation by Nazi Germany. For one person to redefine his superiors' misplaced perceptions of a changed reality required extraordinary steps, yet if Dallaire could have found those steps, the outcome might have remained a costly civil war rather than a catastrophe on a par with the killing fields of Cambodia.

Lesson in Leading Up

Redefining an institution's reality is one of the upward leader's greatest tests. Well-established worldviews are robustly resistant to erosion, let alone conversion; but the extraordinary difficulty of converting your superiors' definition of reality often suggests the overiding importance of achieving it.

A PREVENTABLE HUMAN CATASTROPHE

The report of the Organization of African Unity asked "What the World Could Have Done," and its blunt answer was that it could have prevented the killings: "The simple, harsh truth is that the genocide was not inevitable, and that it would have been relatively easy to stop it from happening prior to April 6, 1994, and then to mitigate the destruction significantly once it began."

Though the grassroots mayhem was enacted by tens of thousands of peasants, their instigators were relatively few in number and not well armed for defending against a modern army. When the perpetrators felt real international pressure, they tended to suspend their abuses, but they were rarely subject to such pressure. Only when the Rwandan Patriotic Front mobilized its own large-scale forces to march across the killing fields did the killing stop.

In the aftermath, Dallaire would say he had witnessed "Dante devils from hell run amok in what was once paradise on earth." To send the devils back, Dallaire had less than a thousand fresh and willing soldiers at his command. Looking back, he said, "I think I could have done better." If he had been able to instill the will in his superiors that was so evidently missing, he might have obtained the thousands of troops that he knew he needed at the time, and in retrospect we know might well have made an historic difference.

CHAPTER 4

RETAINING THE CONFIDENCE OF YOUR DIRECTORS AND INVESTORS

CHIEF EXECUTIVES AT CBS, COMPAQ COMPUTER, AND BRITISH
AIRWAYS ENTERED THEIR BOARDROOMS WITH A PLAN FOR THE
FUTURE AND LEFT WITH THEIR HEADS ON A PLATTER

A T THE VERY top of the pyramid, leading up takes on distinct form, since your bosses are countless and their responsibilities are diffuse. In a publicly traded company, your superiors may include a dozen directors and hundreds of investors; in a nonprofit organization, scores of trustees; in a government agency, millions of citizens. They own you collectively, and no *one* is your boss.

The crux at the apex is recognizing that you must keep all of your numerous superiors well apprised of what you are doing and, above all, informed in advance of whatever big plans you have for the future. Though directors and investors are scattered across the country and rarely if ever in your office, meeting with them, listening to them, and performing for them are the essential ingredients for retaining their collective trust. If faulty moves in any of these areas undermine their initial confidence in you, they may invent their own temporary leadership whose sole purpose is your ouster. If your good moves in all of these areas reinforce their starting faith in you, they'll give you all the latitude you need for your most ambitious ventures.

This chapter will show the importance of holding the confidence among all those above you who count. It focuses on the person who has reached the uppermost rung of the corporate ladder and who is most directly responsible to the firm's directors and investors.

Your title of chief executive officer says you're king of the roost. Your pay proves it. You have worked a lifetime to earn the pinnacle, and now the perks and power have made it all worthwhile. You run your own schedule, beholden to no one. You define company strategy, vital to everyone.

Twenty years ago, your predecessors were assured of staying at the summit until they decided one day on their own that the mowed fairways and gated communities of Pebble Beach or Palm Beach were even more alluring. They and only they determined precisely when they would abdicate the throne. But with the rise of investor clout and director fortitude, executive command is no longer quite so secure. It now requires the best in upward leadership to remain at the top, as we will see in three top executives who took their directors and investors a little too much for granted. In doing so, they risked having themselves ushered out the exit well before they planned to go anywhere near it.

Thomas Wyman of CBS found himself facing that door at a time when he still thought he owned it. So also did Eckhard Pfeiffer of Compaq Computer and Robert Ayling of British Airways. They had badly damaged their relations with their boards, and instead of retiring one day on their own terms, their upward miscalculations threatened early retirement on terms set by others.

In some cases, top executives are victims of circumstance, casualties of forces far beyond their control, scapegoats for errors not of their making. The ultimate cause could be a faltering economy that gave no quarter or a founding family that allowed no latitude. Certainly such macro factors helped trigger the premature departure in 2000 of the chief executives of blue-chip enterprises ranging from Coca-Cola and Procter & Gamble to Xerox and Lucent Technologies. Yet rarely are such circumstances solely responsible.

Our examination in this chapter of the CEO dismissals at CBS, Compaq Computer, and British Airways will show that executive actions are almost always contributing factors. Each account contains a unique blend of circumstances, but together they will show that a key limitation is insufficient appreciation for the power of superiors and the universal fact that all superiors despise surprises. Add to this a world where shareholders now rule, and the lesson becomes clearer still: Executive success requires not only inspired employees and satisfied customers but also approving directors and appreciative investors who expect to know what you are going to do almost before you know it. In other words, you must lead up as well as down even when you have arrived at the top.

CEO THOMAS WYMAN TRIED TO SAVE CBS, BUT HE FAILED TO KEEP HIS BOARD INFORMED

CBS television stood as one of the nation's great franchises in the mid-1980s. The Black Rock, its towering dark marble headquarters on New York's Sixth Avenue and Fifty-second Street, spoke perfectly of the era's unassailable corporate dominance. And Thomas H.

Thomas Wyman, July 1985

Wyman, CBS's top executive, epitomized the omnipotent chieftain at a time when CEOs answered to nobody.

Thomas Wyman had pedigree. Named one of America's top leaders by *Time* magazine in 1974 and the number two at Polaroid at the fast-track age of forty-two, he had gone on to run the Jolly Green Giant Corporation and from there to Pillsbury, where he served as vice chairman. Now, still only in his mid-fifties, he had reached the pinnacle of an American icon from which Walter Cronkite, Bill Moyers, Edward R. Murrow, and Dan Rather had told us the news. Wyman presided over a workforce of 25,000, and he did so with all the titles that one could garner. He was chairman, president, and chief executive of CBS, Inc.

On the morning of September 10, 1986, with his directors convened for one of their monthly meetings, held on second Wednesdays, Wyman entered the boardroom with a plan to merge his company with Coca-Cola. The plan would provide a sure defense against the hostile raiders who had been circling CBS, takeover artists Ivan F. Boesky and Saul Steinberg among them. Competitors had been circling as well, including Gulf & Western's Marvin Davis. Even U.S. senator Jesse Helms's Fairness in Media group had proposed acquiring CBS to open the airwaves to conservative content. With his own political script and real money to boot, entrepreneur Ted Turner proposed the same. He proclaimed that the major "networks need to be gotten into the hands of people who care about this country," and on April 19, 1985, he had announced he would do that by taking over CBS. The network fiercely resisted, forcing Turner to admit defeat on August 7, though not before Turner had forced CBS into a $1 billion stock buyback with borrowed money.

The raiders and competitors had been drawn by a quarry's scent: CBS's program ratings had plummeted, along with management morale and company capitalization. The firm was undervalued because it was undermanaged, stock analysts said, and new management could extract more. The stock had slumped so far that the company's market value was now estimated at two-thirds its true value.

The company's fading fortunes stemmed in part from the industry's upstart networks, led by Rupert Murdoch's Fox Network and Ted Turner's CNN. With the emergence of cable, the three major networks had seen their traditional dominance drop from 92% of the market in 1975 to 78% in 1983. By the end of the decade, combined market share was projected to reach just 60%.

No longer an oligopoly, CBS needed a new set of management skills if it was to compete in the rough-and-tumble world of deregulated airwaves, but Wyman and his top lieutenants seemed not to be mastering the fast-changing times as quickly as the other majors. During the 1985–86 prime-time season, CBS lost its top-rated place to NBC. On revenue of $4.8 billion, Wyman was turning an anemic profit of just $27 million.

To restore prosperity, Thomas Wyman eliminated 700 broadcast jobs in midsummer 1986. He shuttered *CBS Morning News* and pressed other news programs to become more lively and engaging. His changes produced howls of protest from within the company and across the industry. Journalist Bill Moyers tendered his resignation from the network, saying that "once you decide to titillate instead of illuminate, you're on a slippery slope." *Washington Post* television reporter Tom Shales complained that "broadcasting isn't there just to make money for the damn stockholders."

Wyman went further, pressing the state of New York to pass an antitakeover statute, viewed by vigilant investors as little more than management entrenchment. He wrapped himself in the flag, declaring at the annual stockholders' meeting that "those who seek to gain control of CBS in order to gain control of CBS News threaten its independence, its integrity—and this country." And, most fatefully for his own future, he sought a "white knight," Wall Street parlance for a friendly investor who would unflinchingly stand with management against all would-be raiders.

Laurence Tisch, chairman of Loews Corporation, had earlier told James D. Wolfensohn, a CBS board member and investment banker with whom he played tennis, that he didn't like seeing CBS pushed around by extremists. Senator Helms had sent a fund-raising letter to a million conservatives, urging them to buy CBS stock to "become Dan Rather's boss." Tisch offered to help CBS resist the ideologues, and now Wyman had come to him for precisely that: Just imagine if Helms were indeed Rather's superior. Tisch agreed to purchase a large block of CBS stock as an unmovable stake in the ground, and Wyman further embraced his white knight by inviting Tisch onto the CBS board. When Tisch became a director in October 1985, Wyman explained that it was because of his "well-deserved reputation as a successful, long-term investor in publicly traded companies." Wyman had the reputation right without fully appreciating its implications: Tisch was indeed an investor and not a broadcaster, far more concerned with making money than delivering the news.

By mid-1986, Tisch had raised his holding in CBS to 24.9% of its shares. That was such a commanding position that it would thwart any unwanted takeover, since his consent would be essential to any deal—and he simply would not give it. "This is an investment we [are] going to keep," Tisch declared. "It's not for sale." Nor would he heed any of the outside calls to break up CBS, affirming that "we certainly have no interest whatsoever in dismembering the company."

Tisch repeatedly pledged that his stake was purely an investment that portended no conquest of his own. On June 12, he even wrote Wyman a reassuring note: "I've been concerned in this period of various articles in the press regarding Loews interest in CBS. I want to reiterate to you that I continue to have full confidence in you and your management." He concluded his note by restating his pledge to acquire no more than a quarter of CBS's shares and that "there has been no change at all in our intentions."

Others were not so sure. The *Wall Street Journal* observed that without "spending a dime on lawyers or investment bankers, Laurence A. Tisch may have accomplished what Ted Turner and an $18 million roster of takeover advisors couldn't do: de facto control of CBS, Inc."

In fact, Tisch had not yet succeeded, but the network's independence remained precarious and its performance deleterious. To protect its integrity and bolster its fortunes, Wyman devised a radical remedy. At his initiative, Coca-Cola Co. was prepared to propose a friendly takeover of CBS.

From the pure-play penchant of a decade later, it might look to be an odd couple, but from the vantage of an era still enamored of conglomerates, Coke-CBS had the look of a winner. Loews itself (which was now the company of CBS's biggest stockholder) was comprised of companies that ranged from accommodations (Loews Hotels) and watches (Bulova) to tobacco (Lorillard) and insurance (CNA Financial). CBS, too, had a rich history of diversification: It had published books (Fawcett), made gadgets (Ideal Toys), cut songs (CBS records), produced movies (Tri-Star Pictures), and even owned sports teams (New York Yankees). The results had been equally diverse: The record division earned $8 million in 1984 on a single record, Michael Jackson's *Thriller,* but the Yankees under CBS ownership from 1964 to 1973 fell from first to worst.

Coca-Cola itself had diversified into the amusement business, acquiring Columbia Pictures. With both CBS and Coke in entertainment, creative synergies were sure to be found. With CBS under Coke, hostile suitors were sure to be sidelined.

At the same time, Wyman was already looking over his shoulder. Tisch was tiring of his CEO's performance, and Wyman knew it. By mid-1986, Wyman also sensed that Tisch no longer felt so bound by his earlier pledge to acquire no more than a quarter of CBS's stock, and Tisch's recent behavior seemed to confirm the CEO's worst fears. At a private dinner in July at New York's exclusive Links Club, board members asked Tisch to reaffirm his pledge, but he refused to sign any standstill agreement. Having come into CBS stock as the white knight, Tisch increasingly looked the knight errant.

In building up his position in CBS, Tisch had paid an average of $127 per share. CBS had already declined a takeover offer of $160 from Marvin Davis the prior spring, and Coca-Cola was intimating that it might be willing to pay as much as $170 per share. Shareholders normally expect a hefty takeover premium of the kind anticipated from Coke, but if Tisch intended to increase his stake while blocking even a friendly takeover, as Wyman had come to fear, shareholders would never see their expected premium. As the *Journal* had warned, Tisch appeared to be going for de facto control without spending an extra dime.

Were Tisch to make an outright bid for control of the company, Wyman still expected his board to balk for the same reason that Wyman opposed it: Shareholders would lose. Yet so far Tisch had not tipped his hand. Bringing the Coca-Cola deal into the boardroom might just force it, and if Tisch took the bait and countered with his own bid, Wyman anticipated that the directors would rally to him, the sitting CEO. "He thought that they could go on the offensive against Larry and force him to make his move," explained a CBS executive, and if Tisch then sought company control, "he would break his promise and the board would back Wyman."

Concerned with the same developments, the company's nonexecutive directors were veering down other paths, not yet so well defined but equally fateful for Wyman's future. On Tuesday, September 9, 1986, they gathered on the eve of their regular second-Wednesday board meeting. Wyman had evidently invited his directors to join him for an informal dinner at New York's Ritz Carlton Hotel, but he canceled the gathering at the last minute. (Wyman later denied that he had either initiated or scrubbed the meeting.) One of the outside directors suggested that they convene anyway, and all of the board's members save Wyman and Tisch joined the rump session. The second-floor dining room at the Ritz Carlton filled with the power brokers of America: former U.S. defense secretary Harold Brown and future World Bank president James D. Wolfensohn, former CBS anchorman Walter Cronkite, and future Lucent Technologies chief Henry Schacht.

The directors reiterated their shared commitment to keep the company out of the clutches of hostile suitors, but some angrily itemized the problems that incumbent management had caused or failed to resolve. Walter Cronkite criticized Wyman for his insensitivity to the newscaster's public-interest obligations. Others complained of the firm's financial decline and chronic conflict. Founder William Paley, whom the board had forced out as chairman in 1983 but who still owned 8.1%, baldly urged his successor's dismissal, asserting that the absent Tisch had reached the same conclusion. Some directors, however, objected to any move that would bring Tisch into executive leadership, and at least nine still opposed any ouster of Wyman. Following five hours of animated but irresolute debate, they dispersed at 11:30 P.M.

Wyman Surprised His Board of Directors —
Who, in Turn, Surprised Him

The next morning, Thomas Wyman and his management team joined the board for its 9:00 A.M. meeting on the thirty-fifth floor at Black Rock. Wyman's executive team—including the president of the CBS broadcast group, Gene F. Jankowski; CBS records president Walter R. Yetnikoff; and publishing head Peter A. Derow—opened with a review of the company's flagging figures. A month before, the company had announced that it expected a decline in operating profits for the second half of its fiscal year. Now Wyman revealed that the earnings picture looked no brighter for the coming year either. Though directors were well aware of CBS's financial problems, the revelation of their gravity came, according to one executive, as "terrible" news.

At 11:00 A.M., Wyman's executive team exited, and the chief executive turned to his radical solution. He explained that he had been discussing a takeover plan with Coca-Cola executive vice president Francis T. Vincent, who ran the entertainment unit that included Columbia Pictures. No price for CBS had been offered by Coke, but a substantial premium was expected, and Wyman needed ten days to develop a deal. He also said that Walt Disney Co. was ready to step in with a good price if the Coke negotiations fell through. Wyman would later avow that he had informally let eight of his directors know of the Coke possibility before the meeting. To avoid provoking the anticipated opposition from Tisch and Paley, however, he had not drawn them into his scheme, nor had he informed directors Walter Cronkite, a Wyman critic, or Marietta Tree, a Paley friend.

Wyman's fellow directors sat in stunned silence. Whatever their view of Tisch and his threat, the CBS chief executive had just informed them that he had been seeking a buyer without their formal authorization or even their informal consent. The board had been steadfastly insisting that the network remain independent, and it was more than a theoretical posture, since both ABC and NBC had recently been acquired—by Capital Cities and General Electric, respectively. Moreover, CBS had just spent months fighting off takeovers by Ivan Boesky, Marvin Davis, Jesse Helms, and Ted Turner. Now the directors had learned just how potent the CEO felt and how impotent he evidently saw them to be.

That would all change within the next five hours. A seething Tisch told the board that CBS should stay independent—and that its return to health required not a new owner but new management. He stated that he would not press for Wyman's ouster, nor would he acquire more stock or start a proxy fight: Having come in as a white knight, he would not transform into a malevolent force. But he also made it clear that as the company's premier shareholder, he had lost confidence in its chairman. According to the board meeting's official minutes, Tisch and Paley—who together held more than a third of the company's stock worth more than $1 billion—asserted that Wyman's regime had exhibited "a record of unsuccessful acquisitions, inattention to the talent and creative aspects of the business, particularly in the flagship news division," had shown an "inability to control overhead costs," and had failed "to anticipate declines in operating earnings." Tisch intended no power play of his own, he said, but Paley was less shy. He proposed making himself the new CBS chairman.

The other directors asked Wyman, Tisch, and Paley to step out of the boardroom at noon so that they could deliberate in private. Wyman returned to his office, Tisch and Paley retired to Paley's. Wyman anticipated that the board's anxiety about Tisch's intentions would bring it around to his plan to merge with Coca-Cola. Tisch and Paley expected a very different outcome.

Some directors were described as "shocked" and "flabbergasted" by the Coca-Cola proposal. One asked Walter Cronkite, now the only insider remaining in the room, about company morale, and this "voice of CBS" asserted that Wyman still did not appreci-

Laurence Tisch and William S. Paley after the dismissal
of Thomas Wyman on September 10, 1986.

ate the company's crown jewel, the news division. As the litany of complaints continued, those who had steadfastly remained Wyman's backers now wavered.

By 5:00 P.M. the board concluded that the network would not go better with Coke—and that CBS would be better without Wyman. It dispatched two directors to break the news to the chief executive that any merger plan was off and that the directors had unanimously decided to ask for his immediate resignation. After showing Wyman the exit, the directors told Tisch and Paley that they would get the keys. They unanimously invited Tisch, sixty-three years old, to become interim CEO, and, Paley, eighty-four, to serve as acting chairman.

For informing the rest of the world, the board used its unique asset. Barely two hours after informing Wyman of his firing, the board transmitted its decision to CBS anchorman Dan Rather, who was near the end of his evening newscast. Rather scripted his own words: "The CBS corporate board met today. After that meeting the chairman of the board and the chief executive officer, Thomas Wyman, is reported to be out." Rather turned away from the camera, allowing millions of home screens to go blank without his familiar closing line.

Wall Street applauded: Tisch "is one of the smartest business managers in the U.S.," offered Drexel Burnham stock analyst John S. Reidy. Added Alan Gottesman, an analyst with L. F. Rothschild, Unterberg, Towbin, "You've got to run it more like a business," and Tisch was sure to do that.

In the months that followed, CBS was indeed restructured as a business. Tisch ousted 200 members of the CBS News staff of 1,200 in what became known as "the slaughter on Fifty-seventh Street," he cut the corporate personnel office from 120 to 50, and he sold the records and publishing divisions. By the time Tisch finished his remake of the business, CBS's total employment ranks had been halved. He also eliminated what he deemed corporate waste, ranging from a medical department and a company store to private copiers, rented typewriters, first-class travel, and philanthropic contributions. Tisch removed Wyman's FOR SALE sign but then restructured the company far more radically than Thomas Wyman and the hostile raiders could have imagined.

On January 15, 1987, just four months later, the CBS board unanimously dropped the "interim" from Tisch's CEO title and the "acting" from Paley's chairmanship. Tisch would run the business indefinitely, as Paley would the creative side. Wyman had worried that shareholders wouldn't benefit from a CBS takeover. Now, Tisch and Paley's silent takeover had brought Wyman's worst fears to pass. The average per-share cost of Tisch's stake in the network was $23 less than Ted Turner's offer, $33 less than Marvin Davis's, and $43 less than Coke's likely bid. A year after Wyman's ouster, a reporter wrote that Tisch's "bagging of CBS is the steal of the century. An all-timer."

Wyman Courted Disaster in Believing He Controlled the Board

"In the ultimate analysis," the *Wall Street Journal* editorialized five days after the firing, "the big reason Thomas Wyman lost his job as chairman was not bickering with CBS News, or infighting with company founder William Paley or overspending on soaps. Rather, it was his inability to deal with the company's depressed share price." In an era of investor power, share price is all, and a sustained failure to put air under it can be deemed a fatal shortcoming. Researchers have found that a 50% drop in stock price doubles a CEO's likelihood of exit.

Still, Wyman was working with probabilities, not certainties, and though the company's dismal earnings had put him on notice, other executives had faced worse setbacks and still survived, even prospered. Lou Gerstner of IBM was a case in point; he had faced plummeting share price when he took over in the early 1990s but was never ousted. Indeed, leadership depends on persistence and courage despite dispiriting days, but it also requires a board that stays on board, and here Wyman came up short.

Two days before the fateful directors' meeting on September 10, a *New York Times* writer had warned of its pending significance: "CBS's management is facing a crucial board meeting this week that may prove to be a test of the leadership of Thomas H. Wyman." The chief executive didn't see it that way, however, contending that the speculation and turmoil should have no effect on the event. He believed that a solid majority of his directors—at least ten of the fourteen— was still in his column.

Moreover, Wyman was not only chief executive but also chairman of the board, a post that previous CEOs of CBS had not held simultaneously. Wyman had personally invited Tisch onto his board in the first place. Paley had personally handpicked Wyman to become president. Reviewing Wyman's annual performance just five months before its fateful September meeting, the board had praised his tough leadership against Ted Turner's tender. It complimented his restoration of CBS's credit line despite its deep indebtedness, and it bestowed an 11% raise. As he walked into the boardroom on September 10, Wyman's future felt troubled but still secure. It was, after all, his board—or so he thought.

If business writers on the outside sensed such serious trouble on the inside, the key person on the inside should have more than appreciated how far the board's confidence had eroded. Ordinarily, directors offer nothing to inquisitive writers, yet newspaper columns were filling with stories that the coming CBS board meeting could be a "test" of Wyman's leadership. Despite the swirling commentary, Wyman walked into the meeting with a surprise proposal so radical— the merger with Coke—that only a board still very much on board was likely to embrace it.

Yet Wyman perceived or appreciated none of this. As his directors took their places around the boardroom table, they knew little or nothing about the Coke proposal, but, for his part, Wyman knew even less of the depth of his directors' reluctance to embrace any outside acquirer. He simply "misread the board," said one director. "If Tom hadn't taken his position, nothing would have happened at that meeting."

It can be blinding when you think that you are at the top, so blinding in fact that you sometimes fail to realize exactly where you are. Even if you are chief executive and board chair, your outside board members and owners may retain the upper hand—a power often not evident until push comes to shove.

That potential for a shove is most likely when your performance falters. That's when you will most need to appreciate who is really the boss. That's when you wish you had consulted and otherwise cultivated those who do count. If you have, they and you will know the story and appreciate the rescue plan; if not, they may feel blindsided by an action that is perfectly sensible to you but cannot be readily appreciated by them. The board was shocked by Wyman's plan, but he was even more shocked by its reaction to his plan.

As long as you report to directors and investors, remember that you're not on top, no matter how many perks of office might flow your way. If you keep your real bosses in the dark, surprise them at will, or slight their intelligence, they'll be on top of you before you know it.

Lesson in Leading Up

Overconfidence in your governing board's confidence in you is sure to blind you to the moves you should be making to ensure you retain its trust. Poor profit performance and declining share price are enough for your directors to question their confidence, and that is when your upward work with them will become most critical.

Wyman Misjudged His Founder's Lingering Power

In retrospect, of course, one might have viewed the power situation differently. After all, it was director and former board chairman William Paley himself who had launched CBS in 1928 with $400,000 of his father's money, and he was known to be an arch defender of professional newscasting. Paley was also notorious for not letting go of his creation. When Wyman became president in 1980, he was the fifth to hold that post in the past nine years and the third in just the past four years. Most of his short-lived predecessors had been brought in and then promptly ushered out by Chairman Paley.

By 1983, however, Wyman thought the shoe was finally moving to the other foot. On his initiative, the board forced Paley out to make way for Wyman's accession to the chairmanship. Adding salt to a wounded ego, Wyman also ousted Paley from any personal say in the selection of prime-time programs, one of the founder's life-long passions. Wyman froze Paley out of other decisions of which he had been a part for more than half a century. Wyman deferred to

Paley in his presence, but in private he no longer sought his counsel. Nor did he refrain from mocking what he saw as Paley's infirmities of age.

The reactions were predictable. William Paley began to openly criticize Wyman's decisions, from his sale of the company's executive jets to an alleged overpayment for a magazine empire. Paley voiced his anger over the network's poor ratings and the decline in hard news. The former chairman needled his successor at board meetings, pestering him with small points and reopening resolved issues.

During the days leading up to the September 10 board meeting, Paley had telephoned many of his fellow directors, tipping his hand to any perceptive insider. His blood was up, the adrenaline flowing. He told a friend that he would be unavailable on the several evenings prior to the fateful board meeting, since he was on a crusade to "save my company." In Paley's mind, CBS was still his company. Even if his status as founder didn't command the respect it used to, his 8% stake in the network made his voice impossible to ignore, and he had found common cause with a director whose even greater stake guaranteed a very attentive audience.

It was a dangerous moment for a chief executive to enter a board meeting with a momentous proposal to end the firm as its founder knew it. Paley was already out of sorts, partly because he had trouble letting go, but also in part because the chief executive stoked his resentments. Wyman had cut Paley out of his lingering prerogatives, and while it may have made perfect management sense, as upward leadership it made far less sense. Moreover, though all directors might take umbrage from such treatment, this one happened to be the company founder and second largest stockholder. Paley's anger was already showing in his open criticism of Wyman at board meetings, a rare event in the normally placid culture of the boardroom. Add the CEO's cynical expressions about Paley's shortcomings behind his back, indiscreetly offered in a world of few secrets and much gossip, and it would seem that this chief executive was playing with a loaded gun.

Lesson in Leading Up

Working well in- and outside the boardroom with your directors—
especially your most powerful directors—may not always make for the
best management of the company, but it will almost always certainly
make for good leadership with the board.

A Failure to Maintain Alliances

Wyman had invited Laurence Tisch to join the CBS board because he
viewed Tisch as an ally, but Tisch's investment of $951 million had been
going steadily south. Like Paley, Tisch began to openly doubt whether
Wyman possessed what it took to restore a creative business like CBS,
though unlike Paley he also questioned whether Wyman's cost-saving
cutbacks were severe enough to restore prosperity. At his very first
board meeting, Tisch had asserted that management looked top-heavy,
especially in its sacred news division. It was an early warning, and the
more Tisch learned in the days ahead, the broader the criticism grew.

By the spring of 1986, just months after Tisch had come on the
board, he and Paley began weekly telephone conversations about the
company's management, an unusual degree of dialogue for two outside directors. Tisch publicly declared that he was "100% in agreement"
with Paley's "philosophy," and in board meetings, Tisch began adding
pointed questions about what he implied were optimistic revenue and
earnings predictions. Despite his early criticism of news costs, Tisch also
joined Paley in challenging Wyman's drift away from hard news. On
September 5, only five days before the decisive board meeting, Tisch
told a reporter that "whether the news loses money or makes money is
secondary to what we put on the air. I can't picture any point at which
profit becomes the main thought in deciding on a news program."

So intense was the behind-the-scenes dissent that it surfaced in
public speculation on Tisch's intentions given Wyman's perform-

ance. In April 1986 a *Los Angeles Times* writer had observed, "Unless CBS regains first-place standing in the next year or two, some industry sources wager that Wyman's administration will be replaced by one of Tisch's choosing." In the months that followed, neither revenues nor ratings regained premier status. Wyman sent a memo to board members in July warning that CBS revenues in 1996 were unlikely to exceed $235 million, far below his earlier forecast of $385 million. On August 2, he learned that CBS had registered the lowest prime-time ratings in its history.

At Paley's initiative, he and Tisch began holding a series of private luncheons to consider removing their chief executive. Having earlier avowed only passive interest in CBS, Tisch now suggested himself as a possible successor, and since Tisch and Paley together controlled more than a third of CBS's stock, it was not an unrealistic scenario. All they required was a pretext.

Tisch had begun as a Wyman ally, but he migrated into enemy territory. As a company director and its largest stockholder, his advice about news policy and warning about earnings projections had deserved utmost attention. They certainly drew Paley's notice, and if Wyman was not listening, Paley was. Tisch and Paley formed a new alliance that would prove threatening unless Wyman found the means for working more effectively with each. Personal time and a stronger ear with both directors might have seemed a poor investment of management time given the programming and financial problems plaguing the company. Yet as an investment in upward leadership it might have preserved the original alliance between Tisch and Wyman whose decline would finally prove fatal for Wyman.

Lesson in Leading Up

With a dozen or more directors, working with each and listening to all can be essential for assuring their abiding allegiance to you and averting any alliance with one another against you.

CEO ECKHARD PFEIFFER OF COMPAQ COMPUTER: FAST GROWTH AND SUDDEN OUSTER

Thomas Wyman was ultimately fired by the CBS board of directors because he failed to keep them informed of how he was trying to save the company from the grip of unwanted suitors. The fact that hostile suitors had been circling, however, was itself a product of the company's lackluster performance and skidding share price. Compaq Computer chief executive Eckhard Pfeiffer should have paid attention to the CBS saga, because a decade later he would face his own share-price disaster.

During the 1990s, under the leadership of German-born chief executive Eckhard Pfeiffer, Compaq Computer became a wunderkind in an exploding industry. When Pfeiffer took over as CEO in October 1991, Compaq ranked a lowly eighteenth in a field dominated by IBM, Fujitsu, Hewlett-Packard, and NEC. In 1992, it climbed

Eckhard Pfeiffer five days before his
dismissal on April 18, 1999.

to sixteenth; in 1993, to eighth; and in 1994, to seventh. Four years later, on April 18, 1999, Pfeiffer's board sent him packing.

It had been a remarkable decade for the executive prior to his abrupt dismissal. In a 1991 coup, venture capitalists on the board of Compaq had ousted cofounder Joseph R. "Rod" Canion and installed Pfeiffer. Pfeiffer was the natural insider choice: Canion had recruited him from Texas Instruments in 1983 to build a European operation, and by 1990 Europe accounted for 54% of the company's revenue. Canion elevated Pfeiffer to chief operating officer in 1991, and within the year Pfeiffer had Canion's job.

Over the next eight years, the directors' decision to topple the company's founder seemed nothing short of brilliant. On taking office, Pfeiffer vowed to make Compaq the leading maker of personal computers worldwide by 1996. Pfeiffer hit his target in record time, vaulting from third to first place in a single year. By 1996, he had grown the company's revenue from $3.3 billion to $14.8 billion, a fivefold multiple in just five years.

Nothing fuels future ambition like past attainment, and Pfeiffer declared in 1996 that he would catapult Compaq and its 17,000 employees from fifth in total computers sales worldwide to third. He also asserted that he would double its revenue to $30 billion by the year 2000, and he later revised that goal to $50 billion. *Business Week* named him one of the nation's top twenty-five managers of 1997, placing him in the company of such luminaries as Dell Computer's Michael Dell and General Electric's Jack Welch.

Pfeiffer drove his black convertible Porsche to Compaq's headquarters near Houston as if he were still on a German autobahn, sometimes nearing 100 miles per hour, and he drove the company in much the same way. Speed was everything, he exclaimed, several years before the Internet forced that maxim on everybody. He also ran a lean operation, insisting on a personal staff of a single secretary and producing the highest revenue per employee—nearly $1 million—in the industry. Fellow managers described him as competitive and relentless, supremely confident, and remarkably unflappable. Investors loved their payoff: A share purchased at $30 in October 1991 when Pfeiffer became CEO was worth $425 by January 1998. By 1998, Compaq had become the world's second largest computer manufacturer behind IBM. By 1999, with its earlier acquisitions of Tandem Computers (1997) and Digital Equipment Corporation (1998) consolidated, Compaq and its 66,000 employees had become a premier Internet provider as well, its equipment servicing six of the eight leading portal sites, including America Online.

The 1991 coup removing Rod Canion had been masterminded by board chairman Benjamin M. Rosen, a legendary venture investor whose other marquee successes included Lotus Development Corporation and Silicon Graphics. He had funded Compaq's start-up in 1982 with a $20,000 investment in three Texas Instrument engineers led by Canion, and in 1999 Rosen still held 5.5 million shares in his progeny. It was less than 1% of Compaq's stock, but the stake riveted Rosen's attention on the firm's quarter-to-quarter performance. Rosen, who had served as Compaq's chairman since its inception, also knew the industry well, and he served as a frequent confidant and sounding board for the managers he had backed or installed in it. Pfeiffer and Rosen telephoned each other several times a week. By early 1999, however, those calls were becoming strained as Compaq's results went from incline to decline.

Falling Short of Investor Expectations

On Friday, April 9, 1999, Compaq Computer warned shareholders of slowing revenue and declining profits: First-quarter earnings would be less than half of those expected—$250 million instead of $560. Though this was a bombshell to the investment community, Pfeiffer refused to hold a conference call with investors and analysts to explain why he had fallen so short of their expectations.

That evening, the bad news seemingly behind him, Pfeiffer attended a glittering fund-raiser at the University of Houston. He was the center of attention, with contributors pitching in $3 million to endow a professorial chair in his name. The evening's program included the unveiling of a bronze bust of him, and chairman Ben Rosen lavished praise on him.

When Pfeiffer finally did speak with investors and analysts the following Monday, he blamed the product market for the revenue decline, telling them that the shortfall resulted from "an industry-wide problem of very competitive pricing." His explanation, however, seemed at sharp variance with industry reality. Hewlett-Packard and Dell Computer Corporation were still selling personal computers like hotcakes.

Moreover, Pfeiffer's voice during the conference call was faint and many questioners were inadvertently cut off, ordinarily minor glitches had it not been for the widespread fury on the listening end by then. Given "that many institutions have continued to question management credibility," complained James Poyner, an analyst with CIBC Oppenheimer, "Compaq's handling of the announcement was extremely disappointing behavior." Symptomatic of the Street's reaction, one analyst asked, "If the question is, do you trust the information coming out of Compaq," his answer was an unequivocal "no." By the end of the day, investors had removed 22% of the company's value in extremely active trading.

Less than two weeks after Compaq's share price plunged, IBM announced that its personal computer sales were up more than 50%. Gateway's chief executive said bluntly that "there's a crisis at Compaq, but not in the industry." The inevitable conclusion, then, was that Compaq alone was suffering the industry's ails. In the view of Merrill Lynch analyst Steven Milunovich, Compaq's "rugs" were "being pulled out from underneath them" by direct sellers like Dell and Gateway that were offering better, cheaper, and faster products. If so, there was nobody to blame but top management itself. Ashok Kumar, an analyst with US Bancorp Piper Jaffray, remarked that "someone should take responsibility for this."

Chairman Rosen consulted with the outside directors—all directors on the twelve-member board except Pfeiffer were outsiders—and he told Pfeiffer on Saturday, April 17, that he and the board had decided Pfeiffer must resign. Pfeiffer did so on Sunday, April 18, just nine days after dropping his bombshell on Wall Street. By then, explained analyst Ashok Kumar, with "so much bad blood between the old management and the Street, there was nothing they could do to fix it."

On July 23, the board elevated Michael D. Capellas, already Compaq's acting chief operating officer, to serve as CEO, and the internal promotion proved prescient. Capellas moved Compaq solidly back into the black by mid-2000, posting a second-quarter profit of $387 million. From a low of $18 a share, Compaq's stock nearly doubled in value.

Benjamin Rosen one day
after the dismissal of
Eckhard Pfeiffer.

A widely dispersed stock base can seem to give management the upper hand, but institutional investors have learned to use their clout, even if each owns no more than a fraction of a firm's shares. Together they collectively control a large minority if not a majority of a company's stock, and when unhappy with its performance, they have mastered the art of telling the directors that either the board intervenes or the directors themselves may be voted out. Rarely will this happen, but the conjunction of three factors can almost ensure it will: a substantial drop in performance, even if just a quarter's worth or two; a significant surprise that the setback was coming; and an executive approach of keeping those who own the company at arm's-length. However stellar the company's past performance, when these three factors are so aligned, a prior record counts for little, and the only issue is what the chief executive can credibly promise for tomorrow.

Lesson in Leading Up

Stockholders hate shocks. To keep your board on board, you'll need to keep your investors informed and their expectations in line. Otherwise, disparate shareholders and lofty directors are likely to form an unholy alliance around a single momentary purpose—your ouster.

Disappointing Director Expectations

Benjamin Rosen explained the board's decision to fire Eckhard Pfeiffer: "The company is so much more complex than it was a couple of years ago. It takes a different skill set in managing the company as successfully as it should be." Among those skills was faster movement than even what Pfeiffer had been demanding, and greater appreciation for the power of the Internet. Implementation also was key: "We need to execute better," asserted Rosen, "and improve the speed of our decision making."

Yet the way Pfeiffer saw it, he was a casualty of Wall Street vengeance rather than his own corporate mismanagement. So extensive was investor anger, he said, that it required a head—in this case his own: "If you want to appease the financial community, you create a shake-up." Pfeiffer said that he had been moving with speed and focusing on the Web, pushing the company into a "100% focus on the Internet." In response to criticism that he had been slow to consolidate his acquisition of Tandem and Digital, he asserted that the board simply "did not comprehend" how challenging had been his task to incorporate their 55,000 employees. In reaction to the suggestion that the board had been blindsided by the quarter's unexpected shortfall, he asserted that the directors had actually been informed of the figures before their announcement—and that some had even reviewed and approved the details of the announcement. He said in a television interview, "The Compaq board should hang their head in shame."

But the board had been evaluating the CEO's performance for more than eighteen months, and its decision was only triggered by the earnings shortfall surprise. Several directors had already been suggesting Pfeiffer's replacement, and their dissatisfaction derived as much from his inside management as his financial performance. Most salient was Pfeiffer's record of forcing out or losing many of his own top executives over the years. Chief strategist Robert Stearns had departed, as had manufacturing director Greg Petsch, chief financial officer Daryl White, North American head Ross Cooley, server chief Gary Stimac, and several general counsels. During one eighteen-month period in 1996–97, five of his eleven vice presidents had resigned.

Pfeiffer explained his high executive turnover: "I delegated authority and responsibility to a point that exceeded some people's ability to fully live up to that expectation." The fired managers, however, saw it very differently. Robert Stearns, for instance, complained at a regular senior staff meeting in April 1998 that the company's top team was being undermined by a CEO who treated his top executives as if they were divided into "an A team and a B team." The first enjoyed ready access and choice assignments; the second sat hours waiting to see the chief executive. Pfeiffer caustically responded that "if there is a B team," it was "because you have put yourselves on it."

With many ex-executives having a grudge to settle, Pfeiffer created a minefield around him, and when his financials faltered in early 1999, Rosen began to ask why so many top people had left. In Pfeiffer's view, Rosen spent too much time talking with Compaq's disgruntled ex-executives. For Rosen, the conversations with Pfeiffer's victims were a revelation. Their fingers pointed at Pfeiffer's style. "In retrospect," Rosen said, "it would have been better if we acted earlier."

Investors rarely hear employee complaints, but directors often listen, and in this case they had not liked what they were hearing. For a chief executive to dismiss a few top executives comes with the territory. A CEO who alienates much of his top management team, however, raises red flags about whether he is building what is required for company leadership in the long run. Enterprise performance depends more on the quality of the top team than on the individual who heads it, and if a CEO cannot keep the best members of his team, the directors naturally worry about the future.

While not a failure in upward leadership per se, a manager's inability to keep the best employees in the ranks is essential for keeping the directors on board. So long as performance is stellar, as it had been for Pfeiffer, directors may look the other way; as soon as performance falters, as it did for Pfeiffer, directors will look your way. Leading up depends on meeting director expectations, and they expect that you'll keep your best talent. Underappreciating that principle, as Pfeiffer evidently did, is a prescription for an early exit.

Lesson in Leading Up

Addressing director expectations is as important as meeting investor hopes, and directors expect that you'll develop a talented top management team to ensure not only short-term results but also long-term success. Investors care little how you achieve your results, but your directors do care how your ranks respond, even when the results are fine. Keeping the board in your column requires keeping your employees on your side, too.

CEO ROBERT AYLING OF BRITISH AIRWAYS: A NEEDED RESTRUCTURING RESULTS IN A SURPRISING SACKING

Eckhard Pfeiffer had presided over a period of unprecedented growth for Compaq Computer: Under his tutelage, the company had grown in revenue from $3 billion to $31 billion in just eight years. If effective upward leadership was vital for keeping his place at the helm, it is even more critical for the chief executive whose company is not enjoying such growth and must restructure to achieve it. Changing company strategies and redesigning corporate architecture are inherently stressful undertakings, and when restructuring is required, leading up with the board of directors and the investment community becomes all the more critical—as British Airways CEO Robert Ayling discovered in 2000.

British Airways had already completed one of the memorable remakes of the industry—from a money-losing state enterprise in the 1980s into a privatized darling of investors and customers by the early 1990s. Robert J. Ayling had taken the reins of Europe's largest airline in January 1996 with a pledge to continue restructuring the airline into "the best-managed company in Britain by 2000."

Ayling knew both the company and the airline industry well. As a solicitor and undersecretary in Britain's Department of Trade and Industry, he had overseen the privatization of British Airways and then joined it as its legal director. He subsequently directed the airline's human resources, marketing, and operation divisions, and he became a managing director in 1993 and *the* managing director three years later. He had fast-tracked to the top of one of Britain's premier companies, one that had been doing exceedingly well under private ownership.

The Right Restructuring Plan, Faulty Leadership of It

Upon taking over, Ayling knew that the company of 64,000 employees required further restructuring. Its fleet of Boeing 747s were aging, oil prices were rising, the British pound was falling, and hungry competitors were threatening. Observers agreed: "When he began," offered one investment banker, "pilots had limos and stayed in four-star hotels in an industry that was destroying capital." Ayling had inherited a "cost structure that was unsustainable," the banker concluded, and the "board should have backed him to the hilt."

To restore prosperity in a cutthroat market, Ayling would have to curtail costs, and this meant renegotiating the generous union contracts that his two predecessors had allowed. It also meant overcoming a dowdy image and attracting upscale flyers. All this would require courage and persistence, and he made it clear to detractors that he was there for the long overhaul. "I shall leave when I'm sixty, and not before," he had declared in his early fifties.

In pursuit of these goals, however, Ayling made few friends among those most affected. He incensed employees with a hard-line, no-negotiation posture during a 1997 strike of cabin crews. He not only threatened to fire them but also to sue for lost revenue, and he added more fuel to the fire when he outsourced engine maintenance and long-haul catering. He alienated budget customers when he deliberately shrunk the airline's market share—some 12% over three years—by catering to affluent customers at the expense of back-packers. He angered travel agents by demanding a cut in their commissions, and irritated traditionalists by repainting the tail fins of his aircraft fleet with eye-catching ethnic art from around the world.

Robert Ayling believed he had a set of bosses willing to ride out the criticism that was inevitable with more restructuring. The directors of British Airways had backed his remake of the company from the start, and he thus pushed ahead, seeking business passengers and acquiring smaller, more efficient aircraft, such as the Boeing 777 and Airbus A320. He added "flying beds" in first class that Singapore and other airlines soon emulated; his improved seating and personal videos for other classes proved hits as well. He negotiated a bold but ultimately unsuccessful alliance with American Airlines. He announced that 6,000 of his employees, nearly 10% of the workforce, would be eased out.

The restructuring seemed to be working. Ayling had successfully cut more than £1 billion in costs from a £10 billion annual operation, and he retained the support of his two most powerful directors: Lord King, who as chief executive had initiated the airline's privatization in 1987, and Lord Marshall, who as the subsequent CEO had taken it from last to first in customer confidence. King now served as nonexecutive president, Marshall as chairman.

But 1999 was not a kind year for the carrier despite the restructuring. The year before Ayling took the helm, the company had earned pretax profits of £585 million. Now it reported a deficit—the first annual loss since privatization. The company's market capitalization had fallen from a high of £7.6 billion to £3.2 billion in early 2000, a 60% decline. Granada Group, a British hospitality and media company, added the airline to its potential target list, and a line of graffiti on London's Heathrow airport captured the reversal of fortune: "First we had a King, then we had a Marshall, now we are just Ayling."

*Lord Marshall, Robert J. Ayling, and Lord King one day
before Ayling's dismissal on March 10, 2000.*

Despite the bad news, Robert Ayling remained a confident fifty-three-year-old CEO. Yet unknown to him at the time, several nonexecutive directors—including Sir Michael Angus, former chair of Unilever; Lord Renwick, former ambassador to South Africa; and Baroness O'Cathain, former director of the Barbican Centre in London—talked informally of ousting their chief executive. They even secretly interviewed a candidate for his position, but the prospect turned it down. As deputy chairman for the board and chairman of its nominations committee, Angus carried the case to Marshall, who was also becoming convinced that his friend and protégé was not living up to his billing. Marshall informally polled the seven other nonexecutive directors, and their feelings were much the same.

Seemingly oblivious to the gathering clouds, Ayling took a holiday break in South Africa. By the time he returned, relaxed and tanned, the board had turned against him, still confident in his plan but no longer in his person. Marshall conferred with the airline's finance director, Derek Stevens, to review the unhappy forecasts for the coming year, and on the evening of March 6, 2000, he met Ayling in the airline's Berkeley Square office to warn of his likely dismissal. Ashen, Ayling retreated to his town house south of London and the solace of his wife, Julia. On March 10, the board met and its directors unanimously voted to remove their chief executive.

Ayling was "baffled" by the board's sudden reversal. "The board had stuck with me" during the stressful turnaround, he said, "and I thought they would stick it out. Having gone through the worst, I thought they would stay with me." Indeed, he thought he had achieved the turnaround that everybody wanted. Just two weeks before his firing, he was telling money managers and stock analysts that the airline expected to double its operating margins within three years through cost cutting and new services for business travelers. He announced that he was putting the Internet at the center of the airline's relations with both suppliers and customers, and online ticketing was to be ramped up from 1% in 2000 to 50% by 2004.

While pulling the carpet from under Ayling, the directors reiterated their support for his strategic redirection. "For a long time we believed that there remained a reasonable prospect that Bob was going to pull it off," said Marshall just after the board's decision. "It was only in the last couple of weeks that the nonexecutive directors, individually and then collectively, decided that the time was now" for his ouster. The nonexecutive directors also decided that Ayling's restructuring was right and must be continued if British Airways was to retrieve its past luster as the world's favorite airline.

Poor performance catalyzed the board's decision, but poor relations with the board explained its action. Ayling had never groomed a successor, possibly as a buffer against his own replacement, and his autocratic, stiff, and sometimes contentious style had alienated many of those around him. The board, Marshall asserted after the sacking, "believes that there is a need for a greater emphasis on the employee relations side of the business." An analyst was more blunt: "When he came in, he had to be ruthless, but he went at it like a bull in a china shop."

Ayling was known to be warm and generous in personal dealings but could turn cold and ponderous with groups. Ayling's legal pedigree may also have limited his outside effectiveness. Karel Van Miert served as the competition commissioner for the European Union when Ayling sought approval for his alliance with American Airlines. Ayling was convinced that there was no legal logic for the EU to block the merger. But with little stroking from Ayling and much contentious challenge, Miert's back went up, and he proved more adept at working the Brussels bureaucracies than did his adversary.

On April 25, 2000, the board brought in Rod Eddington as Ayling's replacement. Eddington, age forty-nine, was an experienced aviation hand: He had served as managing director of Hong Kong's Cathay Pacific Airways and chairman of Australia's second airline company, Ansett Holdings. In pointed allusion to the past, Marshall announced that Eddington, a Rhodes scholar, had a well-deserved reputation for "his leadership, people and management skills." Said Eddington: "People are the lifeblood of any airline." Salomon Smith Barney placed an "outperform" rating on the airline, saying that Eddington "has good communication skills, is personable, has a good track record," and that those qualities would be essential when he sets out to "reverse the abrasive culture between management and cabin crews." Within two weeks, British Airways shares were up more than 20%.

Downsizing, cost cutting, and streamlining are the gritty components of company restructuring in increasingly cutthroat markets. British Airways was due, and the person who knew he had to do it was chief executive Robert Ayling. He appreciated that the process would of necessity be wrenching, but he underappreciated how the widespread human stress below could come back to nip him from above unless he handled it with compassion and care. A cold, harsh, and arm's-length method can force the change required, but for a manager to survive the process, it is also imperative that the affected employees appreciate the need for the change even if personally aggrieved by it, and that the directors can support the manager's method of the change.

Lesson in Leading Up

Corporate restructuring places a premium on upward leadership: that is when the stress is greatest and the risks are largest, and that is when retaining your directors' support is both most difficult and most vital.

STANDING ON THE THREE-LEGGED STOOL OF DIRECTORS, INVESTORS, AND EMPLOYEES

Thomas Wyman of CBS was unexpectedly dismissed by a board of which he was chairman. Eckhard Pfeiffer of Compaq Computer was abruptly shown the exit of a company he had grown tenfold in eight years. Robert Ayling of British Airways was sacked at a moment when he should have had complete control.

Unique events precipitated each firing, but behind all were distressed directors emboldened by irate investors and unhappy employees. Recognizing that you do have bosses, even if you are at the top, is a first step to self-preservation in a world of increased investor power. Appreciating what your bosses want and when they want it, and delivering on both, is also essential. If you are coming up short on either, it is past time to give special attention to those above you. Otherwise, they may be gunning for you, and you may be the last to know.

Thomas Wyman was unaware of the CBS directors' revolt he was about to face as he walked into his boardroom on Wednesday, September 10, 1986. Eckhard Pfeiffer was as shocked as anybody when the Compaq chairman handed him his walking papers on Saturday, April 17, 1999. And Robert Ayling was confident enough about his future to have vacationed abroad just before the British Airways board ousted him on March 10, 2000.

Preserving directors' confidence can be especially critical among companies engaged in organizational restructuring or strategic redirection, as seen at British Airways. That is when company conflict is most pitched and resistance most fierce. When jobs are threatened, divisions slashed, and rules rewritten, those on the short end hit back with whatever means available, however necessary the changes may be. Outside owners hear little from the ranks, but directors are not out of earshot, and though you are in between, disgruntled employees have no problem going around your back if they are unhappy enough and your back is turned. Your effectiveness in leading up therefore depends in part upon your success in leading down. If you have not done the latter well, your board is likely to know it. Even though your directors have pledged not to interfere with your management of the company, and even if they have promised to back your restructuring of it, they may choose to pull the plug. This is especially true when they hear frequent and unhappy messages about your downward leadership, and those messages parallel what they already see as shortcomings in your upward style. Then, even a stellar performance may not save the day, and declining results may end it.

Wyman's dismissal of staff and his leavening of the news created enemies within CBS who were able to carry their opposition into the boardroom through Walter Cronkite. Wyman's exclusion of William Paley from management decisions, even if appropriate, created another powerful opponent on the board. Pfeiffer's churning of his executive ranks in a search for the right people to manage a changing enterprise created a cadre of disgruntled ex-managers whose critical voice readily reached up to the boardroom when Chairman Ben Rosen reached down for it. Robert Ayling's callous cost cutting engendered widespread hostility within the ranks, a condition no board could ignore. When their boards' support was most vital, it was, in fact, most lacking, and the chief executives had only themselves to blame.

True, the three executives faced exceptionally powerful overseers. Wyman reported to two directors who together owned a third of the company; Pfeiffer reported to a chairman who had seeded the company and served as chairman since its inception; Ayling reported to two directors who themselves used to run the company. Many executives will never have to contend with such commanding figures. But as boards become more sovereign worldwide, executives can expect to face more demanding directors than in the past.

A first principle, then, is to remember that you have superiors, even if your business card combines both *chief* and *executive*. A second is to remember the cardinal tenet of the capitalist universe, on a par with nature's abhorring a vacuum in the physical universe: Never ever surprise your directors. That is when you are most vulnerable, as Wyman found when he startled his board with a takeover proposal, and as Pfeiffer and Ayling discovered when their rosy financial projections turned to ash.

A third principle is to remember that retaining your directors' confidence depends on maintaining credibility with your investors and faith with your employees. Languishing short-term performance had weakened the investor support for Wyman, Pfeiffer, and Ayling. Troubled internal relations damaged their employees' confidence as well. Both developments undermined the ample director support with which each had started.

Effectively leading up with your directors thus simultaneously requires leading out to the financial community and leading down through the management ranks. Executives always sit on a three-legged stool, supported by directors, investors, and employees. If the stool lacks either investor or employee support, the directors will find it difficult to keep it upright with their leg alone.

CHAPTER 5

KEEPING YOUR HEAD WHEN YOU HAVE SEVERAL SUPERIORS

GENERAL PETER PACE OF THE U.S. MARINE CORPS
REPORTED TO SIX COMMANDERS AND COULD DISAPPOINT NONE

BUSINESS HAS OFTEN looked to military models for lessons in leadership because of the seemingly impervious top-down authority system. Yet the military also offers invaluable lessons in just the opposite—the requirement that subordinates challenge their commanders before their orders go into effect. By encouraging those below you to tell you what's right and wrong with your orders before you give them, and by telling those above you what's good or bad with their plans before they impose them, you may save your own life and protect those of many others.

From the football field to the flight deck, America's armed forces have long defined what friendly competition is all about: same goals, different paths, rival cultures. During the late 1980s, however, the nation concluded that it could no longer permit the jousting of the Army-Navy game to reach beyond the stadium. In 1986, Congress enacted the "Goldwater-Nichols" Defense Department Reorganization

Act, requiring improved joint service operations. To ensure that the country's war-fighting doctrine, strategy, and soldiers worked together in common cause, President Clinton in 1993 ordered an integration of military operations under the U.S. Atlantic Command, and the Department of Defense in 1999 transformed that authority into the U.S. Joint Forces Command.

For Marine Corps lieutenant general Peter Pace, the reorganization amounted to a seismic shift. With three stars on his epaulets, Pace had reached a level where formal performance reviews were no longer required. In overseeing the 92,000 Marines and 1,000 aircraft under his command, he simultaneously had to please no fewer than six immediate superiors, all of them four-star generals or admirals. Pace knew that his bosses' bosses—the chairman of the Joint Chiefs of Staff and the secretary of defense—were watching as well.

"If I try to be all things to everybody," Pace warned himself, "I'll be nothing to anybody." And thus his challenge: how to meet the demands of multiple superiors, each with a distinct agenda.

In navigating the turbulent waters around multiple superiors, Pace developed several personal guidelines. One: Ensure that his own performance was above reproach. Another: Fully inform each of the bosses of what he was recommending to all the others. And a third: When in doubt on how to resolve the commanders' conflicting requirements, act on principle. Knowing who you are and what you stand for provides sure guidance when your several superiors have divergent imperatives.

Pace's personal guidelines were reinforced by a powerful culture that is both top down and bottom up. It guides every U.S. Marine and is reinforced daily by officers like Pace. Command and control are at a Marine officer's fingertips when required. But challenge and confrontation are at the subordinate's fingertips when needed. If you receive a direct order, you are of course obligated to follow it. But if that order detracts from the military mission—and everyone is trained to discern what does and does not contribute to a mission—you are also obligated to take issue with your commanding officer. The military might appear to be the last place on earth where upward leadership is tolerated, but in fact such leadership is obligatory, as we'll see in this chapter.

Peter Pace's experience also points to the critical importance of an encompassing culture for stimulating and rewarding upward leadership. Many individuals like Pace learn to lead through a natural process of solving problems and achieving missions. Others come to appreciate the art of leading up only if the organization fosters it. Once you have personally mastered the art, building a culture around you where all are inspired to lead up can vastly leverage its impact.

A Sergeant in Vietnam Questioned Authority but Saved Lives

Born in Brooklyn and raised in the town of Teaneck, New Jersey, Peter Pace had always wanted to attend the U.S. Naval Academy, but he hadn't intended to become a U.S. Marine. In fact, he became one with little forewarning at all. Between his first and second years at the academy, he and his fellow midshipmen spent three weeks in an amphibious warfare program run by the Marines, and he liked what he saw. Upon graduation in 1967, he volunteered for the Corps, and

General Peter Pace

after six months of training, he arrived in Vietnam, just as the war there had reached one of its great turning points.

On January 30, 1968, the eve of the Tet Lunar New Year festival, an estimated 84,000 Vietcong and North Vietnamese troops attacked thirty-six major cities and towns, including Da Nang, Hue, and Saigon, transforming a rural struggle into an urban nightmare. In the fierce fighting that followed, U.S. and South Vietnamese soldiers managed to force back the invaders. More than 30,000 Vietcong guerrillas died in the counteroffensive. None of the territory seized in their attacks remained in enemy hands. But the violence of the Tet Offensive so unnerved the American public that the battlefield victory would become a wartime defeat, with most Americans now convinced that the insurgency could not be crushed and that America had become trapped in a quagmire.

One of the most fiercely contested terrains was the ancient city of Hue, the capital of Vietnam until 1949, not far from the border that then divided South Vietnam from the North. In the opening moments of the Tet Offensive, Vietcong and North Vietnamese troops seized the Citadel, a fortress surrounding the Imperial City. Ensconced behind its seven miles of moats and ramparts, the insurgents held out for twenty-six days until finally dislodged by the U.S. Marines.

Marine Corps lieutenant Peter Pace arrived in Hue to take command of a rifle platoon still mopping up from the carnage left behind. Inwardly a "scared puppy" but outwardly cool, Pace and his platoon were soon patrolling the precarious countryside. As they walked the landscape, Pace knew that any faulty decision could send them down a path from which many soldiers might never return. At one point, his platoon was serving as an advance party for a company of 160 men on patrol when Pace came to a fork in the road in an area crawling with enemy forces. He radioed his company commander, Charles Meadows, for advice: "Do you want me to go left or do you want me to go right?" Captain Meadows barked back, "Go left." When Pace faced a second split, he asked again for advice. The third call for the same purpose brought him a tongue-lashing from his commander: He was a lieutenant, the guy in front, and he was there to take action.

Pace learned on the spot that when they were his problems to solve he would make his own decisions and not run them up the chain of command. "That was a lesson," recalled Pace, "that I never forgot." The decisions would be case by case, but he grasped the singular importance of being clear minded about which were his and which were his commander's calls to make. He also resolved to err on the side of confidence over diffidence, of solving more and asking less.

"I promised myself that I would get in trouble for going too far," he said, "not for holding back." Pace thought to himself: Okay, you want me to lead, I'm leading. If you don't want me to lead, you'll have to walk the length of the column to come up here and find me to stop me. He also knew he had hit on a formula for action: "Freed up to do what I thought best, I would make mistakes, but I'd get a whole lot more done."

The Marine Corps reassigned Pace and his men to the rice fields outside Da Nang, a welcome change of scenery but with little improvement in security. Snipers positioned themselves in the tiny villages dotting the rice paddies, and when Pace's platoon approached one of the hamlets near Liberty Bridge on July 30, 1968, an enemy marksman found a mark: Lance Corporal Guido Farinaro, a nineteen-year-old from Bethpage, New York. As Pace approached his fallen comrade, he saw a chest wound so severe that death was certain and imminent. Outraged by his first fatality, Pace resolved that the sniper would pay the same price. He seized the radio to call for an artillery barrage, but as he was giving the village's coordinates, he looked up to see his platoon sergeant, Reid B. Zachary, staring at him. The sergeant was on his second Vietnam tour, and Pace had come to place great trust in his judgment in their months together since Hue.

The sergeant said nothing, but his eyes said it all. "I knew that he was right, that I was about to do the wrong thing," Pace recalled. Recognizing that he had nearly "crossed over the line," he canceled the artillery and swept the village instead. The platoon found only women and children in the hamlet, many of whom would have perished in an artillery pounding.

Pace had been jarred into clearer thought by his noncommissioned officer: "Before you go into combat," he reflected, "think through who you are, what you will allow yourself to do, and what you will not allow yourself to do, because the time to decide whether or not to drop the bombs is not when the pilot flying next to you has been shot down. The time to decide whether or not to take out the village is not when you've had one of your guys killed by a sniper. You've got to have an anchor that you can hold on to when the overwhelming emotions wash over you. I had that anchor but I almost let go. Just looking at my platoon sergeant got me recalibrated."

For Pace, it was an early lesson in learning from below, in accepting upward advice even when volunteered with little more than a questioning look. Ensuring that you have the right anchor beforehand was important, Pace argued, but without a nod from under, any anchoring would have been moot.

Lesson in Leading Up

There's no better place to point your antennae than at what your subordinates are implying or communicating through other means. Because their stake in you is so large, they often appreciate you and your situation better than you do yourself.

SEEING UP TO LOOK DOWN

Pace's recalibration would be tested again before leaving the Vietnam countryside. In fact, he faced several near-fatal experiences of his own, and they later reinforced his own resolve to remain a lifelong career military officer.

One of these experiences occurred when he was encamped near an old French fort in midsummer 1968. The battalion commander assigned his platoon to assist with security, and the chief of security asked Pace to help improve a defensive plan for the perimeter, already fortified with two lines of barbed wire. Pad and pencil in hand, Pace meandered several hundred feet between the inner and outer lines of wire to acquire a better fix on the ground that he was to protect. The security chief came screaming at him not to move: "You're in a minefield, Pete!" Frozen in place, Pace clearly saw what he had no reason to notice before. The trigger for a three-pronged "bouncing Betty" pierced the soil just to the right of his foot. If touched, it would have propelled an explosive four feet upward to detonate in his face.

An equally providential brush with fate came several weeks later when on patrol west of Da Nang in the province of Quang Nam on August 18. Pace had done what officers wisely did, removing his bars, carrying a rifle, walking among the foot soldiers. He would not so visibly be the commanding officer, the perfect target for any guerrilla. Still, village children proffered a hardy "Hi, boss!" as he passed, and enemy sharpshooters intuited his rank as well. As his company approached the village of La Thap, it began taking fire from the settlement, and Pace knelt down to consult with several Marines, including acting company gunnery sergeant Freddy Roosevelt Williams from Plains, Georgia. They discussed how to seize La Thap, and as they stood back up to move off, Williams, age thirty-three, stepped between Pace and the village tree line some 500 meters distant. Just as he did so, he took a rifle shot from the trees in the side, a fatal hit that would have otherwise hit Pace squarely in the chest. Whoever had pulled the trigger seems to have had the "unmarked" officer firmly in his crosshairs.

It would be a bloody patrol. As they moved across a stream and rice paddies toward the village, three more of Pace's men were fatally hit: Corporal Michael D. ("Chubby") Hale, Lance Corporal William O. ("Whitey") Travers Jr., and Lance Corporal Michael R. Witt. Hale and Witt were both age twenty-one, and Pace was with them when they died. Travers was nineteen, and Pace saw where he lay.

Peter Pace hadn't yet reached his twenty-third birthday when he wandered into that minefield. He served his entire thirteen-month tour operating in the field before shipping back to the States in early 1969. Another five years would pass before the United States completed its withdrawal from a war that had cost the Marine Corps 13,000 dead and some 88,000 wounded. Of the 158 Marines in the company that Pace had joined in Hue in early 1968, fewer than a dozen left the country unscathed.

Peter Pace's moments of tempting fate had sealed his fate. "After the possibilities of Hue City, the minefield, and the firefights—and never getting wounded—it seemed to me," he recalled, "that there was something the good Lord wanted me to do." The something was not yet clear, but the intent seemed evident.

In the U.S. Marine Corps, only eighty officers hold the rank of general: half bear one star, twenty-five display two, eleven carry three, and four show four. For every sixteen colonels, the highest rank below the single star of a brigadier general, only one will move up. Once the Corps selects its generals, it invests heavily in their development, and the outlay won't be repaid for years. The U.S. Marine Corps promoted Pace and invested in him.

Peter Pace added one star to his lapel in 1992, the second star of a major general in 1994, and the third, of a lieutenant general, in 1996. By then, he had entered the select ranks of flag officers who presided over the nation's 170,000 Marines. Anywhere along the way, Pace might have been passed over for promotion, and if so, he would have retired. But if he exited for personal gain—lucrative private-sector opportunities that were beckoning some fellow officers—he would have violated his vows of selfless service. If "I'm going to walk away, for whatever reason," he said, "then I have really done my service a disservice." His would be a lifetime commitment. Once you are selected to be a general, he explained, you "forfeit your right to voluntarily leave."

Having reached the select ranks, Peter Pace felt his career choices were now dictated as much by what the Marine Corps needed as by what he might want. The Corps is not a corporation that can fill an executive vacancy from the outside. It only promotes from below, and if you walk away before your time, you hurt the organization twice: You create an unanticipated void, and you deny an opportunity to a great colonel who otherwise would have become a capable general instead of taking retirement. As a result, Pace came to view his own options as if he were looking down on them from the perch of the Marine commandant. He could visualize so clearly to the top that he could appreciate what they expected of him.

The military is a unique institution, but whether the arena is armed combat or product competition, a capacity for seeing up to look down—a vital component of leading up—can be generated by most organizations if they give their new managers early exposure to frontline responsibilities and risks. Ever since his life-testing moments as a twenty-two-year-old field officer in Vietnam just months after commissioning, Pace had a firm fix on his priorities. "If I was going to serve in combat at all," he said, "I was fortunate to do it in the first tour as a Marine officer because it crystallized for me what's important and what's not."

A chance to sink or swim early in a career may not inspire life-long loyalty to the institution—few organizations besides the United States Marine Corps can expect that—but it can instill an enduring obligation to the principle of viewing the organization as if you owned it. Leading up from below depends on looking down from the top, and there are few better ways for developing this capacity than by placing officers and managers on the line early in their careers.

Lesson in Leading Up

By never forgetting what those below have done for us and what those above expect of us, we can help ensure that everything from our daily actions to our career decisions remains true to their sacrifice and to our mission.

MAINTAINING FACE-TO-FACE CONTACT WITH YOUR SUPERIORS

What's the day-to-day job like for a man in charge of 92,000 Marines and 1,000 aircraft, with six bosses scattered across two continents? Pace maintains a headquarters office in Norfolk, Virginia, but as this typical (and only partial) schedule from the six weeks beginning February 1, 2000, shows, the general is rarely there:

February 2: Miami: Pace met with his Florida-based staff for the Latin region.

February 3: Miami: Pace briefed one of his six bosses, General

Charles E. Wilhelm, commander in chief for the Southern Command, on training military forces in Peru to combat drug traffic in South America.

February 7: Stuttgart, Germany: Pace's staff briefed him on developments in the Balkans, where thousands of Marines were stationed.

February 8: Pace and the three other "component commanders" (i.e., generals representing the Army, the Air Force, the Marines, and the Navy) focused on Bosnia and Kosovo during a meeting with General Wesley K. Clark, commander in chief, United States European Command, and NATO's supreme allied commander for Europe since 1997.

February 9: Camp Lejeune, North Carolina: At this Marine Corps base Pace hosted a display of military firepower for 150 generals and admirals from the Air Force, the Army, and the Navy.

February 12: Pace attended a black-tie annual birthday ball for the Navy Supply Corps, the only Marine able to attend.

February 15: Pace met with another of his six superiors, Admiral Vern Clark, commander in chief for the Atlantic Fleet. When Pace shipped Marines across the Atlantic, he did so on Admiral Clark's ships. The subject of this meeting: the future of the Atlantic Fleet and the preparation its people required.

February 24: London: Pace joined a seminar for U.S. ambassadors and business executives from throughout Europe and hosted yet another superior, Admiral James O. Ellis Jr., commander in chief for the European Fleet. The focus of this seminar: furthering American interests in Europe.

February 25–27: Quantico, Virginia: Pace gathered with a group of twenty senior commanders at the Marine Corps base here, to prepare a strategic plan for the decade ahead.

March 1: Pace met with U.S. secretary of defense William Cohen.

March 6: Stuttgart: Pace convened his European staff.

March 7: Pace met with U.S. ambassadors to a dozen European nations.

March 8: Bosnia: Pace visited Marines based here.

March 10: New Orleans: Pace met with the Marine general officers responsible for the 42,000 Marine reserves under Pace's command.

These were less than half of Peter Pace's stops during the six-week period, but to the unaided eye it would still appear to be a schedule from hell. The schedule might have been less onerous if he had farmed out some of his obligations to others, especially as he was not short of staff members and his office included a one-star deputy commander. Pace also could have lightened the load by letting others represent him at the frequent meetings with Wesley Clark in Europe. Of the four component commanders reporting to Clark, three already resided on the Continent. Only Pace had to cross the Atlantic to attend, and during the most violent periods of the Balkans conflict, Clark was convening the group almost weekly.

Despite the hours of air travel, Pace took the view that he had to be in the room when Wesley Clark decided on his European actions. When Clark had something that should be done, he asked each of the commanders around the table, "Can we do it?" And if only three subordinates sat at the table, Pace knew, Clark would only hear three answers. If Pace sent a substitute, the replacement would be a one- or two-star officer in a sea of four stars. Thus Pace would have to be there in person to ensure that Clark received a fourth answer with three stars behind it. It was not a matter of fighting for position at the table nor, by implication, a piece of the action for its own sake. Rather, it was a matter of making sure the boss knew all his options. "If I'm not there to articulate to him what would best serve his mission in the Balkans or elsewhere," Pace argued, "then I'm not serving him the way I should serve him."

Conscientiously attending the meeting to voice a view was only half of his purpose. Accepting Pace's point of view depended on Clark's trust in Pace, and that could only be assured if Pace was consistently in the room. If Clark knew little more than Pace's three-star status, he would respect the rank but have little on which to trust the man. Face-to-face contact became the sine qua non for credibility.

"I want to make sure all of my counterparts know who Pete Pace is and know they can trust me, and that I will not lie to them," Pace explained. "When I tell them I am going to do something," he went on, they know that "I [am] going to do it and they can bank on it." During his several years as Marine commander for the Atlantic, Pace never missed a Stuttgart meeting with Clark. As a result, when the commander in chief for Europe thought about employing the Marines in the Balkans or elsewhere, he knew that Pace was the sure "door" to using the 92,000 Marines under his command. The ultimate objective, Pace said, was to ensure that Wesley Clark "knows that I'd live and die for him."

Being there is a must for communicating up what the boss needs to know. But it can also be essential for building trust so that the boss knows as well that the subordinate means action. Faxes, telexes, and overnight delivery services strengthen the factual foundation for taking action, and surface mail, voice mail, and e-mail bolster the flow, but making a point to see your boss in person engenders the confidence that you are indeed ready for action under his or her direction.

Lesson in Leading Up

For representing your operation's capabilities and requirements to your superior, there can be no substitute for frequent face-to-face discussion and debate.

U.S. SECRETARY OF DEFENSE
WILLIAM S. COHEN

CHAIRMAN, JOINT CHIEFS OF STAFF,
GENERAL HENRY H. SHELTON

COMMANDANT OF THE
MARINE CORPS
GENERAL JAMES L. JONES

COMMANDER IN CHIEF,
JOINT FORCES COMMAND,
ADMIRAL HAROLD W. GEHMAN JR.

COMMANDER IN CHIEF,
ATLANTIC FLEET,
ADMIRAL VERN E. CLARK

COMMANDER IN CHIEF,
EUROPEAN COMMAND,
GENERAL WESLEY K. CLARK

COMMANDER IN CHIEF,
EUROPEAN FLEET,
ADMIRAL JAMES O. ELLIS JR.

COMMANDER IN CHIEF,
SOUTHERN COMMAND,
GENERAL CHARLES E. WILHELM

U.S. MARINE CORPS FORCES, ATLANTIC
GENERAL PETER PACE, COMMANDER

What Peter Pace Saw When He Looked Up

WHAT TO DO
WHEN MULTIPLE BOSSES DISAGREE

The atomic-age arms race brought us the MIRV—the multiple independently targeted reentry vehicle, with ten nuclear warheads programmed to attack ten targets simultaneously. Peter Pace reported to his own MIRV equivalent—Multiple Independently Ruling Voices—and sought to respond to the six as if each were his sole superior. He may "live and die" for Wesley Clark, but he also made identical commitments to the other five.

The principle of simultaneous targeting of multiple independently ruling voices would be put to a thorough test for Pace after the Yugoslav Republic began its tortured disintegration in the early 1990s. The U.S. and European Community had recognized Bosnia's sovereignty by April 1992, but soon thereafter Serbian paramilitary and regular units attacked Sarajevo to open their notorious "ethnic cleansing" of the region. In 1995, when the two sides finally brought their bloody conflict to an end with the Dayton Peace Accords, the European Community placed an international peacekeeping force of 60,000 troops in Bosnia to assure implementation of the agreement.

In late 1998, the European commander in chief, General Wesley Clark, sought the dispatch of additional troops for a sensitive mission in Bosnia. As unified authority for the region, Clark continually probed his subordinates to see which service could best achieve what he wanted done, and for this mission he decided he wanted the U.S. Marine Corps. Clark had graduated first in his 1966 West Point class, studied on a Rhodes scholarship at Oxford University, served as a White House Fellow, earned a Purple Heart in Vietnam, and led the military side of the Dayton negotiations on Bosnia. He asked tough questions and demanded much, and he had a task in Bosnia that he wanted done now. Near the end of a component-commander meeting in Stuttgart, Clark asked the only person who could send what he sought, Peter Pace, to supply the force. "Yes," Pace answered, "I have the Marines to do that."

General Clark was pleased to have Peter Pace's Marines for the Bosnian action, but Pace candidly advised *against* their use in Bosnia. "I don't think your Marines are the best force to do that," he warned Clark, "but if they come here, they can do that mission." Other military forces were sufficiently prepared and well equipped to achieve Clark's mission in Bosnia, and Pace would rather "save the Marines to do the things that Marines were better suited to do." He recommended to Clark that although the mission was important, "Don't spend ten dollars when five dollars will do the trick. Save your ten-dollar bill for the ten-dollar mission."

Wesley Clark decided nonetheless to spend the ten, and he asked the U.S. Joint Chiefs of Staff to authorize deployment. Upon receipt of the request, the Joint Chiefs invited the opinion of Admiral Harold Gehman, the commander in chief for the Atlantic Command, who controlled not only military personnel stationed in the United States but also those deployed in a vast region extending through Europe, Africa, and South America. Headquartered in Norfolk, Virginia, Gehman would take the request to the Marine general who oversaw all the Marines in Gehman's territory and whose office was in a neighboring building no more than a hundred yards distant: Peter Pace.

On the adage that what goes around comes around, Pace had earlier warned Clark that when Gehman later came to him for a feasibility assessment, as he surely would, Pace would oppose deployment of the Marines, even knowing that Wesley Clark badly wanted them.

"General Clark," Pace had warned, "when that question comes down to me, I'm going to say, 'Yes, I have the Marines, but I don't think they should do this mission.' " Pace wanted Clark to know what was next: "When I walk out of my office in Europe and I walk into my office in Norfolk, what I'm going to say in Norfolk is going to be an outside influence on what you want from me in Europe."

Upon returning to Norfolk, Peter Pace knew what was coming,

and it came soon. "Pete, do you have the Marines?" asked Harold Gehman. "Can they do the mission? Should they do the mission?" Pace responded affirmatively to the first and second questions, but negatively to the third. "Oh, by the way," Pace added, "you need to know that I've had a conversation with General Clark," and he informed Gehman that he had told Clark of his opposition. Gehman notified the Joint Chiefs that the Marine force was available but should not be used.

Peter Pace also cast a "third vote" against deployment when another boss, then–Marine Commandant Charles C. Krulak, posed the same question, and Pace conveyed the same response up through this superior, who also happened to be a member of the Joint Chiefs of Staff. Washington declined Clark's request for a Marine deployment, after which Clark obtained the troops from a European ally.

A similar test arose in October 1998 when General Charles Wilhelm of the Southern Command solicited support from Peter Pace after a devastating hurricane left a wide swath of death and destruction in Central America. Hurricane Mitch, the most powerful hurricane ever recorded over the Atlantic, killed 7,000 residents in Honduras alone, destroyed 80% of the country's crops, and left 20% of the nation homeless. The White House ordered the U.S. armed forces to render emergency assistance, and Wilhelm was the executing authority. He asked Pace: How many bridges can you build? How many roads can you construct? How much water can you purify? And how soon can you get your Marines down there?

General Pace would have to muster the people and equipment required for the urgent mission, but he was also mindful that his forces existed to wage the nation's wars, not provide help for its humanitarian causes. If he allowed too many Marines to spend too much time in Central America on a mission of compassion, if he employed too many of his war-fighting assets, he would deplete his capacity for combat. He could always pull his troops from Honduras if hostilities erupted elsewhere, but he knew it would take weeks to extricate them from the mud. Pace thus qualified his response to his boss even though he knew his chief would use everything Pace could give him. "Here's my estimate," he told Wilhelm, "of what I can do for you and maintain my responsibilities for the rest of the world." Wilhelm routed his formal request up through the Pentagon, and once again Admiral Gehman and General Krulak asked Pace for his own independent assessment of what General Wilhelm required. Balancing the immediate requirements of his southern boss against the potential requirements of the other two, Pace advised the use of some troops but not all that were available. Again, his recommendation carried.

"Although I have six bosses," Peter Pace observed, "I try to approach each boss as my only boss and do my work for that boss, not oblivious to the other five but remembering that I owe this boss my allegiance on whatever it is that we're working." A good principle, but the personal allegiance would inevitably become an issue when one superior's missions conflicted with those of the others, and they frequently did. Another guiding principle would be required if Pace were to properly contain the centrifugal forces pulling against him from the multiple independently ruling voices he was sworn to obey. He needed to know how to keep his own head when he reported to several others.

Lesson in Leading Up
When dealing with multiple independently ruling voices, it's best to face and serve each superior as if he or she is your only boss.

TOTAL HONESTY ALL THE TIME WITH EVERYBODY

Informing your superior that you won't make a requested resource available is not the conventional foundation for a long and successful career, but many organizations no longer follow a conventional organizational chart anyway. The traditional pyramid with seven mid-dle managers reporting to a single senior manager—and that senior manager and six others in turn reporting to a single chief execu-tive—has become as much the exception as the rule in industry as well as the military. In response to a world that demands organiza-tional flexibility, the simple device of vertical controls has given way to the complex system of multiple relations.

If commanders and managers were once entirely under the thumb of the all-powerful boss, they are now increasingly responsible to not just one superior but a multitude, as well as to cross-functional teams, shared services, joint ventures, outsourcing vendors, and action projects. This is precisely what the Pentagon had demanded in the early 1990s in transforming the armed forces from service-driven command to crisis-focused authority. That is why Admiral Harold Gehman oversaw all armed forces stationed in the United States, regardless of branch. And that is why Pace had six superiors rather than one.

The new ways of doing business during the MIRV era required new ways of leading up, and Peter Pace knew they must be mastered. The main axiom, he concluded, would have to be one of "total hon-esty all the time with everybody, and making sure that each of my bosses knows what I'm saying to my other bosses when it crosses over onto their turf." *Semper Fidelis,* always faithful, the famed service motto of the U.S. Marine Corps, came to require a leadership corol-lary: *Semper Veritas,* always truthful.

When Peter Pace saw a decision going against what he knew one of his other superiors wanted, he was thus quick to offer an unequiv-ocal heads up: "If I know that one of my bosses, whichever one it is, would like something other than what's going to happen, then I make sure that that boss knows exactly what I've said and whom I've said it to. That won't necessarily make him happy, but it will maintain the trust that we have with each other. He knows that I'm telling the truth even though he might not like my version of the truth."

Preemptive, detailed, upward disclosure may well be the axiom of officers or managers in organizations that require navigating through a matrix instead of reporting up a chart.

A test of Peter Pace's commitment to the principle of truthfulness and transparency came when he was invited to join a meeting of the Joint Chiefs of Staff in "the tank," the Pentagon room where top officers regularly meet on the crisis or policy of the week. America's six ranking commanders—the Joint Chiefs chairman and vice chairman, the Army and Air Force chiefs of staff, the chief of naval operations, and the Marine commandant—faced a major operational decision. The chairman asked Pace to brief those attending on the issue question because Pace—the director of operations for the Joint Chiefs—knew more about the details of the proposal than anybody else.

Going into the tank, several of Peter Pace's superiors supported the operation, and they advocated it inside. Late in the discussion, the chairman turned to Pace, the only three-star officer in the room, and asked his opinion. Pace straightaway explained that he opposed it. He would not have stated his disagreement on his own initiative, but when asked by the chairman, he followed the axiom of arguing for what he thought was right, even if in conflict with his superiors. As the brass filed out of the meeting, Pace turned to one of his superiors and mused that his bald contradiction of the chiefs' position would likely constitute a CSM—a career-shortening move—especially since the Joint Chiefs at the end had agreed with Pace. But Pace also knew in advance how his superior would respond: of course not. Saying that your boss is dead wrong—when you believe that—is an integral component of Marine Corps culture, and there was no reason to make an exception here.

Frank and full upward disclosure is a sound operating principle, and a good test of whether you are complying is to ask yourself if what you are saying to one superior is what you would say to any other. A further test is to check for whether your outward and downward mes-

Peter Pace offering Pentagon briefing, March 14, 1997.

sages are the same as what you've been offering upward. If so, your facts will be consistent, your judgment will be solid, and your reputation will be secure.

Lesson in Leading Up

With several bosses, full disclosure is essential, including frankly informing any boss whose proposals or policies are at variance with your own informed judgment.

FOSTERING A CULTURE OF LEADING UP

When James L. Jones became the Marine Corps' thirty-second commandant in mid-1999, it came as no surprise that he turned to Pace and other Marine generals for their candid comments on a draft document setting forth the commandant's strategic intent. After several drafts, Jones distributed "The Commandant's Guidance" to all

Marines and posted it on the Web. Several months later, the commandant asked all of his three- and four-star generals to report their actions for bringing his "guidance to fruition" and what needed change. Pace in turn solicited responses from all of his own one- and two-star generals, and he routed thirty-nine pages of commentary to Jones.

Among the suggestions that Peter Pace sent up the chain was to convene the Corps' top commanders to ensure that their assumptions and requirements were consistent with one another and clearly communicated to the commandant. An example of the potential inconsistencies was how Pace himself and his Pacific counterpart anticipated future use of the 42,000 Marine reservists. Pace sought to prepare the reserve troops for sudden dispatch to hot spots in Europe and Latin America. To that end, he would use prepositioned equipment in those regions so that he could move the reservists to the equipment when a sudden need arose. In contrast, Pace's Pacific counterpart, Lieutenant General Frank Libutti, commander of the U.S. Marine Corps forces for the Pacific headquartered in Hawaii, simultaneously sought to train the same reservists for rear-area security in Korea if the peninsula erupted in war. Without Pace and Libutti meshing their conflicting plans for use of the same resource, they would not be giving the commandant what he needed in advance to decide on the best worldwide use of his force. Accordingly, Pace suggested that they resolve such conflicts well before they were faced, and the commandant formed the General Officers Futures Group to sharpen Corps priorities.

It was natural both for the commandant to reach down and for his officers to speak up. "Leadership is the heart of our institutional character," offered the commandant in his 1999 guiding statement. And critical to the exercise of leadership, he asserted, was recognizing that "as many good ideas come from the bottom up, as come from the top down."

Looking down doesn't mean abrogating responsibility for action.

Nor is it simply empowering others for its own sake. Indeed, as Peter Pace saw it, the world had two popes: "One runs the Catholic Church and another runs the Marine Corps." When the commandant spoke, his officers made it happen. They pushed back with contention and analysis, sometimes rancorous, "but at the end of the day when the commandant says, 'This is what I want after listening to you guys,' we all get in step."

Peter Pace carried the same authority with his own senior staff officers, but he insisted that they contest his ideas until he had finalized a course of action. The twenty officers carried specific responsibilities for logistics, personnel, intelligence, and the like. He did not want to hear about problems that should have been fixed by the person posing them—he learned that lesson decades earlier in Vietnam. But he did want to learn about all the problems that were indeed his to solve—before it was too late to solve them. To bring that out, he had to set the stage. "Please give me the luxury of thinking out loud," he would tell his staff officers. "Please don't take every word that comes out of my mouth as what the general wants." Though many of the staff officers were colonels, even they were three grades below Pace's own rank, and new staff officers gingerly waited to see if he really meant what he said. To demonstrate that he did, he thanked those officers at their weekly meeting with him when they challenged his thinking or showed him to be wrong.

By insisting on hearing from below and making himself heard above, General Pace was sharing a precept inculcated from the first day of the six-month officer training school that the Marine Corps runs at its Quantico, Virginia, base and repeated in statement and story by officers whenever given the chance. Brigadier General Thomas Draude, an officer who served as an assistant commander for the First Marine Division during Desert Storm, explained to a civilian audience how he had finalized the division's attack plan to help expel Iraq from Kuwait in 1991. He first laid out the assault strategy for the 20,000 troops in his division, he said, and then he asked all of his subordinates to poke as many holes in it as possible, which they readily did. Charles Krulak, the former Marine Corps commandant, described the underlying principle: "You have to have people who will challenge the status quo, otherwise you will die. [Even] a private has an obligation to stand up and say, 'Why are we doing this?' "

Corporate cultures can appear impersonal and immutable, but they are always the product of past actions—whether those actions were self-consciously intended to bolster that culture or not. Current actions can thus do much to build a culture that champions upward leadership. A step by chief executive Wayne Leonard of Entergy, a power company headquartered in New Orleans, illustrates the kind of small measures that together can generate big change. In 1998, he was forging a management team among his top sixteen lieutenants to drive a turnaround, and he knew he had to get the absolute best from them all if he was to achieve the restructuring. For this he articulated thirteen "ground rules," and the thirteenth made unequivocal what he wanted from below: "It is okay to tell the CEO that he is dead wrong."

Lesson in Leading Up

A culture of upward leadership is built, not born. For that, a persistent insistence that all below you examine your proposals and challenge your errors is required. Asking those of lesser rank to say what they candidly think and complimenting them for doing so are small measures that can manufacture a big mind-set.

A VIRTUOUS CIRCLE: SUPPORT YOUR PEOPLE, AND THEY'LL SUPPORT YOU

Peter Pace learned another valuable leadership lesson from early in his career in Vietnam. At the end of a dangerous day's patrol in Vietnam, when he was still Lieutenant Pace, he encamped his men after dark and broke camp before dawn, never placing them two evenings in the same place. On first taking the night's site, Pace devoted himself to securing the position and plotting its coordinates should friendly fire be needed. He slept little, but when he finally did lie down, he found that his men had always dug a hole for him without his ever asking

On leaving Vietnam, Pace recalled, "I felt that I really owed those men who didn't come home a debt that I could never pay them, so I decided I would focus on my next unit," which happened to be a platoon stationed at the Marine barracks in Washington. Here Pace discovered one of team leadership's great virtuous circles: the greater his support for his troops, the greater their support was for him. "I didn't realize this at the time, but the more I tried to give them and take care of them, and the more they realized I was taking care of them, the more they gave me."

Peter Pace found his Marines becoming better at taking care of one another, taking care of him, and taking care of business. And they made sure that their lieutenant "wasn't going to get hung out to dry." If he erred in a decision, his troops were quick to warn him. "If they respect you as an officer," Pace recalled, "as you start to do something you shouldn't, they'll ask you not to do it." Investment in their welfare resulted in rich reward. "You end up looking better than you are because they are literally taking care of you, since they want you to be their leader and they want you to be successful."

As a lieutenant general, Pace relied on the same principle to get a far larger job done. He often spent no more than three or four days in his Norfolk office over the space of a month. With 92,000 troops reporting to that office, the work flow was enormous, akin to that facing the chief executive of a giant corporation, but his staff had learned to manage it so well that "he hadn't a clue," he confessed, "exactly what they're doing" most of the time. With clear instructions to them and then vigorous support for them, Pace found that he didn't need to sweat the details.

During the air war in Kosovo, for instance, the Pentagon asked Pace to station two Marine squadrons in Hungary to fly combat missions. He instructed his staff when and where they were needed, and the staff disposed of all the rest: clearances, ammunition, fuel, family, transportation, and thousands of other steps for moving soldiers to eastern Europe. Pace's officers informed him of the major steps as they executed them, but knowing the mission, none of them needed to ask another question about its execution.

Faith in the boss was the essential prerequisite, and Peter Pace could see this in himself as he thought about his own superiors: "If you know that your boss cares about you and truly wants the very best for you and your organization, and if you see that there's something out there that might somehow adversely impact him, you're going to rally around him and make sure that doesn't happen." That's how a virtuous circle works: Unswerving support for subordinates engenders unswerving support for the boss, and each is thus more able to get his or her respective tasks accomplished. Robert E. Lee, a Marine colonel and onetime director of the leadership school at Quantico, summed it up in a simple formula. "You always have to protect your puppies," he asserted, "even if they sometimes urinate in your boots."

Lesson in Leading Up

Downward leadership and upward leadership are integrally reinforcing; if you are effective at the first, it will beget the second; if you are adept at the second, it can inspire the first.

LEARNING FROM MISTAKES

Not only are successes, coups, victories, and triumphs often potent sources of learning, but mistakes, errors, accidents, and disasters are as well. The Marine Corps places great stress on its moments of glory. Yet it also scrutinizes and learns from its setbacks and losses: for example, the monthlong assault against entrenched Japanese forces on Iwo Jima in 1945 came at a cost of 28,000 Marine casualties, but its ultimate success paved the way for the end of World War II six months later. Leadership training at the Marine base at Quantico builds on what did not work as much as on what did.

In providing this emphasis, the Marine Corps implicitly sets the stage for upward leadership. Reviewing one's mistakes through discussion with both subordinates and superiors is a powerful method for appreciating what went wrong when decisions did go badly. Blunders are to be exposed, dissected, and transcended—not avoided, denied, and concealed. The premise is clear: Fewer gaffs can be expected next time if last time's missteps are acknowledged and appreciated. Marine commandant James Jones underscored the principle in his 1999 statement of strategic intent. "Tolerance for mistakes unleashes creativity and initiative," he wrote, and it "contributes to our warfighting skills by encouraging us to accept prudent risks." When "we are confident that we will not be held to an impossibly high standard, the process of trial and error will enhance the learning process and will encourage us to act with the boldness that should be our hallmark."

Peter Pace relied upon that risk-taking and mistake-tolerating culture to get his own job done. When he sent the two squadrons to Hungary for the air war against the Serbs in Kosovo, he knew his staff would do the job well—but not perfectly well. And that was okay by him. Pace had learned to accept a 90/10 success rate, with 90% getting done as planned. "I'll buy that ten percent," he asserted, because what did get achieved is "ninety percent of a huge amount of work." Besides, he knew he could always retrofix the one thing in ten that did go wrong. "As long as I don't shoot anybody for one of the ten things," he added, "it keeps working."

Lesson in Leading Up

Remember, your subordinates will make mistakes—that's why you're the boss and they're not. But if you treat well-managed risk as tolerable and understandable mistakes as informative, you'll build a capacity below for those to lead up and one day move up.

CONCLUSIONS

In Vietnam, the foot soldiers in Pace's Second Platoon of G Company in the Second Battalion of the Fifth Marines in the First Marine Division had made sure that their green lieutenant, fresh out of Annapolis and Quantico, learned what he ought to do. Not long after arriving in Hue, Pace joined his men in filling endless sandbags, a new officer determined to demonstrate that he was prepared to do whatever he ordered his men to do. But the platoon sergeant was quite ready to tell Pace that filling sandbags was not his job. "Thank you," said the sergeant, "but we need you to be thinking about the next thing."

Later, in the daily patrolling of hot zones near Da Nang, Pace often found it easier to put himself forward than to order others ahead. He was reluctant to risk the lives of others without risking his own. His men, though, were again quick to pull him back: "If we go out there and get in trouble," he was told, "we know you're back here to bring forward the rest of the platoon and to call on the artillery fire. If *you* go out there and get into trouble, the rest of us back here don't have the training that you've got to do the things that you do. Let us go do our job and you stay back here and do your job."

Once again, guidance from below had brought better results above. Imagine the impact of that artillery barrage that an angry Peter Pace had wanted to call in—the one that would have destroyed a Vietnamese village to kill a sniper. It would have neither enhanced a green lieutenant's reputation with his own men nor contributed to the military's mission in Vietnam. Good that Pace's sergeant cast a critical glance as the lieutenant radioed the hamlet's coordinates for shelling. And good, too, that Lieutenant Pace heeded the warning. In acting on that glance, Pace in no way diminished his leadership. He only added to it, and he learned the value of ensuring that those above you do their job the right way.

Sometimes, of course, the boss is not quite so ready to listen or to learn. The superior may even subject subordinates to misdirection or mistreatment, but the culture of the Marines requires that subordinates exercise leadership whether or not any is displayed above—and despite whatever is coming from above. Subordinates must master what is right to do regardless of what their boss wants done.

Marine culture even stresses what most hierarchies abhor: going over your boss's head. It must be done with clarity of purpose, but it can be done without fatal repercussion. Indeed, Marine policy fosters jumping however high you need to go to find a solution. The purpose is not to criticize or undermine the boss, but to resolve the problem.

"If you have a bad boss and it's harmful to the institution, you have to take it up," advised former Marine commandant Charles Krulak, and it is inevitable that you will have to do so sometime in your career. "You *will* face that time," he warned, "and you will face that time before you are ready for it. And when you face it, draw inside and on your character to do the right thing."

Not surprisingly, throughout the ranks the U.S. Marine Corps sees far more responsiveness than stonewalling. It has been described by journalist David Freedman in *Corps Business* as the ultimate bottom-up organization, one that is forced to foster leadership from below if it is to be aggressive and fast acting in a hostile and fast-changing environment. When combat begins, decisions must be made at all levels, and thus leadership must be displayed at all levels.

Leading up for Lieutenant Pace—and later for General Pace— derived from neither management theory nor personal philosophy.

It was simply a product of addressing problems that necessitated such leadership and a culture that supported it. Everyone has to learn on the job, and from the job. But by looking at how Peter Pace's personal experience intersected with Corps values, we also can extract several operating guidelines that should be universally applicable for those who would lead up:

- Ensure that one's own performance is exemplary
- Disclose information and intentions fully to all superiors
- Meet frequently with every superior
- Listen to subordinates and learn from mistakes
- Foster a capacity for every subordinate to challenge up
- Learn how to look down on your own role from on high
- Sharpen your own principles before they are tested

More than three decades after his combat experience in Vietnam, Lieutenant General Peter Pace still knew the names of every platoon member killed and precisely where it happened. He had never lost the sense of absolute obligation to those who would never return. "These are Marines who trusted me, and as a result of doing what I told them to do, they died," he said, his voice pausing. "I know I did the best I could. I wish it would have been better." In seeking to redeem that wish, Pace discovered that he would have to lead not only down but also up.

On July 6, 2000, President Clinton announced that he had nominated Pace to the four-star rank of general with assignment as commander in chief of the U.S. Southern Command, and on August 24, 2001, President George W. Bush nominated Pace to serve as vice chairman of the Joint Chiefs of Staff, the first Marine officer ever to so serve.

CHAPTER 6

GUIDING YOUR GUIDE

BECK WEATHERS AND SANDY HILL PITTMAN DID NOT ASK
THEIR CLIMBING GUIDES ON MOUNT EVEREST WHAT
THEY SHOULD HAVE ASKED

MOUNTAINEERING LORE PROVIDES numerous accounts of leadership on the line, and few are more revealing of the need for upward leadership than that of what happened on the upper slopes of Mount Everest on May 10, 1996. The events of that day, which eight climbers failed to survive, have become well-known, but the importance of how the role of upward leadership contributed to the events that unfolded has been less appreciated. Had the climbers more effectively led up that fateful day, the outcome might have been far different for two of those on the slopes, one who returned with frightful injuries and one who did not return at all.

The first hours of May 10, 1996, found Sandy Hill Pittman and Beck Weathers moving toward the top of Mount Everest. Earlier, the two had rested briefly in tents on the windswept plateau of the South Col. Now they were ascending the final summit ridge in their bid for the ultimate trophy of mountaineering.

Both appeared to be climbing with strong leaders. Pittman's team was led by Scott Fischer, a world-class climber whose prowess and verve were legendary. Rob Hall, Fischer's equal but also his rival, headed Weathers's team. But in the thin air and treacherous terrain on the South Col, appearances are often deceiving.

As the two groups trudged up the summit ridge long before dawn, Pittman believed that Fischer was in fine form. Yet unknown to Pittman, Fischer had exhausted himself several days earlier assisting a distressed client, and he would be moving up slowly and saying little during the hours that followed. His reserves for a summit bid were dangerously low.

Beck Weathers was in trouble as well: Just as dawn was breaking, he realized he was going blind. Not long before leaving for the Himalayas, Weathers had undergone a new form of eye surgery. Now, an unanticipated side effect was causing temporary blindness at the extreme altitude. Weathers told Hall that he planned to descend to the camp on the South Col, but Hall told Weathers to remain exactly where he was until Hall came down from the top.

A killer storm overwhelmed them later that day, and in the hours that followed, five climbers would die on the summit ridge or South Col and three others on the north side of the peak. Fischer and Hall would be among them, with Pittman and Weathers nearly perishing as well. The climbers' fates had hinged on how skillfully they had led one another on this most deadly day in Everest's history, and several had failed the test.

Pittman passed up an opportunity to dissuade her "boss" from a summit bid, just as Weathers passed over a chance to press his leader for clearer instructions. Had Pittman so intervened and Weathers so asked, the experience might have ended less tragically for all. As will become evident in this chapter, their fateful inactions that day on Mount Everest powerfully affirm the paramount duty of rising up when your boss is faltering, whether for reasons of poor health or limited clarity. Confidence in and respect for your superior is essential, but nobody is invincible or faultless. Biding your time and deferring to authority serves no one well when it's clear that the boss would fare far better with your upward help.

THE BUSINESS OF CLIMBING MOUNT EVEREST

Mount Everest straddles the border between Nepal and Tibet, and over the years climbers have attacked it from both sides. The legendary 1924 British expedition of George Mallory and Andrew Irvine ended with their mysterious disappearance above the North Col on the Tibetan side. The equally renowned 1953 expedition of Edmund Hillary and Tenzing Norgay culminated with their conquest of the peak from the South Col on the Nepalese side. Today, more than a dozen paths have been blazed to the summit, but most expeditions use the best-known and least-harrowing South Col passage. The route commences from the Base Camp at 17,700 feet, wends its way onto the South Col at 26,000 feet, surmounts the Hillary Step at more than 28,700 feet, and reaches a snowy apex at 29,035 feet.

Given the fragility of human life at that altitude, a remarkable number of people have tried the ascent. In 1996 alone, more than 398 climbers converged on Mount Everest, and 98 stood on its summit. By March 1999, 764 men and 44 women had reached the world's "third pole"—yet 161 people had perished on the journey up or down.

Scott Fischer and Robert Hall had chosen the South Col for their separate commercial expeditions to Mount Everest. Both charged mightily for the privilege of attempting the summit under their seasoned tutelage. Amateur adventurers had defined the sport of mountaineering for more than a century, but professional alpinists had

Scott Fischer

Rob Hall

muscled in. Commercial rates could run more than $50,000 per person, a seemingly absurd price to pay for several weeks of mortal risk and total misery in what has come to be dubbed the "death zone." But rising numbers sought the services of Fischer and Hall, and exorbitant price proved no barrier. Hall and Fischer asked $65,000, the highest in the business, and they got it.

Scott Fischer headquartered his business—called Mountain Madness—in Seattle, and Rob Hall ran Adventure Consultants from New Zealand. But they conducted their businesses where the customers paid to be—in the Andes, East Africa, or the Himalayas. And whatever the mountain range, a lot of customers wanted Fischer, age forty, or Hall, age thirty-five, on the leading end of their rope. If you were convinced that imperiling your life for fifteen minutes on an icy pinnacle was worth a small fortune, Fischer or Hall were as good a choice as any to get you up there. Their résumés bristled with personal conquests of the world's great peaks; their companies' advertising brimmed with client conquests of the world's best routes. Both owned the business, both booked the business, and unlike more than a few CEOs, both did the business. It was they who shepherded you to the summit. And they offered real prospects. Fischer would tell author Jon Krakauer (who wrote *Into Thin Air,* about his climb up Mount Everest): "We've got the big E figured out; we've got it totally wired. These days, I'm telling you, we've built a yellow brick road to the summit."

In a competitive culture where extreme was supreme, Fischer's iron-man exploits were already renowned. He had ascended Mount Everest without bottled oxygen, a feat achieved by only the mighty few who could force their bodies to function in the rarest of air. He had not only scaled Pakistan's K2, the world's second-highest mountain at 28,250 feet and a more daunting peak than its big brother, but he had done so after dislocating his shoulder. One of Fischer's clients had said of him, "He was the rodeo king of high-altitude guides."

Rob Hall was no slouch either: Not only had he climbed the "seven summits"—the highest points on the seven continents—but he had done so in seven months, reaching the finale, 16,067-foot Mount Vinson in Antarctica, with just hours to spare. But Fischer and Hall were also family men. Fischer had a son and a daughter; recently married, Hall was an expectant father.

Sandy Hill Pittman and Beck Weathers were two of the fee payers. Both had money, but they had not made impetuous decisions in committing a lot of it to get to the top. A New York–based writer, Pittman had already conquered six of the world's seven leading summits and had attempted Mount Everest twice before, once via a far more difficult face in Tibet. Mount Everest remained the jewel missing from a crown already adorned with Kilimanjaro in Africa, Denali in North America, and Aconcagua in South America. Beck Weathers had achieved five of the seven summits. This was the Dallas pathologist's first outing on Mount Everest, but he came with a gritty determination to test the limits of personal endurance.

Beck Weathers had flown from Kathmandu, the capital of Nepal, to a gravel airstrip at the Himalayan village of Lukla (elevation 9,350 feet), the trailhead for most expeditions approaching Mount Everest from its southern flank. Sandy Hill Pittman landed at Syangboche, a lesser but considerably higher airstrip at 12,795 feet. For a week their expeditions wended their way up mountain gorges, visiting the region's trading hub at Namche, seeing a venerated Buddhist monastery at Tengboche, and noting an emergency medical center at Pheriche. By early April, Weathers and Pittman had reached Base Camp, the glacial stopping point where trail hiking gives way to ice climbing.

Days of altitude conditioning followed as they steeled their metabolisms for the rigors above. Hall and Fischer ran their parties up and down the treacherous Khumbu icefall, taking them as high as 23,000 feet and then back to the base, only to send them up again. In this way they prepared their clients for the depleted oxygen and unrelenting punishment of high altitude. Drop humans suddenly into it, and they'll be gasping in seconds, comatose in minutes, dead in hours. Move mountaineers gradually up it, and they'll function acceptably well for days at a time.

THE IMPORTANCE OF FOLLOWING ORDERS

Successful expedition mountaineering also means effective management of supplies and logistics. Camps had to be stocked, safety ropes fixed between them, and oxygen cylinders stashed along the way. Experienced in such expeditions, Rob Hall and Scott Fischer neglected none of the necessities. Each also stressed one more preparatory step, a step that would prove especially critical for the events ahead.

Rob Hall repeatedly instructed his eight clients that they would have to reach the top of Mount Everest by 2:00 P.M. on summit day. Otherwise, even if they were in sight of the top, they would have to turn back. There could be no exception to the "2:00 P.M. rule," since it could prove lifesaving if followed and life-threatening if neglected. This had "been drilled into us over and over," Beck Weathers said.

Jon Krakauer concurred: "Over the previous month, Rob had lectured us repeatedly about the importance of having a predetermined turnaround time on the summit day—in our case it would probably be 1:00 P.M., or 2:00 at the very latest—and abiding by it no matter how close we were to the top."

The day before leaving Base Camp on May 6 for the final push to the summit, Hall assembled his team in the mess tent and laid down the law. "I will tolerate no dissension up there," he declared. "My word will be absolute law, beyond appeal. If you don't like a particular decision I make, I'd be happy to discuss it with you afterward, but not while we're on the hill."

The reasoning behind the 2:00 P.M. imperative was easy to appreciate. Climbers on the way up typically reached the highest camp on the South Col late one afternoon and then, with just a few hours of rest, departed for the summit around midnight. They must swiftly surmount 3,000 vertical feet to the top and then descend back to the Col's protective tents by nightfall. To fail to return before dark risked overnight exposure to a lethal combination of the elements. Oxygen tanks were rationed for the daylight hours but not beyond, and nighttime chill factors routinely reached fifty degrees below zero. If climbers achieved the summit by 2:00 P.M., they had a reasonable chance of returning to the South Col camp before dusk. Any later, however, and they risked falling short. Though some mountaineers stranded on the summit ridge have endured a terrible night out, the odds were stacked against survival.

Beck Weathers knew the drill: "Absolutely no later than two" was the canon, he said. If "you're not moving fast enough to get there by two, you're not moving fast enough to get back down before darkness on the mountain."

The 2:00 P.M. rule contained an Achilles' heel, however. If a client was not far from the summit when the two o'clock turnaround time arrived—perhaps an hour or even less—the urge to press on despite the personal perils could be overwhelming. After all, the client had invested thousands of dollars and months of effort for the singular purpose of standing on the top, and that point was tangibly close. Moreover, it was a one-shot affair: Fail to reach the top on summit day, and there can be no second shot.

"Every moment that you're up there, your body is dying beneath you," recalled Weathers. "The whole point of this exercise is to reach this moment with just enough strength to go to the top and get back down, and then to get out of there."

Tales abound of what it means to fall just short. Swiss alpinist Raymond Lambert had nearly reached the summit of Mount Everest one year before Hillary and Tenzing finally succeeded in 1953. He wisely turned around because of threatening weather, but his obituary in the *New York Times* would later highlight the near miss. In falling short, wrote the *Times,* Lambert "came within 800 vertical feet of immortality."

George Mallory had set a 4:00 P.M. rule for himself and his ropemate, Andrew Irvine, on their fateful stab at the summit on June 8, 1924, and while it remains unknown if they reached the top before, by, or after that hour, others speculated that it would have been nigh impossible for them to reverse course if they had been anywhere near the summit, whatever the time. Fellow climber Noel Odell wrote that Mallory's "craving for victory" would likely "have been too strong for him" to resist, and John Noel, expedition filmmaker, conjectured that once the "goal was in their grasp," how could they "turn back and loose it?"

Even seasoned guides who set the turnaround rule would not be entirely immune to the siren call. Every client that Rob Hall delivered to the summit of Mount Everest was one more jubilant customer, one more living testimonial. If he delivered them all, it was one more notch for a claim that prospective clients should find irresistible: Last year all his clients reached the top. In 1992, he had shepherded six clients to the summit, a year later seven, and during the five years prior to 1996 he had placed thirty-nine on top. His advertising could properly claim that his company was "the world leader in Everest Climbing, with more ascents that any other organization." One early 1995 advertisement even asserted "100% Success!" His failure to back up that claim later that year—none of Hall's clients reached the top during a mid-1995 expedition—made a comeback in 1996 all the more vital. Appreciating that fatal attractions can prove precisely that, his 2:00 P.M. dictum was in place to stiffen his own resolve along with the clients'.

At Rob Hall's suggestion, Scott Fischer adopted the 2:00 P.M. rule, too. One of Fischer's two other guides, Neal Beidleman, recalled that "we decided to enforce a two o'clock turnaround time: Anybody who wasn't within spitting distance of the summit by 2:00 P.M. had to turn around and go down." The policy, however, did not reach everybody on the front line. "I don't know what the prior arrangements were," Charlotte Fox, one of Fischer's clients, would later say. "There was never any talk of turning around." Another client, Lene Gammel-gaard, recalled: "I never heard anything whatsoever about a turn-around time on summit day."

ANOTHER CRITICAL SUCCESS FACTOR: WORKING TOGETHER AS A TEAM

If Rob Hall fretted about a timely return, Scott Fischer seemed more worried about total teamwork. Like people on any commercial tour, Scott Fischer's customers were thrown together; the guide's job was to create camaraderie. "Think of it as a blind date," observed one of the clients. "All you initially have in common at the bottom is the reason you're there, the top of the mountain." Fischer repeatedly reminded his eight clients that they would have to bond as a group if they were to reach and return from the summit, whatever the hour. It was not a maxim imposed, just instilled. "The critical mandate was that we stick together," recalled Pittman, but it was "gentle guidance without coddling." If they worked together, understood one another, and depended on one another, their capacity for success and survival would be formidable. If not, when mutual support became essential—as surely it would on summit day—they ran the risk of being stranded, even abandoned. Adrenaline would propel them up, but only teamwork could get them down. "It's attitude, not altitude," Fischer was fond of saying.

Summit day would be *the* day when teamwork ultimately counted, and for that day Fischer insisted it take literal form. For reaching great altitude, he had allowed his clients great latitude. They made their own decisions on when to climb, they climbed without guides much of the time, and they even picked which camps best suited their own conditioning program. "You're all experienced," Fischer had explained, "and in going up and down, take your own pace and do your own thing because you are experienced." But for the final push, he insisted on a rule as ironclad as Rob Hall's turn-back time. "On summit day," Fischer declared, "we are sticking together like a Cub Scout troop." The eight clients were to remain within visual sight of one another all the way up the high ridge.

Again, the rationale for teamwork was easy to appreciate in a sport where practitioners were roped together and lives literally depended upon one another's actions. The imperative of mutual reliance is well illustrated by one of the most famous moments of mountaineering lore. An American expedition attempting K2 in 1953 had not been far from being the first to reach the summit when one of their eight members, Arthur Gilkey, developed a potentially lethal blood clot in his leg. At grave risks to themselves on what has been called the "savage mountain," the team of seven bundled Gilkey in a makeshift litter and started down. The rescue party was descending a perilous ice slope in a snowstorm when one of the frostbitten climbers lost his footing, pulling four others from their tenuous grip on the ice. Seeing his teammates sliding toward an enormous drop-off but roped to them, climber Pete Schoening cautiously slowed and then stopped the rope, holding them with an ice axe that he had wedged behind a boulder. The fact that all had been connected held all from oblivion.

By staying together on Mount Everest, Fischer explained, the team would detect early signs of a climber's weakening and could intervene before it was too late. If any client began to falter for any reason, others were instantly available to assist. For one climber, Fischer's safety net for summit day required no justification. The mountaineer whose action had saved the day on K2, Pete Schoening, was on the Fischer team.

Lesson in Leading Up

If you expect those below to support your leadership and step into the breach when needed, they will need to understand your strategy, your methods, and your rules. That requires repeated restatements of your principles and consistent adherence to them.

WHAT HAPPENS WHEN NO ONE RECOGNIZES A LEADER'S WEAKNESS?

Near dawn on May 6, with weather holding and anticipation high, the teams of both Rob Hall and Scott Fischer moved above Base Camp for the final time. On the afternoon of May 9, Beck Weathers and Sandy Hill Pittman ascended a wall of ice, scrambled across the rocky ribs of the "Geneva spur" and "yellow band," and sometime between 5:00 and 6:00 P.M. crawled into tents pitched on the windswept South Col, an ice-covered plateau between the summits of Mount Everest and its southern neighbor, Lhotse. More than fifty climbers had reached the South Col for the evening. The wind gusted to sixty miles an hour and more.

Scott Fischer arrived near 5:00 P.M., exhausted but evidently bent on preserving all appearances to the contrary. Despite his iron-man image, he had ample reason to feel depleted. During a 1984 expedition to Annapurna, an 8,000-meter mountain 200 miles west of Mount Everest, a gastrointestinal parasite had entered his system, and he had been unable to shake it in the dozen years since. The parasite's effect would occasionally flare up, resulting in short bouts of acute distress. An associate reported that Fischer had been hit in the 1996 Base Camp sometimes daily with moments of intense sweating and shaking.

"He'd get up in the morning," said Jane Bromet, a publicist who accompanied Fischer to the foot of Everest. "It would take him five minutes to finally stand up."

Lene Gammelgaard, a client from Copenhagen, observed in a diarylike account on April 15 that "Scott's fallen ill again" and on April 19 that Scott's "illness made him pull back."

Adding to Fischer's woes was a faltering client, Dale Kruse. Kruse may have been suffering from cerebral edema—a potentially fatal swelling of an oxygen-starved brain—but whatever his exact condition, he had acclimated poorly. When Kruse barely made it to Camp One at 19,500 feet on May 6, Fischer concluded that his client had come to the end of his line and walked him back down to Base Camp. The next day, Fischer had to reverse course yet again to reunite with the rest of his clients, all of whom had spent the night at Camp Two, at 21,300 feet. Another professional guide, Henry Todd, who passed Fischer early on May 7, was surprised to see how slowly Fischer was moving, but Fischer managed to reach Camp Two by evening.

Late May 9 found Hall's and Fischer's teams both perched together at Camp Four, at 26,000 feet on the South Col. During the evening hours, clients dozed fitfully, waiting for the midnight wake-up call that would mean they were starting their final assault. When the guides had arrived on the col just hours earlier, the howling wind seemed severe enough to cancel departure, but by 10:00 P.M. the blow abruptly abated. "Guys, saddle up, we're going for it," beckoned Rob

Hall to one tent, and to another, "Be ready to rock and roll at eleven-thirty!" By midnight, the members of Hall's team had pulled on their clothing layers, climbing boots, and oxygen masks and were out of the tents and on the move. The night, said Weathers, was "exquisite."

Fischer beckoned the four climbers jammed in his own tent, including Pittman, to get moving as well. "I slept like a baby," he declared, and then added in his characteristic high-spirited style, "We're going to pop this one!" Fischer's group started thirty minutes after Hall's, but by 4:00 A.M. the two teams became entwined in the single-lane pathway that the mountain permitted to the top. In the clear, calm, moonlit sky, they could discern a faint white ridge rising high above them. It was not terribly cold by Everest standards, just ten below zero without a breath of wind.

"The stars looked just incredibly clear," recalled Pittman.

As the teams moved across the South Col's ice toward the summit ridge, Pittman did not sense that Fischer was off his game. Fischer, though, had begun to leave a trail of clues. He had risen at 10:00 P.M., but his preparations for departure were so slow that he finally left the high camp sometime past 1:00 A.M., long after all of his and Hall's clients, guides, and sherpas had set out.

WHAT HAPPENS WHEN A LEADER FAILS TO GIVE ADEQUATE INSTRUCTIONS?

Beck Weathers had departed for the summit ridge soon after midnight, but he decided not to divulge his own special concerns to his guide either, or anybody else. He climbed steadily in a "slow, rhythmic, metronomelike gait" that climbers prefer until the first hint of dawn, but then the sky's faint light confirmed his worst fears—he had become virtually blind. On his way up to the South Col the day before, he was already losing some focus, but not fatally. He could discern the shape of the ice step just in front of him, and he stayed

Sandy Hill Pittman and others ascending Mount Everest, May 10, 1996.

on track by quickly kicking his own boot into the step vacated. Now his vision was disappearing as the route was toughening.

"We start up the summit face and it's pretty straightforward climbing," Weathers recalled. "It's just vertical. All you've got to do is put one foot in front of the other. It's step and rest, step and rest, hour after endless hour until we're about halfway up the face and we have to move and traverse to the left. This is inherently a more dangerous kind of move. It's harder to protect, and you've really got to be able to see where you're putting your feet. As I get there, I realize that I can't see the face of this mountain at all."

Weathers would later learn that his eye surgery some two years earlier had brought on the temporary blindness: Low atmospheric pressure at extreme elevations distended the eye after the procedure, resulting in a momentary but debilitating loss of focus. But he needed no understanding of the medical cause to appreciate that his $65,000 fee might get him no higher. Still, he hoped the rising sun would dilate his pupils into focusing pinholes. Until then, he had to move very cautiously. He was fourth among the thirty-three climbers moving single file up the slope, but he stepped out of line and dropped back to dead last, sharing pleasantries with others as they traipsed past. Three teams of climbers were on their way to the summit, brought together by a window of good weather the day seemed to promise.

Despite the early morning's warming light, neither of Beck Weathers's eyes found sufficient focus. Finally, he confessed his condition to Hall. "Rob, you guys go ahead and boogey on up the hill," said Weathers. "At the point that I can see, I'll just wander up after you." At first Hall insisted that Weathers return to the South Col with one of the sherpas, but Weathers hoped that the searing sunlight might soon contract his pupils. Fine, Hall said, but he would tolerate only limited delay: "I don't like the idea. You've got thirty minutes. If you can see in thirty minutes, climb on. If you cannot see in thirty minutes, I don't want you climbing." Five days earlier, a day before leaving Base Camp, Hall had warned his clients to stick together on the summit ridge. Until they reached a point midway up the ridge, "everyone needs to stay within a hundred meters of each other," he had insisted. "We will be climbing in the dark, and I want the guides to be able to keep close track of you." Now, still short of the midpoint on the ridge, he was violating his own dictum. Weathers would stay behind, the rest would go on.

Weathers appreciated Rob Hall's logic, but he harbored scant hope for swift recovery and proposed his own contingency plan: "If I can't see in the first thirty minutes that you've given me, at the point that I can I'm just going to head back down to the high camp." Hazardous slopes lay below, however, and Hall nixed the plan. "I don't like that idea any better than the last one. If I come off this hill and you're not standing here, I'm not going to have any idea whether you've gone safely down to that camp or you've just gone off for an eight-thousand-foot looper." Hall's expedition counted only two guides beside himself and four sherpas on the ridge, and none could be spared to wait the thirty minutes. Weathers would simply have to remain right there until Hall came back from the summit to accompany him down. Hall extracted a fateful commitment: "Now I want you to promise me, Beck, I am serious about this—I want you to promise me that you're going to stay here until I come back." Weathers acquiesced. "Rob, cross my heart, hope to die. I'm sticking."

In moments Hall was gone, pursuing his other clients upward, and Weathers sat down for what would prove to be a very long stay near a rock promontory at 27,600 feet known as the Balcony. He wondered if he should have asked for more detailed guidance. What should he do in case Hall's plan for return did not unfold quite as intended?

FISCHER'S AND WEATHERS'S PROBLEMS CATCH UP WITH THEM — WITH TRAGIC RESULTS

The day's sunrise, indeed, seemed to forecast a perfect day for the summit climbers. The sky was almost cloudless, the mountain massifs of Makalu and Kangchenjunga stood clear, and the wind and temperature were merciful. Late morning congestion, though, had slowed many of the climbers seeking the summit, especially at the famous Hillary Step, the near-vertical forty-foot slab constituting the route's great bottleneck. Only a single person at a time could negotiate the cliff, and doing so required as much as ten to fifteen minutes for each to surmount it. Hall's and Fischer's climbing parties alone would have meant a crowd, but a third group, this one of Taiwanese climbers, had converged on the same point at the same time. By noon, climbers had backed up below the foot of the step for an hour or more. The result was a massive operations problem well familiar to manufacturing managers: A single choke point can stymie an otherwise brilliant production line. (So perfect was the step's stranglehold on this day that it now serves as a teaching case in the Wharton School's M.B.A. program.)

As the lead climbers surmounted the Hillary Step around 1:00 P.M., clouds filled the valleys to the south, transforming high points into island peaks. Above the step, thick overnight snow further slowed the first climbers as they fought their way through knee-deep drifts, but Anatoli Boukreev, the lead guide for Scott Fischer, finally topped out at about 1:07 P.M., with Jon Krakauer and Andy Harris, one of Rob Hall's guides, just minutes later. To the trained eye, however, all was not well. When Martin Adams, a Fischer client and private pilot versed in clouds and weather, reached the summit at 1:25 P.M., he fearfully reckoned the rising vapors to be the crests of thunderheads. "When you see a thunderhead in an airplane," he said, "your first reaction is to get the fuck out of there. So that's what I did."

By two o'clock, only six climbers had reached the summit: Anatoli Boukreev and Neal Beidleman, the two guides working for Scott Fischer; Andy Harris, the guide for Hall; and clients Martin Adams and Klev Schoening with the Fischer group and Jon Krakauer with the Hall team. Sandy Hill Pittman reached the top at 2:21 P.M., finally notching her seventh summit (only the second woman to do so). She remained more sanguine about the weather, and she would later say about her brief triumph on the top, "If I felt any anxiety up there, it was because we were late, but not because I saw any weather." Assisting struggling clients—some moving sluggishly, others suffering from severe oxygen deprivation—delayed Rob Hall's arrival on the summit until 2:30. It was his fifth time on top, more Everest notches that any nonsherpa mountaineer.

On his way down from the summit, Jon Krakauer passed Scott Fischer still on his way up, and he "looked extremely wasted," recalled Krakauer. Martin Adams and Anatoli Boukreev exchanged a few words with Fischer on their way down, but Krakauer reported that none of them "discussed Fischer's exhausted appearance. It did not occur to any of us that he might be in trouble." Accompanying four clients down from the top at 3:10 P.M., guide Neal Beidleman came upon Fischer twenty minutes later, just above the Hillary Step.

"He just sort of raised his hand," Beidleman recalled. "He looked like he was having a hard time, but he was Scott, so I wasn't particularly worried. I figured he'd tag the summit and catch up to us pretty quick to help bring the clients down."

In fact, all of Fischer's clients who had reached the top were now well on their way down. Seeing him as he trudged toward the top would be their only encounter that day with the expedition leader.

As she passed Fischer, Sandy Hill Pittman perceived nothing out of order, though oxygen masks can hide much. Fischer had planned to serve as summit "sweep," and to Pittman his tail-end position now looked like expedition policy, not private pain. Fischer finally tagged the summit at 3:40 P.M., half an hour after the last of his successful clients had started back down. On the summit, Fischer repeatedly complained to his chief sherpa, Lopsang Jangbu Sherpa, that he was feeling ill, saying, by Lopsang's recollection, "I am too tired. I am sick, need medicine for stomach."

Meanwhile, Beck Weathers never even came close to the summit. He remained immobilized on his icy perch far below, but the site offered one compensation to the otherwise disappointed climber: The midday's modest warming finally returned some focus to his eyes. For hours he savored what has to be one of the world's most exclusive vistas.

None of those who did reach the top that afternoon lingered long, save Rob Hall, who had stayed to welcome Seattle postman and client Doug Hansen. Age forty-six, Hansen had almost summitted with Hall a year before, coming within 330 vertical feet of the top, half again as close as Raymond Lambert. That time, Hall had turned Hansen around at 2:30 P.M. within sight of the top. Now, well past the turnaround moment he had insisted on—and therefore obviously not even following his own orders—Hall waited on the summit for Hansen to arrive.

More than twelve hours earlier, just three hours after leaving the South Col, Doug Hansen had stepped out of the line of climbers and reported that he felt cold and poorly, and had decided to turn back.

After talking briefly with Rob Hall, he reentered the climbing line and continued to trudge slowly upward, becoming the last climber of the day to reach the top. Hansen seemed close to the summit when Hall looked down after reaching the top himself at 2:30 P.M., but Hansen would not finally attain the summit until after 4:00 P.M. Only Rob Hall, who must have exchanged some lost final words with his fellow team leader, remained to extend Hansen a hand.

Many small decisions had added up to the now risky dispersion of the mountaineers on the mountainside. By 3:55 P.M., Weathers sat below, waiting for Hall's return, Hall sat on top waiting for Hansen's arrival, and Fischer had just left the summit. Nearly two hours had passed since the turnaround time, a dangerous situation in its own right but a potentially fatal exposure if the weather or a leader's condition turned from good to ghastly. The warning signs that it might just do that had registered on clients Martin Adams and Jon Krakauer, but evidently less so on the guides themselves. Organizations are only as good as the intelligence they gather and their response to it, and members of the Hall and Fischer outfits had more information than their leaders appreciated or were prepared to use.

Lesson in Leading Up

Tracking the terrain, the threatening conditions, and the physical and mental states of both the boss and the team members is everyone's responsibility. So is transforming that market and internal intelligence into a responsible course of action.

WHAT HAPPENS IF THERE IS NO CONTINGENCY PLAN?

Much earlier in the day, three climbers in Rob Hall's group had turned back after they concluded that the backup at the Hillary Step would give them no chance of summitting by 2:00 P.M. On the way down, they came upon Weathers's lonely lookout at about noon.

"Beck, come on down with us," one pleaded.

"Well, guys, I did something kind of dumb here," responded Weathers. "I put myself in a box where I promised Hall that I would wait for him. We have no radio and I have no way to tell him I've left. It would be as if I never honored the commitment at all. I just don't think I can do that." He didn't. The hour Weathers had told himself to expect Hall, 3:00 P.M., came and went with no sign of the team leader, and then 4:00 P.M. and even 5:00 P.M. without any sign. What eyesight had been earlier restored by the sun's brilliance now faded. Clouds had billowed up the valley below soon after 3:00 P.M., and snowflakes floated by soon thereafter.

Another of Weathers's party—Jon Krakauer—stumbled upon him around 5:00 P.M.: "Beck, what are you still doing up here?" Krakauer implored him to descend. "Come down with me," Krakauer said. "It will be at least another two or three hours before Rob shows up. I'll be your eyes. I'll get you down, no problem." But when Weathers warned that his limited eyesight required that he be escorted, Krakauer suggested that he wait for Michael Groom, the other of Hall's two guides, just twenty minutes back, who was then escorting an exhausted client, Yasuko Namba. No problem, thought Weathers to himself. What possible difference could twenty minutes make?

When Michael Groom appeared right on schedule, Beck Weathers was finally ready to descend the 1,600 feet to the South Col, some twelve hours after he had taken up his lonely vigil. Sandy Hill Pittman had been descending with guide Neal Beidleman when they overtook Groom, Weathers, and Namba. As a member of Rob Hall's team, Namba was not Beidleman's responsibility, but Beidleman nonetheless placed her on his rope, since Namba and Weathers were so near incapacitation. Pittman waited for what seemed an eternity as Beidleman roped up the spent climbers. As they proceeded down,

Namba lurched and stumbled, and with the storm brewing, their snail's pace became alarming. Until now the descent had progressed well, Pittman recalled, but she was becoming "very concerned." Still, she could see the tents below, and the safe haven looked no more than an hour away.

Beck Weathers moved little better than Yasuko Namba. "Beck was so hopelessly blind," recalled Groom, "that every ten meters he'd take a step into thin air and I'd have to catch him with the rope." The icy descent had become far more perilous in the fading light and blowing snow, and by the time they neared the South Col, the storm unleashed its full fury. Two lightning strikes exploded nearby. Still, Weathers estimated that it should not take long to reach the campsite. In "another forty-five minutes, maybe an hour, of fairly easy walking we're going to be at those tents, in the sleeping bags, drinking hot tea and putting the day to bed," he thought. We "can't see the camp but it is so close, it's just right over there."

The gathering storm transformed the upper ridge from a predictable pathway to a death trap. Rob Hall remained near the summit with client Doug Hansen, who had become so drained by his final push to the summit that he was no longer able to move in any direction. If the client could not move, Hall could not either. Scott Fischer had managed to get himself far below, but not far enough before the storm unleashed its full fury. Out of gas, he collapsed, and though only 1,200 vertical feet above the South Col, it mattered little where he was because he, too, had become utterly immobilized. By nightfall, about 6:30 P.M., winds howling at seventy miles an hour and plummeting temperatures soon combined to create a windchill of seventy degrees below zero.

By the time Beck Weathers reached the edge of the South Col, his near blindness had become the common condition. A complete whiteout—a featureless condition in which visibility is reduced to the hand in front of you—had settled over the col. Weathers joined with other equally lost climbers, including Sandy Hill Pittman, all desper-

*Climbers descending summit ridge below the Hillary Step, about
4:00 P.M. on May 10, 1996, as storm clouds are forming.*

ately searching for the lifesaving shelter of their tents. But the intensifying storm and descending darkness obliterated any hints of where
the tents might be pitched. With no landmarks to guide it, the
group—now numbering seven clients, two sherpas, and guides
Michael Groom and Neal Beidleman—lurched about, wandering
dangerously close to the col's huge drop-off into Tibet before simply
hunkering down for the night at 10:00 P.M. Formed into a huddle—
a "dog pile," as guide Beidleman later termed it—they pushed and
punched one another to remain alert. "We tried to keep warm by
pummeling each other," Weathers recalled. Those still alert knew full
well that if anyone drifted off, it would be to a final slumber.

Miraculously, the sky momentarily parted in the middle of the
stormy night, revealing the summits of Everest and Lhotse long
enough for Klev Schoening, a client on Fischer's team, to calculate

the camp's direction, some 300 yards to the northwest. He, guides Michael Groom and Neal Beidleman, another client, and the two sherpas walked toward the tents. They left five clients, four too weak to move, including Beck Weathers and Sandy Hill Pittman, for a subsequent rescue party. Within twenty minutes the six staggered into camp. It was now 12:45 A.M.

Guide Anatoli Boukreev, well rested at the camp, returned to find the five abandoned clients. Just before Boukreev arrived, one of the stranded clients—Tim Madsen—heard Beck Weathers say, "Hey, I've got this all figured out." Weathers stood up, but a gust of wind blew him beyond Madsen's flashlight beam, and Madsen assumed that Beck Weathers had become a "lost cause." Yasuko Namba looked too frozen to be resuscitated, lying unconscious on her back with a glove missing and snow drifting across her face. In two separate trips, Boukreev brought Madsen, Pittman, and a third client back to Camp Four, arriving with the last at 4:30 A.M. Beck Weathers and Yasuko Namba were left for dead.

The next morning, physician Stuart Hutchison, a client on Rob Hall's team, organized a second effort with four sherpas to rescue Weathers and Namba. He found Namba and Weathers alive, but he reached the same ghastly conclusion that neither could be saved. "Their faces and torsos were covered with snow," he recalled; "only their hands and feet were sticking out. The wind was just screaming across the col." Weathers seemed to be mumbling, Hutchinson reported, but "his right glove was missing and he had terrible frostbite. I tried to get him to sit up, but he couldn't. He was as close to death as a person can be and still be breathing." After consulting with one of the sherpas, Hutchinson made a triage decision, abandoning the dying to concentrate remaining resources on rescuing the living.

Left for dead again, Weathers's body refused to die. In midafternoon he woke up, stood, and walked straight into the South Col camp at 4:35 P.M. He returned from the dead, or in terms he prefers, he was reborn. The expedition had radioed word in the morning to

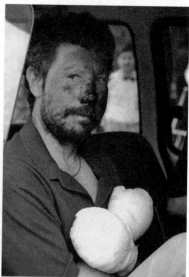

Sandy Hill Pittman   *Beck Weathers*

his wife, Peach, in Dallas that he had died, only to tell her later the same day that he was no longer dead. Weathers often spoke afterward of May 11, 1996, as his new birthday, making him an early bloomer. "On that eleventh of May, I was granted a second chance at life. I'm now a year old," he said in 1997. "I regard myself as reasonably precocious for one so young." But the night before the rebirth had done grievous damage to his body. Irreversible frostbite led to the amputation of the right hand and all the fingers on the left. A widely reprinted photo snapped just after the descent showed Weathers with blackened nose and cheeks, and many rounds of reconstructive surgery lay ahead. Yasuko Namba, the other client left for dead with him, got no such second chance.

Robert Hall and Scott Fischer were both still alive but frozen in place on the upper ridge. Hall had stayed only a few minutes on the summit after Hansen arrived near 4:00 P.M., and on the way down he radioed at 4:30 and again at 4:41 to report that they needed oxygen. Hall managed to guide Hansen to the top of the Hillary Step but then radioed that he didn't think he could lower Hansen down the step without oxygen. Hearing him in these and subsequent radio transmissions into the early hours of May 11, others on the mountain urged Hall to leave Hansen and descend below the Hillary Step to the South Summit, where several full oxygen bottles had been cached. At 4:43 A.M., Hall reported that he had finally reached the South Summit, evidently without Hansen, but also said that he had become "too clumsy to move." At 5:00 A.M., those at Base Camp connected their radio to Hall's wife's in New Zealand, and they briefly talked. At 9:00 A.M. Hall reported he was finally moving with oxygen. More than nine hours later, he told his wife in a final radio transmission at 6:20 P.M. not "to worry too much," but he was still near the South Summit and would move little farther.

Scott Fischer had descended well below the Hillary Step, but by the time Lopsang Jangbu Sherpa overtook him at 6:00 P.M. near the Balcony, Fischer was badly faltering. He told Lopsang, "I am too sick, too sick to go down." By 8:00 P.M., Lopsang has managed to move Fischer some 300 feet below the Balcony, but Fischer could no longer move under his own steam, and he urged Lopsang to leave him. Still some 1,200 feet above Camp Four, Lopsang abandoned Fischer at 9:00 P.M., vowing to return with a rescue party. A rescue party of two other sherpas reached him the next afternoon, and though Fischer was still breathing, he was unconscious and unresponsive, and, as others had done with Yasuko Namba, they left him where they found him. Like Dale Kruse, Fischer may have been stricken by cerebral edema. The next day, Lene Gammelgaard recorded the anguished comments of Lopsang: "Lene, he was ill already at the top. He came up to me saying he was so tired, so tired." Lopsang reported that he had "never seen Scott like that before. He just gave up."

The clients had done what they had come to Mount Everest to do, which was to push themselves to the summit. So daunting was the job that they were predictably obsessed with their own execution of it, taking one hard step after another until no more steps remained.

Guides were paid to make the big decisions about turning around and menacing weather; the clients' job was just to move themselves up and down the summit ridge. Yet some of the clients had also appreciated that they and their team faced ever more ominous conditions. Most saw that the backup at the Hillary Step would delay them from reaching the summit until well past 2:00 P.M.; some recognized that the billowing clouds were a portent of a storm to come. A few concluded without instruction from above that the wise decision was to descend, but most plunged on, focused on their personal task of summiting and oblivious to the growing threats around them. Had their guides earlier insisted that everyone carried responsibility for their own success and the survival of all, more clients might have forced themselves down the summit ridge before all hell broke loose.

Lesson in Leading Up

If you are to expect productive questioning from below, it is essential to encourage upward challenges from your subordinates and to test the principle with practice well before your organization is forced to confront harrowing conditions.

HAVING THE CONFIDENCE
TO CHALLENGE YOUR BOSS

During the raging storm on the night of May 10, the selflessness of the guides, sherpas, and fellow clients in the huddle kept Sandy Hill Pittman alive, and the actions of still another climber ultimately pulled her to the safety of Camp Four. Without their aid, provided at great peril to themselves, she would surely have perished on the South Col. And without Fischer's insistence on teamwork for success and survival, their assistance might not have been so fully rendered.

"In my head, I heard Scott's voice saying, 'Stay together as a team.' And we did," Pittman said. When those in the huddle complained of freezing hands or feet, others massaged circulation back into their limbs; when some became too still, others pummeled alertness back into their heads. Above all, they stayed together, making the subsequent rescue feasible. Pittman concluded: "It is a testament to the power of teamwork that members of our team survived. Scott's leadership brought us all back alive."

What about Fischer himself, though? In speculating on Fischer's condition as he and his team climbed toward the summit in the wee hours of May 10, Pittman has said that she should have rendered assistance to *him*. She had not thought to question her leader, she said, because she had assumed that he had been in complete control, that his command of reality matched his reputation for invincibility.

Yet signs of Scott Fischer's faltering had been evident to others for days. When he walked through Rob Hall's Camp Two halfway up to the South Col on May 7, Fischer had looked uncharacteristically haggard. The day before, he had retreated down the mountain with the stricken Dale Kruse, doubling his energy outlay at a time when all his reserves would be needed above. Others were visibly hammered by the high altitude, but Fischer normally should not have been. Yet Jon Krakauer noted that Fischer moved with a "clenched jaw" and looked "anxious and extremely tired."

Still, Sandy Hill Pittman had not seen it herself. Earlier, she'd had extensive contact with Fischer in Base Camp and above as she dispatched daily bulletins by satellite to NBC, and in none of those conversations had he outwardly complained. She had shared a tent at Camp Three on the exposed Lhotse face with Fischer and Neal Beidleman on the night of May 8, and though short on food, all three had joked and laughed as if each were fit as a fiddle.

Weathers reported that Hall's leadership in preparing him for the summit bid would have been successful were it not for his own failing eyesight, but Weathers's leadership lapse nearly resulted in disaster for himself. When Weathers told Hall of his incipient blindness, Hall had insisted firmly but simply—too simply as Weathers would learn—that Weathers remain near the Balcony until Hall came down. When some twelve hours later Hall had not returned, Weathers was still parked high on the ridge as the storm hit, and his delay nearly proved lethal. Had he descended with the three fellow clients who passed him at noon, he would have spent the afternoon comfortably ensconced in a tent at Camp Four, in his words "drinking hot tea and putting the day to bed." Had he followed Jon Krakauer down at 5:00 P.M., Weathers might still have reached the South Col before the camp was lost in the whiteout, as Krakauer himself had done. Instead, in honoring his pledge to Rob Hall until Michael Groom finally roped him down the slope at 5:20 P.M., Weathers risked all and almost lost.

On separate occasions, I have found opportunity to ask both Beck Weathers and Sandy Hill Pittman what decision they most regretted—aside, of course, from the decision to go for the summit in the first place. The critical mistake, Weathers said, was not to have asked Hall for more detailed and contingent instructions if Hall should be delayed in his own descent. "I did something really stupid" in not asking for more contingencies, Weathers said. "What never crossed my mind—and what was clearly the worst decision I made that day—was what was going to happen when the sun started to go down."

Sandy Hill Pittman responded that it was really a nondecision that was her most regrettable act: In not recognizing that her boss needed assistance, she may inadvertently have missed a life-preserving moment. I had asked that question when Pittman met with a group of Himalayan trekkers near a Buddhist monastery at Tengboche in Nepal, with Mount Everest towering over her shoulders. Our nineteen assembled hikers were mainly graduates of Wharton's Executive M.B.A. Program, and we were on a "leadership trek" through the Khumbu region that I annually organize with colleague Edwin Bernbaum. For the next several days as we wended our way up to a vista point near Mount Everest of more than 18,200 feet, Pittman's comments kept coming home in a pleasant way. Every few hours, one trekker or another would solicitously ask me, "How are you doing?"

Lesson in Leading Up

Asking your boss to elaborate and clarify inadequate instructions can make the difference between survival and success. So can checking on your boss to ensure no faltering at the helm.

Asking the two bosses for more clarity on May 10—and pausing to make sure the bosses themselves were up to the challenge—might well have helped lead those on the summit ridge down a less catastrophic path. But it is also useful to consider what the bosses themselves might have done to have fostered a penchant for challenging up by the ranks below. For this question, consider what Jon Krakauer regrets he did not do on May 10: "My actions—or failure to act—played a direct role in the death of Andy Harris."

Andy Harris, one of Rob Hall's two guides, had been on the summit of Mount Everest with Jon Krakauer at about 1:15 P.M. Krakauer departed soon thereafter, but on reaching the top of the Hillary Step fifteen minutes later, he was stalled for an hour by the up-climbing traffic, and for most of it he suffered hypoxia, since his oxygen tank had finally emptied. He had left a fresh canister in a cache at the South Summit not far below, and as he neared the storage spot, he spotted Andy Harris already there.

Although Harris declared there were no full canisters in the cache, Krakauer found at least six. Harris, however, rejected the discovery, and nothing could convince him otherwise. With a replenished oxygen supply, Krakauer proceeded down, but Harris did not.

At 4:30 P.M. Rob Hall radioed from above the Hillary Step that he desperately needed oxygen for Doug Hansen, but Andy Harris, still at the South Summit, again insisted that none was there, when in fact two full bottles were stashed there for Hall and Hansen. At 5:30 P.M., perhaps finally realizing that oxygen had been at his feet all along, Harris climbed back toward Hall and Hansen. At some point after that, he disappeared. A subsequent expedition found his ice axe some fifty vertical feet above the South Summit.

In reflecting on Andy Harris's behavior at the South Summit, Jon Krakauer later concluded that the guide must have been oxygen starved or worse. "In hindsight," wrote Krakauer, "Andy was acting irrationally and had plainly slipped well beyond routine hypoxia." But just as Pittman failed to recognize signs of weakness in Fischer, Krakauer, in his own impaired state, did not recognize what in retrospect should have seemed obvious. Had they been of equal authority on the team—and they had equivalent technical experience—Krakauer believes that Harris's debilitating condition would have registered. But Andy Harris "had been cast in the role of invincible guide," recalled Krakauer, "there to look after me and the other clients; we had been specifically indoctrinated not to question our guides' judgment. The thought never entered my crippled mind that Andy might in fact be in terrible straits—that a guide might urgently need help from me."

For good reason, the culture of the climb had stressed *compliance* with the guides' authority. When critical decisions must be fast and binding, the guides normally did know what was best. Yet without a counterpoint in the culture that stressed *independence* when the guides either could not or would not understand what was indeed best, they could not capitalize on the still discerning judgment of those around them. Had Jon Krakauer thought he could more quickly act on Andy Harris's plight, had Sandy Hill Pittman more fully appreciated Scott Fischer's faltering, and had Beck Weathers more swiftly challenged Rob Hall's instructions, subsequent events might have taken a very different course, and so many climbers might not have died on that tragic ascent.

For the rest of us, then, the events of May 10, 1996, point to the importance of staying alert for wavering leadership and stepping into the breach without being asked to, or even better, understanding *why* your boss's leadership may be wavering before it worsens. A companion point is to ask your boss for clarification or elaboration of underdeveloped instructions before it is too late. For organizations seeking to foster better leadership in everyone, the tragedy on Mount Everest is a reminder to instill an understanding that although authority is to be respected, self-reliance, initiative, and upward intervention—leading up—must have their place, too.

CHAPTER 7

DESIGNING A FUTURE YOUR BOSS
CAN'T QUITE ENVISION

CHARLENE BARSHEFSKY NEGOTIATED THE U.S. TRADE AGREEMENT
WITH CHINA ON BEHALF OF HER BOSS, PRESIDENT BILL CLINTON,
AND DOMINGO CAVALLO STABILIZED THE ARGENTINE CURRENCY
FOR HIS BOSS, PRESIDENT CARLOS MENEM

STRATEGIC THINKING IS a defining capacity of downward leadership. If the topmost people do not understand where a company or a country should be going and how to get there, the workforce or the public is sure to feel rudderless. Though ready to row, they'll be without purpose or direction for pulling ahead. Great insights on what the organization should achieve and the best path ahead, however, are often far from obvious, even to those who rule. Strategic thinking is one of the greatest challenges of all for those at the top, and most of those at the top can use all the help they can draw from below.

Learning how to give strategic assistance to those above is thus a defining quality of leading up. It depends upon diverse experience, broad thinking, and insightful appraisal. It requires a tenacity of purpose to render what is needed in the future even when the boss can't visualize it or is unprepared to endorse it.

To illustrate such upward leadership, we turn to two public officials who fashioned a future that their superiors needed but could not quite see. One served the president of the United States of America, the other the president of the Republic of Argentina; one fought for the end of trade barriers, the other for the end of hyperinflation. Both received a broad authorization from their president to redefine the future, but neither was given instructions on how to get there. Through skillful application of their upward leadership skills, each devised a way forward, giving their presidents what they needed and their nations what they deserved.

Charlene Barshefsky confronted the challenge of negotiating American terms with China for its entry in to the World Trade Organization. For China, it was a tough but necessary pill. WTO membership would help to reform what had often been seen as a rogue economy, and without such reform, it would not be sustainable in a globalizing market. For the United States, membership would also be tough, for it would require congressional approval for the normalization of trade relations on a permanent basis, something that Congress had always refused to grant.

By April 1999, the two sides had largely completed their negotiations, and Chinese premier Zhu Rongji arrived in Washington on April 7 to complete and sign a deal. With little support in Congress from Democrats leery of offending the union movement, however, the president himself balked at the last minute. Barshefsky had warned the Chinese premier that Clinton was ambivalent, but Zhu Rongji had nonetheless expected to fly back to Beijing with a bilateral trade agreement in his hip pocket. He went home, instead, empty-handed.

Despite this setback, Charlene Barshefsky had no intention of giving up. However difficult the Chinese were to deal with, they still constituted the world's largest marketplace, one the United States stood to be shut out of at a time when the rest of the world was about to enter. But if the negotiations had been hard before, they would be even more strenuous with a premier who now felt humiliated. To win the second time around, Barshefsky would have to hold the deal together and bring it to a signing. She would have to persuade not only the Chinese to agree, but also her own boss to accept.

Domingo Cavallo confronted a challenge of a very different character when he became economy minister of Argentina in early 1991, but it was a leadership challenge of the very same kind that faced Charlene Barshefsky.

Growth was negative and prices were haywire. With hyperinflation soaring past 5,000% annually, residents of Buenos Aires, a sprawling metropolis of 11 million residents, debated whether to travel across the city by bus or taxi. Since they paid bus drivers at the trip's start but taxi drivers at the end, the real cost of the taxi fare could prove less than a bus fare paid an hour earlier.

Cavallo had taken the reins of the Economy Ministry with a mandate to fix the problem. He believed that privatizing state enterprise and ending import tariffs would contribute, but what was really required was the unprecedented step of fixing the country's currency to the U.S. dollar. And that would take some fancy footwork. His president, Carlos Menem, had risen to power as a Peronist, and as the standard-bearer for the populist party of Argentine workers, Menem had been elected to overcome the military and business elites who had bankrupted the country. He was the charismatic heir to a nationalist tradition of government control and welfare protection—the antithesis of the cure Cavallo was prescribing.

Cavallo, though, firmly believed that if he could not apply his bitter medicine, the ravages of stagnation and inflation would leave all Argentines behind in a global economy that was lifting most others. Cavallo would have to exercise the kind of broad-based thinking that his superior required if the faltering economy were to be resurrected.

Charlene Barshefsky and Domingo Cavallo faced historic opportunities to make a profound difference in their countries' futures. They also faced superiors whose political instincts and party roots ran contrary to the very course they knew they would have to follow. Moreover, as we'll see in this chapter, Barshefsky and Cavallo would have to write their own road maps, charting a path to a destination defined by their leaders but with no past precedents and plenty of political obstacles along the way.

The road maps that Barshefsky and Cavallo crafted tell us to keep a laserlike focus on the ultimate purpose of our enterprise. Keeping the prize in mind can carry us past personal hardship and dispiriting setback, even belligerent opponents and wavering superiors. Surmounting those obstacles depends as well on ensuring that our plan is airtight in conception and precise in formulation. It will require, too, that we mobilize support among our superior's constituencies, whose backing will be essential for whatever is proposed. Above all, Barshefsky and Cavallo show us that when our institution is presented with an historic opportunity and our superior has asked us to take advantage of it, strategic thinking, precise analysis, and determined advocacy are the ingredients of historic change.

SETTING THE STAGE FOR TRADE
NEGOTIATIONS WITH CHINA

In 1993, newly elected U.S. president Bill Clinton had placed one of his confidants, Mickey Kantor, in charge of the Office of the U.S. Trade Representative. Kantor needed help and asked attorney Charlene Barshefsky to talk with him about international trade. She promptly said that she had no plans to leave private practice. Fine, Kantor replied, he just wanted to pick her mind. And it was a good one to pick.

After graduating seventh in her class in 1975 from the law school of the Catholic University of America in Washington, D.C., Barshefsky had joined one of the capital's premier law firms, Steptoe & Johnson, where she became a trade specialist and partner; by 1993 she was cochairing the firm's large international practice. With eighteen years of private practice and an income of more than half a million dollars, Barshefsky had little incentive for government service. Because she had two young children—ages four and nine—doing any extensive travel for any purpose was near the top of her list of undesirables.

Charlene Barshefsky

Mickey Kantor, though, wasn't easily dissuaded. He arranged for one more discussion seemingly focused on trade, and then he popped the question: Would she serve as his deputy and ambassador for Asia and Latin America? Barshefsky was "basically paralyzed," and she worried whether acceptance would be "the right decision" or "a dreadful mistake" for her family. Sensing her ambivalence, Kantor gave her time to mull it over. For some, a ranking position in the new administration would have required ten minutes' reflection before getting to yes; for Barshefsky, days passed without resolution.

Barshefsky and her husband, Ed Cohen, a fellow lawyer who later served as deputy solicitor for the U.S. Department of the Interior, were driving together to work ten days later when Barshefsky decided she could waver no more. "I've just got to call Mickey Kantor," she told her husband, who had been encouraging her to take the job, "but I don't know what to do about it. I really have to say yes or no. I wish I had a 'sign.' " When a car passed several minutes later with the vanity plate Go4It, Barshefsky had the omen she was looking for. "That's a 'sign,' " she exclaimed. "I'm going to say yes!" Barshefsky arrived at her office, sat down, inhaled, called Kantor, and did just that.

For a job she had never sought, Barshefsky took to it well. Kantor promoted her to be his principal deputy in 1994, and China became a large part of her responsibilities. Among her first tasks was the negotiation of a Chinese crackdown on pirated products, a wide-spread and officially tolerated practice that was costing U.S. makers of music, films, and software more than $2 billion annually.

During her November 1995 visit to Beijing, Chinese officials reiterated a long-expressed interest in becoming a member of the World Trade Organization, the group that sets the rules for international commerce. Membership had its privileges: China's exports were likely to be boosted. But membership brought obligations as well, and Barshefsky cautioned that U.S. support would not come "cheap." She reminded Wu Yi, who was then Chinese trade minister, that international trade depended on market openness and domestic responsibility. Without the latter, she said, any discussion of WTO membership was pointless. The government still was not fully cracking down on its illegal CD makers, and Barshefsky warned at a Beijing press conference that "China cannot expect the American people to support new agreements if existing agreements are not enforced." She outlined an arduous "road map" for the Chinese to follow if they hoped to gain U.S. support in their bid for WTO membership.

Upward Service Requires Vision but Can Entail Hardship

Charlene Barshefsky knew that opening trade with China would be an arduous path for the United States as well, but she also saw it as an essential one. It was not a front-burner issue for her president, but she believed a swift normalization of trade with China was unequivocally in the interests of the country that Bill Clinton had sworn to protect. It was that overarching vision that would drive her through the many months of international flights, grueling negotiations, and family absences that were required to achieve it. It would serve her well in working for a president who wanted more export-driven growth and a more productive relationship with China but whose own political party contained elements strongly opposed to both.

For Barshefsky, the driving concept was one of expanding economies and growing security. She saw her role as pursuing "Roosevelt's overarching vision that countries that send goods across borders don't send armies." What her job came down to, she said, was a "bringing together of nations that were adversaries, an opening of the trading system to help ensure peace, stability, and prosperity." In the final analysis, she felt she was contributing to "policy making at its best for the broadest good. It may lead to inequities along the way, which have to be rectified, but I think it is the broadest vision for the greatest number of people."

The past record was clear to Barshefsky: Since 1950, world economic production had grown sixfold, per capita income had risen threefold, infant mortality had dropped by two-thirds, and world life expectancy had lengthened by twenty years. Nations from Albania to Mongolia were embracing market economics. And all these developments, Barshefsky believed, were driven in part by a fifteenfold growth in global trade, and she intended to make them all that much stronger by catalyzing even greater economic exchange. For that, normalizing American trade relations with China and bringing China into the World Trade Organization were essential.

A trade agreement with China would strengthen American security as well. "It is not in our interest to keep a fifth of humanity out of a more integrated world," Barshefsky explained. But China "won't move toward international norms if it feels isolated and repudiated." It is "by opening China's markets and integrating China into the modern global economy" that the United States can "help ensure that a nation of 1.2 billion people plays its proper role as an import market, as a source of economic growth for its Asian neighbors, as a reform-minded country, and ultimately as a China that plays a different and healthier role in the Pacific."

Barshefsky needed no instruction from the president to know what the future should look like or to understand both the economic and security payoffs that would come with China's full incorporation into the global economy. Upward service requires one's own development of a vision and then helping one's superior to appreciate and act on it, not waiting to be told. It entails not just appreciating it intellectually but also personally resolving to making it a reality. On both fronts, Barshefsky was already out front.

But the great challenges of building an overarching vision invariably require great energy and investment, and they inevitably take their personal toll. Charlene Barshefsky traveled the world but rarely saw much of it. Most of her time abroad was spent in meetings where the exchanges were never easy, since each side knew that billions of dollars were at stake. Sometimes the meetings became grueling.

When a team of Japanese negotiators tried exhaustion as a tactic, Barshefsky dueled with them for fifty-one hours straight, broken by a single twenty-minute catnap. If they are going to stay up all night, she said to herself, so will I. She decided that she could stay with the best in a war of attrition. When a Japanese negotiator asked her if she would like a break from another exhausting session, Barshefsky retorted, "I'm never tired."

It was a game for which she had given up three-quarters of her pay and a significant portion of her family life. Barshefsky called her two young daughters daily from whatever world capital she was visiting, but a lot was lost in transmission. On top of the personal losses, she had to endure attacks by protectionists, and though she had acquired a thick skin, it was never quite thick enough. All that and more would have to be tolerated, however, if Barshefsky was to reach a WTO agreement with China.

Lesson in Leading Up

Whether you work for a private company or a government agency, you need to be clear minded about the organization's overall purpose, and you should make your decisions so your actions are clearly directed at that purpose. Your obligation is to build your own vision and to act strategically on behalf of your superior, whatever personal hardships may be encountered.

Building a Base for the Boss

Barshefsky's responsibility for achieving her vision on behalf of the president would be suddenly expanded on April 3, 1996, when a U.S. Air Force jet carrying Secretary of Commerce Ron Brown and an entourage of business leaders crashed into a mountainside near Croatia's Dubrovnik airport. President Clinton asked Mickey Kantor to become his secretary of commerce, and in his place the president appointed Charlene Barshefsky to his cabinet as the acting U.S. trade representative. The Senate formally confirmed Barshefsky's appointment on March 17, 1997.

The president knew he had an able negotiator in place. "She's tough as nails and her reputation precedes her," observed Robert Reich, a former labor secretary for Clinton, and that "makes her a more formidable negotiator." Elsewhere in Asia, Japanese trade representatives had publicly named her "Stonewall." President Clinton had taken to introducing her as a "brilliant trade negotiator for our country" and "our toughest negotiator."

For a negotiator, those were high accolades—no nation wants a soft touch representing its side. But this negotiator was required not only to craft the deal but also to sell it, and that, Barshefsky knew, required a whole different set of skills. The president would have to steer any trade deal with China through a political minefield. A negotiated document simply wasn't enough to guarantee success. Whatever arrangement Barshefsky and her Chinese counterparts arrived at would have to create its own compelling arguments among widely divergent constituencies, without giving aid and comfort to those who could never be brought around to the cause. Barshefsky needed to be certain that her side incorporated the issues that really mattered on the home front while steering clear of the red flags that could kill it, especially since a red flag would stand on top of it.

Barshefsky's upward leadership task was therefore not only to negotiate a mutually acceptable deal, but also to build a base of support for the deal that the president would require if it were to stick. The undertaking was not only technical, calling upon her best negotiating skills, but also political, requiring her best persuading skills. In working on behalf of the president, she appreciated that widespread support for the deal would be essential for the president, and it was her job to help generate it. Building public backing for a change in national policy was not at the core of her job description, but it was at the center of her cerebral cortex.

In her prior push for intellectual property rights in China, Barshefsky had conferred extensively with industry leaders to identify precisely what they were losing and whether they were ready to support the tough deal she was considering. Her conscientious consultation had brought such corporate chieftains as Chrysler CEO Robert Eaton on board to support her initiatives. "Charlene and Mickey do not declare victory if nothing happens, and they do not sign an agreement that doesn't have teeth in it," he observed. "She wants teeth in it."

A WTO agreement would require far more political support than had the intellectual property rights agreements, since the WTO issues were far more sweeping and momentous. As Barshefsky began the arduous process of negotiating with the Chinese government, led by premier Zhu Rongji, she opened a parallel campaign with all of the domestic constituencies most affected. She met with business associations and trade unions, she talked with official supporters and political detractors, and her staff painstakingly reviewed several hundred letters received from members of Congress, many from organized labor, and close to a thousand from trade associations and business firms.

Most of the input, some of it unsolicited, recommended that Barshefsky incorporate provisions into the accord very specific to a constituency or industry. For example, the United Auto Workers feared that any deal would foster manufacturing jobs in China while having the opposite effect in America, and it urged that the agreement prohibit any requirement that a proportion of a product's content be locally made in China. The semiconductor industry feared that the government would continue to force technology transfer as a price of admission, and it opposed any such requirement.

Barshefsky fine-tuned her provisions to meet these and hundreds of other tightly honed preferences and objections. Not every preference made the final cut—some were lost to internal conflicts, others at the bargaining table—but the agreement that finally emerged was authored more by American industry and other trade-related constituencies than it was by any government person or agency. And that, Barshefsky said, is exactly as it should be. "We had to ensure that when we brought the agreement back it would be essentially unassailable," she explained. "Any deal that doesn't have the seal of approval of the business community and other constituencies isn't a deal worth doing."

To the same end, Barshefsky insisted that any completed agreement be made public. It was an unusual requirement that angered her Chinese counterparts, but she knew that total transparency was essential if the worst suspicions of the president's domestic foes were to be allayed.

The agreement would also have to be comprehensive, covering virtually all manufactured goods, all services, and all farm products. Barshefsky believed that nothing of importance could be left untouched. The deal would have to remove industry barriers, slash import tariffs, stop discriminatory taxation, assure trading rights (the right of U.S. companies to import and export), terminate export subsidies, and guarantee product distribution. It needed to address the concerns of all business sectors—ranging from aircraft to banking and brokerage, from autos to wine and wheat. It also would have to prohibit forced technology transfers and protect American wage earners. And all measures in it would have to be enforceable.

Barshefsky had in effect negotiated on two fronts. She sat at the table with her Chinese counterparts to hammer out the detailed formal language of agreement. But she also sat at hundreds of domestic tables to ensure that the formal language incorporated all of their concerns. In doing so, she had appreciated that her task was both bilateral and very political, and that building a successful policy for her president required conscientious dialogue with both the Chinese and the American people.

Lesson in Leading Up

To ensure that your superior can institute a controversial policy that you have been asked to develop, make certain the policy is comprehensive, inclusive, and built on a foundation that is responsive to the genuine concerns of all major concerned parties.

Remaining Unshaken in Conviction Even When Shaken by Setback

During the spring of 1999, Barshefsky's negotiations with the Chinese gained momentum. With all parties narrowing down the most contentious issues, the hours lengthened and rancor intensified. When the Chinese negotiators seemed close to walking out, Barshefsky cautioned publicly on March 25 that the chances of success were now no better than "fifty-fifty."

By the end of March, the two sides had finally resolved many of the most divisive issues, and a mutually acceptable draft was nearly ready, though several thorny issues remained. In a visit to Beijing, Barshefsky impressed on Premier Zhu Rongji the importance of resolving the outstanding issues and cautioned that President Clinton had yet to make a final decision on the agreement because of opposition within his own party. She appreciated that communicating information well beyond the technical aspects of trade relations was part and parcel of her upward leadership.

Still, Zhu appeared ready to make the necessary concessions to complete the deal, and he departed for Washington to conclude and confirm the accord. President Clinton signaled his readiness to receive him: "If China is willing to play by the global rules of trade," he declared, "it would be an inexplicable mistake for the United States to say no."

But when the Chinese premier arrived at the White House on April 7, President Clinton himself was not yet ready to play. He faced

Chinese Premier Zhu Rongji with Charlene Barshefsky
in Beijing on March 30, 1999.

intense resistance from his own liberal Democratic base, and he was wavering between approval and rejection. Behind closed doors, Charlene Barshefsky still argued that the agreement be finished and signed, but other advisors cautioned Clinton against the prospect of a fight with his own political constituency.

The president finally concluded that the timing was not right, and on the very day of the Chinese premier's arrival in the capital, Clinton told Zhu Rongji that the deal would have to wait. Stunned and humiliated, Zhu voiced his displeasure. "Surely the American side realizes that the time has come to end negotiations which have already gone on for thirteen years," the premier complained. At a private meeting with members of Congress, Zhu went further. Clinton, he said, lacked the "courage" to press the case with Congress.

Not surprisingly, the U.S. trade representative found herself in a cross fire of recriminations. "Barshefsky cut one of the strongest trade deals the U.S. has ever negotiated," wrote the *Wall Street Journal,* but she "couldn't sell it to her most important client, Clinton" (though other advisors couldn't sell it to the president either). White House insiders who had opposed concluding the agreement implied that she had entered the final round of negotiations without a suffi-

Chinese Premier Zhu Rongji with President Bill Clinton
at the White House on April 8, 1999.

cient mandate from the president. Others pointed out that she lacked the partisan networks that two of her predecessors, Robert Strauss and William Brock, had brought to the office as party leaders. Even the Chinese premier chided her, saying that the United States "made public many documents and said we had agreed to them, but in fact we have not agreed."

President Clinton immediately appreciated the devastating effects of his public rejection of the deal. He called Premier Zhu several times to get negotiations back on track. While Zhu declined, Barshefsky was determined to negotiate with her Chinese counterpart in Washington to lock down what had already been agreed upon, and she used documents that she had earlier insisted on making public—for which Zhu had chided her—to now help avert any backsliding. Barshefsky worked through the night of April 13 to negotiate a statement memorializing the progress to date that would be signed the next day before Zhu left the United States. "I had to keep the deal together," she recalled. "To lose what we had when we were so close to getting it done would have been tragic." The United States would "have lost an absolutely historic opportunity." The next morning, the two sides signed the memorializing statement.

Undaunted by the larger reversal, Charlene Barshefsky within days was back in Beijing to jump-start the negotiations again, only now with the President Clinton's determination to conclude. This time, though, a tragedy of a different sort in almost the same place where Ron Brown had died would test her resolve. On May 7, the United States mistakenly bombed China's embassy in Zagreb, killing three Chinese citizens. Beijing broke off all discussions.

By September 1999, however, China's freeze was thawing, and Chinese president Jiang Zemin and President Clinton agreed to restart negotiations. New talks accelerated swiftly, and by early November the two sides were once again tantalizingly close to an accord. When anxious days stretched into a week and more, and the remaining tough issues were yet to be settled, Barshefsky began to suspect that the Chinese had decided to tread water, unable to make the further concessions that she knew the U.S. Congress would need if it were to approve the accord. At one point during a break, she told her team at the U.S. embassy in Beijing that the negotiations felt like an episode of the TV series *Seinfeld:* "It may be of some interest," she explained, "but it's content-less and not nearly as funny."

To test the Chinese resolve, Barshefsky packed her bags on November 15 and sent them on to the airport for the long flight back to Washington. On her way to the airport she stopped for a final courtesy call with the Chinese negotiators. Shocked by her abrupt walkout, the Chinese pleaded with her to stay, but Barshefsky told them it was too late: Her vans were already on their way to the airport. When Barshefsky rose to leave for her flight, State Counselor Wu Yi suddenly emerged to say, "Premier Zhu has come to the building. It is unprecedented. Never in the history of the ministry has someone of that rank come here. We always go there. He is here and wants to see you."

The brinkmanship had worked. The premier unstuck the final sticking points, and the two sides consummated the deal on the spot. Zhu told Barshefsky that President Jiang wanted the American team to stop by once the agreement was signed, and Barshefsky seized the offer: "Great! How about today?"

The Chinese president was "extremely gracious" during their meeting later that day, Barshefsky recalled. "He was obviously elated and relieved. We had a very cordial conversation. He put on his over-coat and took us across to a pavilion to show us the South Lake in front of which the Empress Dowager in the Qing dynasty used to sit and look at the geese and the swans." It was "his way of saying thank-you and sending his best regards to the United States without ever saying either."

Charlene Barshefsky had thought she had been close to a mutu-ally acceptable agreement in April, so close that it appeared that Zhu's visit to Washington was likely to result in a finished and signed deal. Despite her efforts to ensure that domestic constituencies were sufficiently on board with the provisions negotiated, she was sur-prised to learn that some—especially the president's own political

Charlene Barshefsky exchanges signed agreement in Beijing with
Chinese minister Guangsheng on November 15, 1999.

party—had not been won over. Undercut by a superior who she had thought was ready for the agreement and then widely criticized for the Chinese visit that went nowhere, her immediate response was back to business and full steam ahead. She appreciated that upward leadership on behalf of big causes can encounter big setbacks, and without missing a beat she plunged ahead for the mission she knew was too worthy for anything less. Her relentless pursuit of the goal, whatever the inconsistency from on high, would finally and fully pay off for her superior

---

Lesson in Leading Up

Uniquely rewarding opportunities present themselves rarely, whatever your business. When they do, you need to be both persistent in your pursuit of the opportunity and consistent in your efforts to make those above you understand its uniqueness. Even when your boss resists or fails to get it, the organization and cause you both serve deserves no less.

Lining Up the Backers

Charlene Barshefsky and China's new trade minister, Shi Guangsheng, signed the final agreement in Beijing on Monday, November 15, 1999. Afterward, Barshefsky and Gene Sperling, director of the White House Economic Council, telephoned Bill Clinton, who was traveling in Turkey, to deliver the news. The two placed a call from a women's rest room at the Trade Ministry, the only place they could find enough privacy to make the call. When they reached the president's hotel in Ankara with the good news, national security advisor Sandy Berger pulled the president out of the shower to receive it. A White House aide later dubbed it a moment of "bath-room-to-bathroom" diplomacy.

Barshefsky returned quickly to Washington to convince the many domestic parties of the new agreement's essential soundness. Since establishing diplomatic relations with China in 1979, the United States had annually reviewed and approved trade relations with China. China insisted that this vexing exercise be ended and its normal trade status made unconditional. If the United States did not meet that stipulation, China could still join the WTO, but it would face no obligation to open its markets to American goods. A favorable vote of both the House of Representatives and the Senate would be required for granting China permanent normal trade relations status, China's precondition for the deal to be operative. She knew it was her job to help assure the president got that vote.

Barshefsky found to her pleasure that neither Capitol Hill nor interest groups were pressing for specific changes in the agreement. Indeed, she received no requests for modifications of any kind to the hundreds of provisions in the document. The fact that the "agreement was strong and comprehensive," Barshefsky said, "was the first step in helping to ensure its political acceptability."

Comprehensive the agreement certainly was. Its 250 pages were filled with fine points, each measure intended to neutralize an adversary or convert an agnostic. For example, China prohibited foreign investment in its telecommunications sector, but the agreement required that it open mobile services to 49% foreign ownership within five years. "We're going from 0 to 49%" said Sprint's vice president for Asian business development Bob Becker, and that's "not too bad." Another clause pertained to China's tariff on oranges and lemons, which had been 40%, but the agreement lowered that to 12%. Florida's *St. Petersburg Times* editorialized that the clause on fruit made the agreement one that "should not be held hostage to short-sighted politics." And another provision referred to China's limits on the number of revenue-sharing foreign films, which had been ten per year, but the deal doubled the limit. Jack Valenti, chief of the Motion

Picture Association of America, declared that to "deny China permanent normal trade relations would be a mystifying blunder."

That's not to say that congressional acceptance was assured. While not quarreling with specific provisions, opponents still voiced principled arguments against the very concept of normalizing trade relations with China. Doing so would only benefit the wealthy, they said, while rewarding a despotic regime. Democratic representative David Obey of Wisconsin argued that the issue came down to whether "the investing class, the managing elite, the venture capitalists, the multinational corporations who have so much to gain by further globalization will be willing to see a tiny fraction of that increased wealth used to help those who will otherwise be caught in the prop wash of their incredible prosperity." Democratic representative David E. Bonior of Michigan, the House minority whip, asserted that "the China we're being told to extend permanent, most favored trade status to" is a "China that would do Joseph Stalin proud."

Congressional approval of trade normalization with China required only a simple majority in the House and then the Senate, and Barshefsky set out with other cabinet officials to ensure what they needed from each. If the president were to secure the votes he required, she would have to apply herself on his behalf to bring in the vote. Upward leadership now dictated lateral persuasion, which became congressional arm-twisting at its best.

With the vote up first in the U.S. House of Representatives, a far more difficult vote than expected in the U.S. Senate, Barshefsky helped ensure that a strong team of presidential advisors was armed and ready. She and the team divided the representatives among themselves and went one-on-one after the most persuadable. She brought small groups to the White House Yellow Oval Room, the more intimate meeting place in the president's residence just above the famous Oval Office. There she argued that the Chinese market was critical for American prosperity: How many more refrigerators can U.S. manufacturers sell at home, she asked, and how many millions more could be sold to 1.2 billion consumers who are still largely without home appliances? She highlighted agreement features that had been added in response to specific industry and labor concerns. She explained how each representative's district would prosper from expanding trade with China. She contended that economic freedom could inspire social freedom, then political freedom, and ultimately religious freedom. What's more, she said, Internet access and American companies would help bring Western values to China, laying the foundation for a less belligerent attitude and more peaceful world.

Barshefsky engaged in personal politics in the extreme—cajoling, coaching, and consoling representatives and senators who were still hearing constituency and lobbyist arguments to the contrary—and she helped ensure that industry advocates were heard on the Hill as well. The movie industry's Jack Valenti testified before the Senate Commerce Committee on April 11 that "the Chinese people love American movies," that the "agreement struck by Ambassador Barshefsky opens up new opportunities in the Chinese market for American visual entertainment," and that a yes vote was essential for U.S. filmmakers. When Democratic representatives like Thomas Allen of Maine proved reluctant to go against the many constituents who opposed the measure, Barshefsky met with him several times and arranged for him to see both President Clinton and Defense Secretary (and former Maine senator) William Cohen. "She's smart," said Allen of Barshefsky. "She knows her agreement. She has a very quick mind. I got what I needed from her." And with that, he said, "I became persuaded that—on balance—it would be helpful to bring the Chinese under the rule of law in international trade."

Barshefsky couldn't ask the premier business lobbies—the National Association of Manufacturers, the U.S. Chamber of Commerce, and the Business Roundtable—to coalesce and collectively press for passage, but the lobbies furnished plenty of ammunition on their own for making the case to Congress. The Business Roundtable alone allocated $9 million to promoting the pact, and a group of business leaders—including the CEOs of IBM, Kodak, and Monsanto—told the president that they were "ready to work with Ambassador Barshefsky" to secure "timely, bipartisan approval of unconditional" trading status for China.

Charlene Barshefsky assiduously worked public opinion as well, viewing it as essential for the president to get the vote he needed. Lateral action was again an essential component of her upward leadership. From late January to late May, she met on forty-three separate occasions with journalists from CNN, *Congressional Quarterly,* NBC, the *New Republic,* the *New York Times,* TheStreet.com, the *Wall Street Journal,* the *Washington Post,* and countless others. She delivered forty-six speeches to groups, including the National Conference of State Legislators, the National Governors' Association, and the Women's National Democratic Club. Barshefsky also sat with hundreds of members of Congress on fifty separate occasions, and she testified repeatedly on Capitol Hill, arguing that U.S. trade in the past had "promoted reform and opening within China" and characteristically concluding that China's accession to WTO "will be the most important such step in decades. Let history show that we had the wisdom, the confidence and the vision this moment of danger and promise requires."

Much of the labor movement, a key constituency of the president's party, remained in fierce opposition, equating free trade with job destruction. The United Auto Workers, the Teamsters, and the United Steel Workers, whose members could be most affected, campaigned vigorously and helped move the AFL-CIO into opposition. Barshefsky had met with union leaders during her negotiations and even incorporated all of what labor sought in the final agreement, but it did little in the end to defuse their anger or mute their opposition. AFL-CIO president John Sweeney declared, "It is disgustingly hypocritical of the Clinton Administration to pledge to 'put a human face on the global economy' while prostrating itself in pursuit of a trade deal with a rogue nation that decorates itself with human rights abuses as if they were medals of honor."

With just weeks until the House vote, organized labor brought 14,000 unionists to Washington to lobby the fence-sitters in Congress. Teamsters president James P. Hoffa exhorted thousands of workers at the capital rally, "Let's go to the Hill and give 'em hell." Reform Party presidential candidate Patrick J. Buchanan declared from the same platform that if he were in the White House, "it won't be Charlene Barshefsky sitting down in Beijing, it will be Jim Hoffa."

A year earlier, the union pressure might well have been enough to buckle the president's resolve, but this time Barshefsky and her colleagues were marshaling more than enough momentum the other way. On April 3, the White House distributed a letter signed by nearly 200 CEOs, including those of Compaq, Lucent Technologies, and Microsoft, urging approval of the China deal. On April 4, it announced that forty-two governors, including George W. Bush of Texas, backed the normalization of trade with China. Three weeks later, it released a letter signed by 149 economists, including liberal Robert M. Solow, conservative Milton Friedman, and eleven other Nobel Prize winners, backing China's WTO entry. At a White House press briefing, Solow said that "it's such a simple proposition" for China's accession that he "could not generate a hard exam question" about it.

Coming back in spades after Zhu Rongji's failed visit a year earlier, Barshefsky would savor unequivocal success on this second round. She and her administration colleagues had built the support required for the deal's approval to sail through a previously reluctant Congress. On May 24, 2000, the House of Representatives, where opposition has been strongest, voted 237 to 197 for permanent normal trade relations with China.

It was then up to the Senate, where Barshefsky was more confident that the administration had the needed votes. On September 19 the Senate voted 83 to 15 for normalizing trade with China, signaling the biggest change in U.S. relations with the world's largest nation since President Nixon's historic visit in 1972.

Steven Ricchetti, the White House deputy chief of staff who had served as one of the president's point people for passage, observed, "This thing didn't get done because of happenstance." A "helluva lot of things went into getting it done." And many of those things had stemmed directly from the vision and initiative that Barshefsky had brought to the office. It may never have flown without her several years of dogged pursuit of an agreement, and without her appreciation for the fact that her boss would only back it and Congress would only approve it if she negotiated a deal they needed. And then she had to persuade them of that simple truth. Leading on behalf of a superior through trying times requires not only an enduring upward commitment but also persistent lateral persuasion.

Lesson in Leading Up

Building the lateral backing that your superiors need to implement a contentious but otherwise sensible initiative is an essential precondition for ultimately making it happen. The indispensable elements for success: a judicious combination of compelling concepts, detailed prescriptions, and retail persuasion.

DOMINGO CAVALLO CONFRONTED A COLLAPSING ECONOMY

Charlene Barshefsky's goal in 1999 had been to produce a trade agreement that her president wanted and a reluctant Congress would approve. To get there, she successfully navigated a political minefield. Domingo Cavallo's goal in 1991 was to turn around a ruinous economy that had driven his president and congress to the brink of desperation. To succeed, Cavallo would have to pull off a rare political hat trick, and do so in a nation not notable for the flexibility of its governmental ways.

For Barshefsky's upward leadership on behalf of the American president to succeed, she had to have a vision of what should be achieved, what could be realized, and what would be required. For Cavallo's upward service on behalf of Argentine president Carlos Menem, he would have to have that and more. Barshefsky had come to office in an era of great economic prosperity; Cavallo took office on the eve of a complete economic collapse. It would demand of him a solution that was totally outside the box and one that was utterly antithetical to the precepts of his president's party. It would require creative thinking and strategic action of exceptional intensity, and few contemporary examples more clearly reveal how upward leadership can spell the difference between economic demise or national prosperity.

To appreciate the crisis that Cavallo was called upon to resolve in 1991, one must glance back a decade in Argentina's history. A decade of national mismanagement had plunged the country into a tailspin. In 1981–82, President Leopoldo Galtieri committed the colossal blunder of seizing Britain's Falkland Islands. Public revulsion over the disastrous venture—323 seamen died when a British torpedo sank the *Belgrano* on May 2, 1982—forced General Galtieri and his military junta back to the barracks, but the elected president who followed, the Radical Party's Raúl Alfonsín, fared little better, inheriting deep-lying problems from his predecessors. During his six years in Casa Rosada—the presidential palace—Alfonsín had put the economy further in reverse. With a well-educated population of 33 million and abundant resources in an area eight times the size of Germany, Argentina had earlier been poised to join the First World. Alfonsín's policies had steered it toward the Third. At the start of the 1980s, Argentina had been manufacturing 240,000 motor vehicles annually; ten years later, the total was just half that. During

Domingo Cavallo

Carlos Menem

Alfonsín's last year in office, the economy shrank 6% and inflation at moments topped 5,000%.

From the political chaos of military humiliation and hyperinflation emerged a presidential candidate who promised an end to it all. During the campaign of 1989, Carlos Saúl Menem drew hundreds of thousands to street rallies around Buenos Aires. "For the hunger of the poor children," he exhorted, "for the sadness of the rich children, follow me! For the tables without bread, follow me!" Only he could undo what his predecessors had done—"I'm not going to deceive you! Follow me!"—and what he promised was government largesse, an honored tradition of his political movement.

As the standard-bearer for the Justicialista Party, Menem carried the legacy of no less than Colonel Juan Domingo Perón, the charismatic politician who had single-handedly transformed the role of the Argentine state. During Perón's two presidential regimes from 1946 to 1955 and 1973 to 1974, the government enlarged welfare and nationalized industry. Peronism had survived Perón's death in 1974, embodied in millions of fervent followers and now a convincing contender who promised a comeback.

Carlos Menem's near rout of the Radical Party's candidate in the May election represented a political turning point: It was the first time since 1916 that elected presidents of opposing parties had succeeded each other. But this triumph for democracy and civilian rule promised disaster for business. As former governor of La Rioja Province, Menem arrived with an established reputation for featherbedding and corruption. Worse, he led a party of the masses, a movement standing for workers' rights and government guarantees. Company managers and private investors were appalled at the prospect of more regulations and handouts. The magnetic Carlos Menem was being compared with Juan Perón in more than just personality.

Just before Menem's 1989 election, the Argentine austral had traded at seventeen to the U.S. dollar. During his first year in office, the austral plummeted to 5,000 against the dollar, and in the first month of 1991 it lost another 40%. Currency exchangers began demanding 10,000 australs for one American dollar, and beleaguered banks responded predictably, raising interest rates to 600%— per month! The absurd daily consequences of the hyperinflation could be heard in restaurants when departing patrons argued not over who paid the check—a credit card charge would be nearly worthless by the time it was paid weeks later—but who furnished the cash tip, since it was paid on the spot.

Domingo Cavallo Takes Charge

On January 28, 1991, a frantic Carlos Menem telephoned his foreign minister, Domingo Felipe Cavallo, at a foreign emissaries' conference in Venezuela. None of the three economy ministers that Menem had appointed during the first eighteen months of his administration had been able to reverse the deepening crisis. Nor had four central bank presidents that Menem had tried out in just seven months. So Menem called his foreign minister back to Buenos Aires to do what the president and all his financial experts had so far failed to do.

Cavallo's résumé had not made him an obvious choice for the ministry of economy or for an angel of recovery. He had presided briefly—for just fifty-two days—over the country's central bank in 1982, later represented Cordoba in the national congress from 1987 to 1989, and was now serving as the foreign minister, but he had no proven record in what Menem wanted from him. Still, what Menem craved was Cavallo's creative thinking and political savvy, and he needed both immediately. Menem's first eighteen months in office had brought domestic disaster. Real wages were plummeting, a military group had attempted a coup, and Menem's approval rating had fallen to 30%, the lowest since taking office.

The boisterous president and his bookish minister could not have brought more different styles to their political marriage: Menem savored red Ferraris and public appearances; Cavallo favored family gatherings and technical lectures. But that mattered little. Menem gave the new economy minister a powerful brief to remake the economy in the image not of Juan Perón but nearly the opposite, which Cavallo had long been advocating. It was not only a monumental task but also the sort of opportunity for which Cavallo had long been hoping. "For a number of years," Cavallo said, "I thought I could play an important role in the transformation of the country." Now he would have his chance. An official working for him revealed just how far he intended to push: "We are going all the way. This is a very deep transformation of the country. This is not for six months or a year. This will be forever."

Business interests seemed to believe it. The day after Cavallo's appointment as economy minister became public, investors drove the stock index up by 30%. But inflation also intensified—meat prices at the capital's biggest market rose overnight by another third. Clearly, the private sector believed that Cavallo might just be the savior that Menem was not, but the newest master of this declining universe knew that he had little time to waste.

Upon Cavallo's return to Buenos Aires, the president's brother and senate president, Eduardo Menem, was waiting at the airport along with the president's chief of staff. The two drove Cavallo directly to Casa Rosada, where they grilled him about who he would like to keep or replace in the president's cabinet if a radical remake of the Argentine economy were to succeed. Minutes later in Menem's office, Cavallo said he would only take the economy post if the president would indeed shake up his cabinet and give Cavallo a free hand to pick all of his own ministry officials. "I want a coherent team within my ministry and a coherent team of ministers, a coherent cabinet," Cavallo explained, "because a lack of ability to work as a coherent team, a coherent cabinet, had been the problem during the previous year and a half."

Menem immediately assented, and within one day the president had reassigned his defense minister, Guido di Tella, as foreign minister and outgoing economy minister Antonio Erman Gonzalez as defense minister. Cavallo anticipated that his sweeping measures would require a foreign minister who could persuasively explain them to the international community, and di Tella, a fellow economist and good friend, was just the one to do so. Since the economic changes would also require support of the army despite a tightening budget, Gonzales was right for defense.

Cavallo immediately pressed President Menem to make a completely unprecedented policy move. Cavallo proposed to fix the increasingly worthless Argentine currency to the almighty American dollar. For a nationalist movement rooted in the Buenos Aires working class rather than the Wall Street banking class, such a step was heretical, but Menem was so anxious to end hyperinflation that after a brief explanation and few details, he told Cavallo simply, "Let's go ahead with the idea."

On March 14, with the president's immediate backing and his own team in place, Cavallo drafted the plan in days and presented it to congress, barely six weeks after Cavallo had taken office. For the next two weeks, Cavallo spent his days in the congress, explaining and reexplaining the plan's arcane mechanics. It would fix 10,000 australs to one U.S. dollar and make the two currencies completely convertible. Only an act of congress could change the exchange rate. The government would print no more pesos—the currency's new designation—unless it held the same in dollar reserves. Thus it could spend only what it collected in taxes, ending the long-standing but highly inflationary practice of paying for government deficits by printing new money.

Cavallo drew the vigorous backing of the president and his entire cabinet. Professional economists with whom Cavallo had longtime relations endorsed the plan. Cavallo met at length with a prominent conservative deputy and onetime presidential candidate who had earlier served as economy minister, and the conservative deputy threw himself into convincing his colleagues. The senate voted yes on March 22, and after an all-night debate, the Chamber of Deputies decisively approved the bill on March 28 by a vote of 115 to 64.

Like Charlene Barshefsky, Domingo Cavallo knew that leading up—in this instance to save his country from economic collapse and his president from political ruin—required a far-reaching plan, and that in turn required a presidential cabinet that would support the plan and a congress that would endorse it. Further appreciating that time was not on his president's side, Cavallo insisted on instant changes in the cabinet and immediate action by the congress. He got both, and in doing so he set the stage for one of the greatest economic about-faces ever.

Lesson in Leading Up

Building lateral support for far-reaching change requires a top management team whose members can effectively back and execute the measure. The proper staffing of that team is your responsibility and not just that of the boss. The same is true of mobilizing the support of others whose backing and approval will be required for execution.

Cavallo's Plan for Convertibility Ended Inflation

Cavallo's ministry team had already prepared the necessary regulatory decrees, and he put his "dollarization scheme" into effect just one business day later, on April 1, 1991. The plan almost instantly ended the country's hyperinflation, achieving what his predecessors had failed to do. By the end of April the annual inflation rate had plummeted to 5%, by May to 3%, by August to 1%, and by December, 0.4%. With a monetary yardstick restored, the economy rebounded dramatically. Annual automobile production shot up from 95,000 cars to 155,000. Having contracted by 7% in 1989, the economy expanded by 10% in 1991. Despite the layoff of many state workers, the national unemployment rate declined from 8.8 to 6.4%.

Domingo Cavallo also prevailed upon his president to crack down on widespread tax evasion, a chronic problem that had stoked inflation. During the 1980s, the government deficit had averaged 9% of gross domestic product, but with internal revenues up by half within the year, its deficit dropped to 1.8%. In the fourth quarter of 1991 Argentina even ran a surplus. Cavallo also redoubled the president's resolve to move his nation from one of the world's most closed and coddled economies to one of its most open. "Before, it was very easy to be a businessman in Argentina, with subsidies, speculation, and protection," said the president. Now, "never again will the state rescue companies."

With Cavallo's economic stabilization a resounding success, Menem expanded his political base from a blue-collar constituency to the middle class. In congressional and provincial elections in September 1991, the public voted overwhelmingly for his Justicialista candidates.

Rearguard resistance did flare. When Cavallo announced on September 13, 1991, that a quarter of the workforces of five government-controlled banks would have to retire or transfer to the government's tax-collector ranks, bank workers simply stopped working.

The secretary-general of the association of state workers, Victor de Gennaro, bitterly complained, "The structure of unions, once the base of working-class life in Argentina, is coming apart." But Cavallo retained Menem's ear and confidence despite the anger within the president's traditional political base, and on October 31, the government proceeded to close a host of state regulatory agencies, eliminate exports taxes, prohibit price restrictions, and decentralize wage negotiations. The "execution of government is not a task for the timid," Cavallo would later say.

In a dramatically short time, the Menem government's neo-Peronism seemed to have evolved into anti-Peronism, but ever mindful of the president's political base, Cavallo would spin the story another way: "Peronism has always been a realist movement, and what we are doing is changing with the times." Some party stalwarts agreed. Estela Maris Armentano, secretary of a local branch of the Justicialista Party in a shantytown near Buenos Aires, saw Justicialista populism in the president's liberalization. "Juan and Evita Perón always said the people should come first," she said, "and that's what Menem is doing."

The end of hyperinflation came as a first for many Argentines accustomed only to a currency whose value plummeted by the week, day, or even hour. Stores began advertising prices in print for the first time in years, and customers insisted on receiving their change, too worthless to bother with under the old economic regime. Suddenly automobiles and appliances could be purchased on installment plans, and homes could be bought by obtaining mortgages. Workers no longer demanded continuous readjustment of their wages. Coin-operated telephones and vending machines, for years known only to Argentines who had traveled abroad, now appeared on the streets of Buenos Aires. Even the government that had forced the change wasn't quite ready for it: Although the currency had stabilized, it was still being printed on the same poor-quality paper that had been used when bills became worthless almost overnight. Newly durable in value, the paper currency began to disintegrate with its sustained circulation.

By the end of 1991, the country's stock exchange had doubled in value, and a year later it would double again. Wall Street and the World Bank took note. The managing director of the International Monetary Fund, Michel Camdessus, met with Domingo Cavallo on January 28, 1992, declaring his results "impressive" and urging "early and full support of the Argentine program by the international banking community." In most countries the average person can't name their finance minister, let alone evaluate the incumbent's performance, but a 1992 poll found that 57% of the Argentine public approved of Cavallo, twelve points more than their approval of Menem. *Euromoney* elected him "Finance Minister of the Year," and *Latin Finance* magazine went further, declaring him "Man of the Year." When Domingo Cavallo finally resigned his post in 1996, the *New York Times* editorialized, "Few people get the chance to play so constructive a role in their country's history as Domingo Cavallo."

Cavallo had done what any number of his predecessors had failed to do: He gave the Argentine economy a restorative shot in the arm, and his superior a new lease on political life. Cavallo's strategic insight into what would work and realistic sense of how to work it were decisive for this act of upward leadership. So, too, was his capacity to put all the pieces quickly together to spark his big bang for a new economic universe.

Domingo Cavallo's reputation as miracle worker outlasted his service with President Menem and transcended his service for a Peronist regime. When Menem's successor, President Fernando de la Rúa of the Radical Party, struggled in 2001 with an economy on the verge of falling off a cliff again, he brought Cavallo into his government on March 20 as the economy minister. Once again, the presidential charge was to fix the economy—now not to tame hyperinflation but to crack a deep recession—and de la Rúa left it up to Cavallo to devise a solution. True to form, Cavallo immediately insisted on reshuffling the president's cabinet to ensure support for his emergency measures, and the measures he proposed—tax cuts and deregulation—were precisely the opposite of what de la Rúa had been pursuing.

Lesson in Leading Up

A mandate from your superior to reform an organization is an historic opportunity that calls for far-reaching advice and forceful implementation. The more uncertain those over you are about how to achieve the goal they desire, the more clear minded and determined you will need to be in formulating and executing your strategy.

DEFINING A FUTURE FOR YOUR BOSS

Charlene Barshefsky worked behind the scenes for her president, and she helped deliver what he needed even though he wasn't precisely clear on what he sought. In reviewing Clinton's performance just days before he left the White House, the *Christian Science Monitor* wrote that the WTO deal for China "became a hallmark of Clinton's legacy as a free trader. More-open trade and an embrace of globalization were at the core of both the economic and foreign policy of the nation's first baby-boom president." Domingo Cavallo had done the very same for his president. The hallmark of Menem's legacy was the country's lasting embrace of market principles, a stable currency, and a growth rate during the 1990s twice the average rate of Latin America's twenty countries.

Barshefsky ensured that her boss could stand on a far-reaching trade agreement, and Cavallo guaranteed that his boss could rest on a transformed economy. Both had received general mandates from their superiors, but both had to fill in virtually all of the blanks. It was left to them to define the specifics, and in doing so Barshefsky and

Cavallo furnished their presidents with what they needed, even though what they desired had been only scantly defined in advance. In appreciating what was required, what was achievable, and what it would take, Barshefsky and Cavallo acted on behalf of their nations in ways that went far beyond the specific instructions or thinking of their presidents.

Only rarely are individuals afforded the kinds of historic opportunities presented to Barshefsky and Cavallo. For most of us, the opportunities are far less momentous. Yet our obligation for leading up is no less imperative. Creating the best depends on countless acts large and small, regardless of the scale or global resonance of the challenge we are called to face. If your superiors have been doing what they should be doing—clearly expressing their general intent but delegating its elaboration and execution to you—these are your moments to shine. You may have to clarify ambiguities and seek further guidance, but knowing the intent and knowing yourself should be sufficient foundation for you to forge a path mostly of your own making. Drawing on the experience of Charlene Barshefsky and Domingo Cavallo, six steps will help define that path:

• *Commit to the program:* Whatever your boss's starting precepts or political bearings, you need to drive toward the end goal and bring your superiors along with you by the sheer force of your commitment.

• *Understand the program:* What are the broad goals of the organization? How will your specific program advance them? And what actions are required to achieve them?

• *Elaborate the program:* Remember, it's you, not your superior, who needs to make certain that the program reflects the major concerns, if not the claims, of all the groups and organizations with a stake in its outcome.

• *Press the program:* Even though your boss may not appreciate the personal costs you are bearing, it's up to you to pursue the program and press throughout the organization for what you know to be right.

• *Support the program:* Whether you get to name and control the management team charged with shaping the program or are just a member of it, building a network of support within the organization is vital to its realization.

• *Sell the program:* Finally, you'll need ardent backers who can make a compelling case across the entire spectrum of affected parties for why the program is in the institution's transcendent interest, even when it is not in some groups' specific self-interest. Active opponents always arise, and a weak sell can rarely prevail over them.

Above all, an opportunity to apply such measures will most likely come because you have already developed your own understanding of the overarching problems facing your company or country—and have been cogitating about innovative solutions for them. The chance to make a difference—to "Go4It"—is more likely if you've already studied what will make the difference. And for this there is no better preparation than building your own trenchant conceptions of what should be done, without waiting for instructions to do so.

CHAPTER 8

PERSUADING THE ULTIMATE AUTHORITY

PROPHETS ABRAHAM, MOSES, AND SAMUEL INTERCEDE WITH GOD HIMSELF

FOR MANY PEOPLE throughout the world, no greater authority exists than God. Whatever the form in which the divinity is cast, God's word is *the* word, an offering beyond dispute. Accepting and embracing God's authority is the essence of the Christian and Jewish traditions.

If ever there were a case for *not* leading up, it is surely here. According to the Bible, it was God himself who created humankind—along with its capacity to reason and argue. If God was able to make perfect decisions on his own, why, then, should he even appear to be consulting with his own creation? What can mere mortals say to the deity? How could they possibly pose a challenge? What situation would drive them to argue with God himself? Yet the Bible's prophets have repeatedly felt compelled to do precisely that. A literal interpretation of the Bible's accounts of the prophets, which are among the world's best-studied teachings, provides our concluding lessons on leading up.

The prophets were chosen by God to speak for him and to guide others according to the divine plan. They conveyed God's intentions so that others might know and obey his will. But the prophets did more than just deliver instructions. The Hebrew Bible—or what many know as the Old Testament—offers story upon story of prophets addressing God directly, counseling him on how best to achieve his plan. They argued, pleaded, and interceded with him, often asking to reconsider his divine decree. The prophets reminded him of his merciful self. When it seemed that the virtuous were about to suffer along with the iniquitous, they pressed him to act in a more just manner. When the punishment exceeded the crime, they argued for clemency.

The upward coaching here is more focused than what we have earlier seen in more prosaic settings. In previous chapters, leading from below often entailed helping higher-ups become clearer about their purpose. Here, the prophets are not questioning God's ultimate plan. Rather, they speak from the perspective of those who must live under his decree—and they only ask God to modify or adapt his heavenly plan so that it will be more triumphant down on earth. For the prophet, though, the act of leading up required greater courage, since he was defying not just a team leader or a chief executive or a company director. The prophet was challenging the ultimate authority for not only himself but also the entire universe.

Three episodes in the Hebrew Bible serve to illustrate what it means to help those above better realize what they are seeking to achieve. The first comes from the book of Genesis, the second from Exodus, and the last from Samuel. As these ancient accounts imply, executive prophets can be just as important as executive chiefs in achieving a company's or a nation's true potential—especially when the best path ahead is not evident to those at the top. In witnessing how three prophets found the strength to challenge the most unassailable power of all, we are called to consider the less daunting task of assisting mere mortals, even when they may seem all-powerful.

The accounts in this chapter offer insights into hard choices: whether to obey commands from the top when we realized they are flawed, or to push for a better solution, even if that means convincing those at the very top. Those choices are weightiest when, as with the prophets, we have the chance to influence not just many subordinates but even generations to come. At times, as managers with simultaneous responsibilities to both those who command us and those we lead, we may sometimes feel powerless to intervene in a disagreeable situation. Yet the biblical prophets remind us that interceding with the highest authority may be the best course—even if it is the toughest. Being truly responsible to those below us sometimes means confronting those who lead us. When we're in between, leading down means we have little choice but to lead up as well.

ABRAHAM RESCUES THE RIGHTEOUS BY ASKING GOD TO BE MERCIFUL

In the heat of a Mediterranean afternoon, Abraham sat at the entrance of his tent. He dwelled with his family, servants, and a collection of livestock beside the great oaks north of Hebron, a city that still stands today near Bethlehem, now divided between Israeli and Palestinian authority. Years earlier he had left Haran, the town of his father in Aramea—now a region in northern Syria and northwestern Iraq—when God had commanded him, according to a passage in Genesis, "Go from your country and your kindred and your father's house to a land that I will show you. I will make of you a great nation." God entered into a covenant with Abraham, promising to make his descendants as numerous as the stars; in return, Abraham was to uproot his family in a pledge of obedience to the divine will.

Following his transit to the land of the Canaanites—modern Israel—as God had instructed, Abraham eagerly anticipated the creation of a great nation. Yet nearly a quarter of a century later, he still had no heir, save a child mothered by his wife's Egyptian handmaid. God had promised Abraham that he would be the forefather of a new people, yet he remained heirless and his kin were far behind him in Haran. How could God's promise come to pass?

This question of the promised clan plagued Abraham as he gazed quietly on a drowsy afternoon. Lost in thought, Abraham was surprised to find three men suddenly standing before him. Ancient custom dictated generous hospitality, and Abraham dutifully bowed to the guests and implored them to stay and rest under the trees as he arranged a meal. When the guests obliged, Abraham selected a tender calf for slaughter, and his wife, Sarah, prepared to serve cakes and curds. While the three guests consumed their fine repast in the shade of the trees, Abraham stood close by, wondering who his visitors were and why they had come to see him.

The guests soon came to the point. They announced to Abraham that Sarah, barren until now, would soon give birth to a son. Overhearing the conversation from inside the tent, Sarah laughed uproariously at the idea of her pregnancy: Abraham was nearly 100 years old and she was well past menopause. But the visitors sternly responded, "Is anything too wonderful for the Lord?" They offered their words as the voice of God, and they delivered his message that Abraham's lifelong yearnings for a new generation were not to be in vain.

Having delivered their startling news, the three guests took leave, and Abraham, ever the attentive host, escorted them down the road. As they walked together, the four men gazed southwest toward the nearby towns of Sodom and Gomorrah, independent kingdoms notorious for their crime and corruption. God had already planned a terrible fate for the two cities because of their wicked ways, but he had not yet informed Abraham, his faithful servant who would surely want to know what God intended for his neighbors.

According to the Bible, God now asked himself a difficult question: "Should I hide from Abraham what I am about to do, seeing that Abraham shall become a great and mighty nation?" The covenant between God and Abraham, a sacred agreement forged between the Creator of the universe and a single human being, was meant to last for all time. For it to survive, however, the two parties would have to communicate openly with each other and thereby build a mutual understanding. At least this is what we infer from God's response to his own question. Should he hide his plan to destroy Sodom and Gomorrah from Abraham? "No," he declared to himself, "for I have chosen him, that he may charge his children and his household after him to keep the way of the Lord and by doing righteousness and justice." For Abraham to be a successful prophet, God realized that he would have to keep Abraham abreast of the divine plan.

In this case, God chose to reveal his plan to Abraham gradually, as he stood on the road with the angel-emissaries. First, the three guests shared a rumor that Abraham presumably had heard already: Everyone was complaining, they said, about the outrageous sins of Sodom and Gomorrah. The envoys said they intended to see for themselves if the charges were true, and they abruptly broke off from Abraham and turned down the road to Sodom.

Abraham was left to reflect on these cryptic events. He wondered: Were these surprise visitors angels of God or perhaps even God himself? Either way, their statements about Sodom and Gomorrah seemed strange. If God knew of an outcry against the town, in his omniscience he would surely know of the inhabitants' guilt or innocence without having to "investigate" for himself. Yet

Abraham was close to God. He felt sure of God's presence among the visitors. This inner knowledge helped him finally guess God's ultimate intention: to destroy the two cities. This prospect troubled him deeply.

Abraham's blameless nephew Lot and his family had recently moved to the city of Sodom. If God destroyed the city, what would become of his own family members? Abraham knew that if God obliterated the community, innocent people would perish along with the guilty. He wondered, How could God inflict such an injustice on innocent people? And if God could act so unjustly here, might he also break his promise that Abraham would soon have a son to finally start his new nation? The deity that Abraham had pledged to follow was a purveyor of justice, yet this decision seemed both capricious and unduly vengeful. With these troubling questions in mind, Abraham felt he had but one option: to address these questions to God himself. He pulled himself together to challenge the very force on whom his life depended.

"Will you indeed sweep away the righteous with the wicked?" Abraham asked his superior. "Suppose there are fifty righteous within the city; will you then sweep away the place? Far be it from you to do such a thing, to slay the righteous with the wicked! Shall not the Judge of all the earth do what is just?"

With the words barely out of his mouth, Abraham feared that God might strike him down on the spot. Instead, miraculously, God conceded the argument: "If I find at Sodom fifty righteous in the city, I will forgive the whole place for their sake." Abraham considered responding again, but the awesome task of arguing directly with God made him reticent. How could he challenge the Lord—the Lord who had created him, the Lord who had chosen him for his special path of righteousness? And yet if he didn't, how could he find peace, for Abraham remained acutely distressed by God's great plan? "Let me take it upon myself to speak to the Lord," he humbly told himself, "I who am but dust and ashes."

"Suppose five of the fifty are lacking righteousness," Abraham continued. Once again, remarkably, God accepted Abraham's challenge: "I will not destroy it if I find forty-five." But since Lot's family was no more than a handful, Abraham persisted. Would God destroy Sodom if he found only forty righteous souls? No, God agreed, he would not. And if only thirty people? "I will not do it if I find thirty there," God replied. What about twenty? Yes, he would still spare the city.

Always awed by the Lord's omnipotence, Abraham feared that God was nearing the end of his patience, but he forced himself to speak his own mind yet again: "Oh do not let the Lord be angry if I speak just once more. Suppose ten are found there." God, in his mercy, conceded the point yet again, saying, "For the sake of ten, I will not destroy it." Finally satisfied that Lot's family would be spared, Abraham returned to his tent, the first time a mortal had dared contend with this mighty master of monotheism.

In the end, of course, God chose to destroy Sodom and Gomorrah, raining down sulfur and fire from the heavens. But God had appreciated the main message in Abraham's pleas, and he dis-

Abraham's Parting from the Family of Lot, *Jan Victors*

patched angels to Lot's house, warning him to flee with his family before the destruction began. Abraham had succeeded in convincing God to ensure that the righteous would not be destroyed for the sins of the wicked.

While the events of this 3,000-year-old story, recorded in the Bible's first book, are very familiar to many, its implications are less obvious but startling: A mere human could argue with God—and win. How could this God, by tradition omniscient and all-powerful, accept counterarguments from one of his own creatures? According to the Bible, it was God himself who created humankind, and as Master of the Universe, God would know in advance every word coming out of Abraham's mouth. And if God makes perfect decisions on his own, why, then, should God appear to be consulting with his own creations, and even more remarkably, taking their advice?

This question confronts readers in not only the first chapter of the Bible, but also throughout the Old Testament. God's chosen ones, his prophets, repeatedly interceded with him, asking him to see things from the human point of view. While God's decrees are always just on the cosmic level, they might sometimes appear unjust on the human level. If God wanted his people to understand him as a merciful and trustworthy God, then he might have to modify his plans. Thus the prophets provide God with a crucial "reality check." And amazingly, God himself seems to have designed this system of checks and balances.

Lesson in Leading Up

Even when you report to the ultimate authority, it is your solemn duty—and in this case a sacred one—to give your best counsel, render your best judgment, and persist in the expression of both, whether such upward leadership is specifically sought or not.

Moses Saves the Israelites
by Reasoning with God

As God had promised, Abraham and Sarah did produce many descendants, but in time, famine forced their great nation to give up its homestead. Under the guidance of Abraham's great-grandson Joseph, they migrated south to Egypt, where Joseph became a state official. Escaping one calamity, though, only led to another. While Abraham's people initially found favor with the existing pharaoh, a subsequent pharaoh turned despotic and forced the people of Abraham's new nation into slavery.

One of Abraham's descendants—Moses—was born during this terrible time for the Israelites in Egypt. Fearing a threat to the throne, the pharaoh ordered the killing of all Hebrew children. But Moses was miraculously spared when God commanded his mother to take an enormous risk with the life of her son. Under divine direction she set Moses afloat in a basket on the Nile River. There, floating among the bulrushes, he was discovered and rescued by no less than the pharaoh's own daughter. She took the abandoned infant and raised the child as her own in the royal household. Thus Moses grew up as a prince in the house of the very tyrannical authority, Pharaoh, who had commanded all the Hebrew sons to die.

Though apparently unaware of his Hebrew heritage, Moses was moved by the sad plight of the Israelites. He protested the cruel treatment of the Hebrews at the hands of Egyptian slave masters. One day he saw an overseer beating a slave, and he flew into a rage, killing the overseer with his own blows. Terrified by the thought of the pharaoh's certain wrath, Moses fled north into the Sinai desert, where he started a new life and found a wife among the nomads.

While tending his father-in-law's sheep in the Sinai, Moses saw a startling sight: A nearby bush blazed with fire without being consumed by it. "Moses! Moses!" came God's voice from the burning bush. "Here I am," replied Moses without hesitation, demonstrating the kind of complete and intuitive obedience that all great prophets possess. The voice continued: I am "the God of your father, the God of Abraham." Having established his identity, God revealed why he had appeared before Moses now: "I have observed the misery of my people who are in Egypt. I know their sufferings and I have come down to deliver them from the Egyptians, to bring them up to a good land, a land flowing with milk and honey."

God would mastermind the Exodus from Egypt, but Moses was to be his instrument for achieving it. "I will send you to Pharaoh," God instructed Moses, "to bring my people out of Egypt." Overwhelmed by his divine charge, Moses humbly protested: How could he persuade and organize the people? For one thing, he suffered from a speech impediment. And what if the Israelites refused to believe he was God's emissary? After all, he had grown up in Pharaoh's house. But God refused to take no for an answer. He told Moses that his brother Aaron would help him with public speaking, and he invested Moses with an ability to perform miracles to assure his credibility. So armed, Moses returned to Egypt to undertake his life's calling.

The events that follow are well-known: Moses implored Pharaoh to "let my people go," but God had mysteriously hardened Pharaoh's

Moses, *Carlo Dolci*

heart, and he refused. Despite Moses' repeated entreaties, Pharaoh remained unmoved, but with each rejection God unleashed a plague on Egypt: livestock perished, the Nile turned to blood, houses swarmed with frogs, boils covered the people, flies filled the air, hail crushed the harvest, locusts ate the trees, darkness covered the land, and, finally, every firstborn child and animal died. Pharaoh's grief at losing his own firstborn son finally moved him to release the Israelites, but the liberated slaves had barely left Egypt when Pharaoh changed his mind and set out with his army in hot pursuit, overtaking and trapping the Israelites near the edge of a great lake (taken by some to be the Red Sea). Using Moses' hand, God divided the waters to create an escape path across the lake bed. The Egyptian ranks rushed after the fleeing party, but as they marched between the parted waters, God closed the lake over them, and all the Egyptians were drowned.

The Israelites were elated by their miraculous escape, thankful to God for his deliverance, and grateful to Moses for their freedom. But as so often characterizes such moments of national liberation, the most difficult trials were yet to come. The Israelites found themselves wandering in a great desert east of Egypt with nothing to eat and nowhere to go, led by a man who claimed to be hearing the voice of God. Soon the people complained bitterly to Moses: "Was it because there were no graves in Egypt that you have taken us away to die in the wilderness?" Frustrated by his followers and their lack of faith, Moses cried out to the Lord, "What shall I do with this people? They are almost ready to stone me." God answered with a resupply of essentials: freshwater, quails, and manna, a desert bread that appeared like dew in the morning.

Following three more months of nomadic roving, the Israelites arrived at the foot of a mountain in the Sinai wasteland. To Moses God promised that here he would end his flock's persistent doubts once and for all: "I am going to come to you in a dense cloud," said God to Moses, "in order that the people may hear when I speak with you and trust you ever after." Moses told his people to purify themselves and prepare to meet their God, and three days later thunder and lightning heralded God's arrival on the Sinai mountain. Smoke enveloped the peak and it shook violently, terrifying all who gazed upon it. God called Moses to climb the mountain, and as the only Israelite able to face the fearsome peak, Moses ascended to hear the words of the Lord. "I am the Lord your God, who brought you out of the land of Egypt, out of the house of slavery; you shall have no other gods before me," God thundered. "You shall not make for yourself an idol; you shall not bow down to them." It was the first of ten commandments that God would hand down that day.

The Israelites trembled in awe and pledged their obedience when Moses returned from the mountaintop to inform them of this startling revelation of God's great power and majesty. Yet no sooner had he started back up Sinai—to receive the Ten Commandments now engraved by God on stone—than his people grew restless once again, and their restlessness quickly turned to rebellion.

"Come, make gods for us, who shall go before you," they implored Moses' brother Aaron, whom Moses had left in charge of the community in his absence. "As for Moses, the man who brought us up out of the land of Egypt, we do not know what has become of him." Aaron succumbed to the people's impatience and asked them to fetch all their silver and gold jewelry, much of it plundered in Egypt before leaving. Melting the precious metal, Aaron cast an image of a calf and presented it to the Israelites: "Here are your gods, O Israel, who brought you up out of the land of Egypt!" He declared a festival for the next day.

Up on the summit, God warned Moses of what was developing below in his absence: "Go down at once! Your people, whom you brought up out of the land of Egypt, have acted perversely, they have been quick to turn aside from the way that I commanded them." Allowing Moses no chance to respond, God continued: "I have seen this people, how stubborn they are. Now let me alone, so that my wrath may burn hot against them and I may consume them; and of you I will make a great nation."

Moses was standing atop a mountain at what should have been a moment of glory. He had received God's commandments engraved indelibly in stone, a sign of how enduring the new covenant was to be between the Lord and his chosen people. If only the Israelites would follow the simple commands—to worship only him, to lead pure lives, and to treat one another with love and justice—then the Lord would fulfill his promise and lead them into the land of milk and honey.

But just days after receiving the commandments, the people had broken the first and foremost injunction—that they should worship only one god and make no idols for themselves. No doubt Moses was deeply disappointed with his followers, a contentious and ungrateful lot, and he was surely downcast about his own ability to lead them to the promised land. And now God was telling Moses about the deplorable behavior of "*Your* people, whom *you* brought out of the land of Egypt." God's use of pronouns seemed to lay all the responsibility at Moses' feet, just as when one exasperated parent says to the other: "Look what *your* son has done." Moreover, God was threatening to destroy the Israelites, to wipe the slate the clean, and start a new nation all over again. It was no idle threat: God had wiped out early generations, such as that destroyed by the great flood in Noah's time.

This was a prophetic moment. The people and their corruption had so angered God that he was intent on destroying them. Standing between them was one solitary figure. Moses was intimately acquainted with the shortcomings of the Israelites, yet he could not bear to see his lord destroy them. Caught in this middle position, Moses, like Abraham before him, girded up his strength to address the mighty Creator and plead for mercy.

Moses' first tactic was to remind God who was truly responsible for these Israelites. He turned God's pronouns back in the other direction: "O Lord, why does your wrath burn hot against your people, whom you brought out of the land of Egypt with great power and a mighty hand?" The Exodus was, after all, God's idea and therefore primarily God's responsibility, not Moses'.

Moses then used what one scholar has called the most social of rhetorical arguments. He asked God, in effect, "What would the neighbors say?" if he destroyed his own people. Moses suggested that if God took his proposed course, the Egyptians might well think, " 'It was with evil intent that he brought them out to kill them in the mountains, and to consume them from the face of the earth.' " In other words, would it not look dreadful for the God of Israel if he slaughtered his own people? Moses could be sure of hitting a raw nerve here: in a world of polytheism, the God of Israel was trying to establish himself as the preeminent God. God had earlier told Moses that he would swallow up the Egyptians in the parted lake "so I will gain glory for myself over Pharaoh and his army." If God destroyed the Israelites, his own glory in the wider world would be diminished: Who would want to serve and honor such a wrathful God?

Having run through these indirect appeals, Moses came to the heart of the matter. "Turn from your fierce wrath," he begged. "Change your mind, and do not bring disaster on your people." Finally, Moses played his trump card: He reminded God of the covenant God had made with Israel's righteous forefathers. "Remember Abraham, Isaac, and Israel, your servants, how you swore to them by your own self, saying to them, 'I will multiply your descendants like the stars of heaven, and all this land that I have promised I will give to your descendants, and they shall inherit it forever.' " God had made a promise to the Israelites, and if he wanted the Israelites to obey him, then God would have to keep up his end of the covenant and allow them to prosper. It might seem easy to wipe the slate clean and get a fresh start, just as one might imagine divorcing a spouse to find a better one. The superior road, albeit a harder way, Moses reminded God, would be to stick with his chosen people in spite of their disobedience. Moses kept the "marriage" of God and Israel from falling apart.

As Abraham had done, Moses reminded God of his own promises and pleaded for their more effective application. Through this process, Moses never forgot that he himself was nothing but "dust and ashes" in the face of his Creator and that God's embodiment of justice was vastly superior to any human conception of it. Yet however dwarfed he may have been, Moses didn't shrink from articulating his own sense of justice. If God wanted his name glorified among all nations, if he sought the affection and obedience of his own nation, he would have to keep his covenants. The goals remained unquestioned. The means of achieving them on earth, however, were open to argument.

Ultimately, Moses was successful. As we read in Exodus, "The Lord changed his mind about the disaster that he planned to bring on his people." The true "winners" were not just Moses, but also the Israelites, whose lives were spared, and God, who sought an enduring relationship with his people on earth.

Lesson in Leading Up

However wrathful your superior, however merciless the message, the well-being of those in your hands must remain preeminent. Pushing up against a vengeful policy coming down from above sometimes requires all the upward leadership you can marshal, but when the purpose is transcendent, the value of your intercession extends well beyond you.

SAMUEL EXECUTES GOD'S SOMETIMES MISTAKEN INSTRUCTIONS IN ANOINTING A KING

Prophecy can be likened to the situation of directing traffic at a busy intersection. The prophet serves as traffic cop, now letting some people's cars pass, then allowing God's trucks to thunder by, all the while never forgetting who assigned him the job in the first place. Working amid high-speed traffic lanes moving in opposite directions requires exceptional fortitude and skill: one must know exactly when to allow one group to have its way, and when to hold another at bay. Maintaining this middle ground is not easy, and the story of the prophet named Samuel demonstrates this principle well.

Samuel was commissioned by God to guide the people of Israel through a difficult transition period; under his prophethood, they would move from a loose band of tribes to a nation united under God's chosen monarch, King David. Charged with such a weighty and complex task, Samuel often found himself caught between the demanding realities of the divine command and the human weaknesses of the people who were meant to carry it out. As a result, the prophet often found himself painfully alone. Yet his fidelity in these moments of crisis—fidelity not only to God's decree but also to his own role as prophet—sustained him and led to the success of God's new plan for the temporal leadership of his chosen people. Leadership in the Samuel mode requires a willingness to question orders and a simultaneous willingness to obey them. The challenge his story presents is: How do you know when to resist and when to submit?

After the Israelites finally reached and settled the promised land under the guidance of Moses' assistant, Joshua, the twelve tribes formed a loose confederation, each governed by a "judge" whom God had elevated to resolve specific problems as they arose. When the tribes asked one such judge, Gideon—who had waged a successful military campaign against one of Israel's enemies—to become king over them all, he refused: "I will not rule over you; the Lord will rule over you." Without a willing and able contender, Israel was to remain a direct theocracy, God himself the adjudicator. But this state of affairs would not last long.

During this time of political restlessness, a boy named Samuel was born miraculously to a previously barren woman named Hannah. As a way of thanking her Lord, Hannah consecrated her son to priestly service at Shiloh, the site of Israel's first permanent temple in the promised land. There Samuel served under a priest named Eli, whose sons—designated to inherit the office of the priesthood—were corrupt, greedily appropriating the best part of the food sacrifices at the temple and consorting with the female attendants.

One night when Samuel was asleep in the temple, he heard a voice calling him: "Samuel! Samuel!" Assuming that it was the voice of Eli calling him, Samuel ran to the priest and presented himself, saying, "Here I am." But Eli said, "I did not call you; lie down again." Samuel went back to bed, but the voice returned: "Samuel!" Once again the boy went to the priest. Again the priest sent him back to bed, saying he had not called him. Samuel, a mere boy of twelve according to Hebrew tradition, was too young to recognize that this was the voice of the Lord calling. But when the call came a third time, and Samuel went into Eli a third time, the older priest perceived the presence of God. He commanded Samuel: "Go, lie down; and if he calls you, you shall say, 'Speak, LORD, for thy servant hears' "

Samuel followed these instructions. But when he said "Speak Lord," the Lord responded by delivering the most dreadful prophecy that the young boy could imagine. God told him: "I am about to do something that will make the ears of anyone who hears it tingle." The house of Eli would be destroyed: His sons would die violent deaths, and his lineage would be banished forever from the priesthood, on account of their blasphemy and corruption. Worse, none could intercede on their behalf: "The iniquity of Eli's house shall not be expiated by sacrifice or offering forever." God's decree was final, and Samuel could do nothing to change it.

The boy lay trembling through the night, imagining with horror how God would execute his command. What would become of his beloved teacher? Samuel had lived with Eli since he was a small child, growing up under his care and learning from him the ways of the priesthood. And although Eli's sons were wicked, Samuel knew that the elderly Eli was himself a righteous man. How could he tell him this frightening news? Indeed, what if Eli didn't believe him? Or believed him and then vented his anguish on Samuel himself?

Yet Samuel was too young to know anything but obedience toward God's word. He did not plead for God to have mercy on Eli's family, as older prophets like Abraham and Moses might have done. This decree from God was Samuel's first lesson in prophecy, and the message was clear: Samuel would first have to find the courage to deliver God's terrifying message before he earned the right to question that message.

When dawn arrived, an anguished Samuel rose from his sleepless bed, opening the doors of the temple as he did every morning. Eli called to him: "Samuel, my son." The boy responded with the simple words of obedience that mark all the great prophets: "Here I am," he said to Eli. "What was it that he told you? Do not hide it from me," Eli commanded. Samuel, overcoming his great fear, told Eli everything the Lord had told him.

Miraculously, Eli recognized the decree of God in Samuel's words and was not angry with him. He said only: "It is the Lord; let him do what seems good to him." Shortly after Samuel's prophecy,

Samuel before Eli

the Israelites went into battle against a neighboring group, the Philistines. When the battle was going badly for the Philistines, the Israelite commanders called for the sacred ark of the covenant, which was housed at Eli's temple in Shiloh. In times past, the presence of the ark—a potent representation of God's favor toward the Israelites—had assured victory, and though Eli's two sons accompanied the ark to the battle, the Philistines struck against the Israelites, felling 30,000 troops, slaying Eli's sons, and capturing the sacred ark. When Eli learned this awful news, he fell over backward, breaking his neck and dying. Samuel's prophecy had come true.

Samuel had successfully overcome his own distress to faithfully deliver God's message. This difficult test had initiated him, and afterward Israelites throughout the land recognized him as a prophet. The trial also foreshadowed even greater tests that lay in Samuel's future.

After the destruction of Eli's house, Samuel came to serve all Israel as judge, rotating among the twelve tribes to govern them all. But Samuel's sons, who were to have inherited their father's office, became as corrupted as Eli's, and Samuel now experienced the same family disgrace that had befallen Eli.

The people of Israel complained that they did not want Samuel's sons to inherit his position as judge. They demanded of him: "You are old, and your sons do not walk in your ways; now appoint a king to lead us, such as other nations have." The reference to other nations came as a stinging rebuke to Samuel, since God and the prophets were constantly exhorting the Israelite people to walk a different path. The surrounding nations worshiped false gods and idols; borrowing their political structures or even intermarrying with them could infect the society with the virus of polytheism.

Acutely distressed, Samuel prayed to God for assistance. God responded, taking much of the rebuke on himself. "They have not rejected you," he consoled Samuel, "but they have rejected me from being king over them." That is, if the people were demanding that

Samuel install a mortal king over the Israelites, then the people were implicitly rejecting the kingship of God. Samuel was not to blame for the Israelites' lack of faith. Yet as God's emissary on earth, he was the one who bore the brunt of the people's shameful demands.

At the heart of the matter was a question of leadership. In the memory of God, Israel's finest moments were in the desert, when the tribes depended completely on God for their survival: He was their supreme monarch. But now the twelve tribes had arrived in the promised land and were spreading out, settling, expanding. Could they continue to live as they had in the desert, without a formal structure of leadership, without a single human leader who could unite them? This question had no easy answer. To the ears of God, the calls for a human king sounded like blasphemy, little more than an attempt to imitate the polytheistic tribes that surrounded Israel. Yet developments in the promised land seemed to move inexorably in the direction of a new model of leadership.

God himself appeared conflicted about these developments. He told Samuel that he would grant the Israelites' request for a sovereign—but they would pay a terrible price for making such a request in the first place. God instructed Samuel to tell the people that one day their own king would force their sons to serve in the king's army, and would make their daughters into royal servants. Samuel prophesied: "He will take the best of your fields and vineyards and olive groves and give them to his attendants. . . . He will take a tenth of your flocks, and you yourselves will become his slaves. When that day comes, you will cry out for relief from the king you have chosen, and the Lord will not answer you that day." In other words, the people would get exactly what they were asking for: a centralized government that would inevitably extract labor and resources for its own glory.

Yet even as God condemned the people in their request for a king, he set about looking for a righteous man to lead the kingdom. God selected the most handsome young man in all of Israel, a shepherd named Saul who "stood head and shoulders above everyone else." Saul had come to Shiloh in search of a lost donkey, and when he approached Samuel for assistance, God said to Samuel: "Here is the man of whom I spoke to you! He it is who shall rule over my people." Samuel first hinted to Saul that he would become king, and Saul protested that he came from Israel's smallest tribe and a little-known family. Such humility, a quality required of every divinely appointed leader in the nation of Israel, only confirmed to Samuel that Saul was meant for greatness. Samuel broke a vial of oil over Saul's head, anointing him as king and announcing God's intention for him to rule all of Israel. One of Saul's major tasks would be to fight back the encroaching Philistines.

In spite of this auspicious beginning, both God and Samuel soon found themselves bitterly disappointed with this first monarch of Israel. Not long after Saul became sovereign, he flagrantly disobeyed the directives of Samuel and thus the command of God. In one instance, Saul was preparing for battle against the Philistines. But before he could begin his campaign, he would have to offer a special sacrifice to God. Samuel instructed him not to make the sacrifice until Samuel himself arrived from another part of Israel, but when Samuel appeared late in coming, Saul offered his sacrifice. When Samuel finally did arrive, he rebuked Saul, warning that the Lord might revoke his kingship.

Whether through lack of discipline or deliberate disobedience, Saul seemed unable—despite Samuel's feedback—to follow the will of God. Samuel later sent Saul into battle against the Amalekites, an enemy tribe from the south, instructing him to slaughter every person and animal captured. Though Saul defeated the Amalekites, he spared the enemy king and took the best animals for himself.

Seeing that Saul more often followed his own whims than divine guidance, the Lord spoke to Samuel: "I regret that I made Saul king, for he has turned back from following me, and has not carried out my commands." Samuel was himself frustrated by Saul's conduct, yet he could not bear to watch the humiliation of his own protégé. Saul was Samuel's creation: He had lifted Saul out of obscurity, installed him as king, and guided him through his early reign. How would Saul take this news of his dethronement? Samuel had promised Saul greatness, and now he was delivering him disgrace. Would the other Israelites lose confidence in Samuel as a prophet? How could Samuel execute God's will if God himself seemed to change his mind and undercut the very orders that Samuel had struggle to implement? The Bible speaks plainly of Samuel's distress. "Samuel was angry. He cried out to the Lord all night." Samuel was caught agonizingly between God's own conflicted feelings and Saul's short-comings as a leader. Yet even in his anger and frustration, Samuel remained loyal to his ultimate authority.

When morning arrived, Saul again defended his decision to retain the Amalekites's livestock, explaining that he intended not to keep them for himself but rather to offer them as a holy sacrifice. Samuel doubted the explanation and reminded Saul that, in any case, "it is better to obey than to sacrifice." Saul asked forgiveness, but God's directive was clear: Saul had to go. So Samuel said to Saul: "You have rejected the word of the Lord, and the Lord has rejected you from being king over Israel." He then pronounced the devastating final judgment: "The Lord has torn the kingdom of Israel from you this very day, and has given it to a neighbor of yours, who is better than you." Deposed, Saul sank into resentful obscurity. He never again saw Samuel. In the aftermath of a later battle injury, he took his own life.

Though Saul's dethronement was decreed by God, Samuel found it difficult to reconcile himself to the forced firing of a figure he had installed. "Samuel mourned over Saul," says the Bible, "even though the Lord had regretted that he had ever made Saul king over Israel." A lesser person might have resigned his calling by now, yet Samuel still placed allegiance to his superior above his own anguish generated by the conflicting commands of his superior.

Samuel's trials were not yet over. The divinity had another wrenching task in store for him, and he urged Samuel to get beyond the pain of the past. "How long will you grieve over Saul?" God asked him. "I have rejected him from being king over Israel." God gave new instructions, telling Samuel to fill a horn with oil and anoint a new king from among the sons of Jesse the Bethlehemite. This decree came as still more bitter medicine: Not only had Samuel been forced to unseat his own selection, but now he would also have to anoint a new king not of his own choosing. But Samuel was ever the prophet, and he did what the Lord commanded, anointing Jesse's youngest son as king.

Samuel's upward leadership came at great personal expense. He had been given the prophetic job of executing God's will at a time when God himself seemed unsure of what was best for Israel. At the same time, Samuel had to cope with the weaknesses and failings of God's chosen people, Saul in particular. Serving on the front line, he personally faced all the disgrace when God's will seemed to fall short.

Though his reputation with his own people had been shattered by the mistaken actions his superior had forced upon him, Samuel never lost faith in his superior, nor did he ever consider quitting. Caught in the middle, he remained steadfast, knowing that God's vision for Israel was ultimately correct and coherent, even if it sometimes appeared chaotic and contradictory. Samuel knew that all affairs lay in the hands of the Almighty, and that when things got rough on the ground, he had no recourse but to ask God for a clearer directive.

Ultimately Samuel's compliant execution of God's will for a new king was one of the greatest prophetic acts in the history of Israel. The son of Jesse, of course, was none other than David, the boy who would head Israel's most glorious kingship. On behalf of his superior, Samuel had navigated a traumatic transition between judgeship and kingship, ushering in David's reign and Israel's golden age.

Lesson in Leading Up

Even ultimate authorities make many mistakes, and your obligation is to recognize them as such and to resist any impulse to resign when those below criticize you for failing policies forced from above. The upward leader's calling is to remain steadfast on behalf of superiors who are recognizably superior, faithfully understanding their intent and executing their mission.

RECRUITING THE RIGHT PROPHETS

Readers of the Old Testament usually imagine the prophets calling the Israelites to follow the path of God, rather than exhorting God to adjust that path. Yet these upward acts of intercession between God and the people were an integral part of the institution of prophecy. The prophets appreciated both sides of a conflict and reached their own judgment on whether to plead with the Israelites or with God himself. Abraham and Moses astutely argued up, and Samuel wisely carried out God's instructions. But they did so only after examining the context and making an independent determination. They appreciated the two-edged role of managing in the middle, of skillfully adjudicating between conflicting demands from above and below. When they did their job well, the prophets retained the respect of both their followers below and the towering figure above.

Drawing on the analysis of biblical scholar Yochanan Muffs, we see that in the Hebrew Bible a prophet was far more than one who simply obeyed the command of God—though this itself was no small feat. Rather, a successful prophet maintained a disciplined independence of mind *in the context of* absolute obedience. The ability to speak one's mind under command from above is crucial not only for the prophet, but by implication for the whole cosmos of God and his chosen people. "The prophet who is lacking in autonomy and bravery of spirit causes the destruction of the world," warns Muffs. But the right role requires great fortitude. "Who can take upon himself this double burden of prophecy?" he asks. "It is enough for one person to be the messenger of the divine court. Is it at all possible for the same man to be the messenger and at the same time to plead with the Lord to rescind the message?" The answer in the Bible is clear, concludes Muffs: "It is not only possible, but essential."

The Old Testament also addressed a question implicit in this principle. If leading up is as important as leading down, how does God know when he has the right person to serve as his prophet? It is much the same question that company executives and executive recruiters face every day. Do they have the right people who can not only help the top lead those below but also redirect the top when the firm and those below deserve better than the present leadership is providing? Four criteria for selecting the right candidate are suggested.

The first criterion was implied in the typical response of those called to prophesy. When God asked Moses to become his prophet, Moses protested his inadequacy for the post. That initial hesitancy was repeatedly expressed by others called to their biblical posts. First spurning the office became a kind of prerequisite for ultimately accepting it. This expressed reluctance constituted an immediate challenge to the ultimate authority, and God's dialogue with his prospective prophets included an opening test of whether the candidate was strong enough to question his superior's decisions. If he did not question them now, before accepting the mantle of prophecy, he was unlikely to do so later. In the same vein, if he was not honest about his own failings now, he was unlikely to be forthright about his own shortcomings or those of others, including God himself.

A second criterion becomes visible in the behavior of those chosen for prophecy. Prophets were uniformly depicted as deeply concerned for the welfare of the people whom they represented before the divinity. A prophet did not simply deliver God's commands and then step aside. If the command brought punishment or destruction to the prophet's own people, he pushed back against the decree. We learn that a good prophet's allegiance must run in both directions, staying true not only to his creator but also to the best interests of his people. A prophet was no longer a prophet if he separated himself from the people he led. The Old Testament prophets knew that their own fate hinged on the fate of their people.

This intimate link is evident in Moses' response on Mount Sinai after God had threatened to destroy those below for their idolatry. Moses vigorously defended his people against the threat, and the power of his commitment was made even more meaningful by the tests it had already survived. The Israelite people had often attacked Moses, and his unruly nation had made his ruling experience so terrible at one point that he had even asked God to allow him to die. (Needless to say, God rejected this attempted resignation.) Moreover, if Moses simply abandoned his now disgraced citizenry, he might find a more promising option in a totally fresh start: God had promised Moses that he would build a new nation through him. Despite the attacks and the alternatives, Moses never wavered in the defense of his people, just as Abraham had done in defending the innocent from destruction.

A third criterion is implied by the way that the prophets accepted complete responsibility for their people's shortcomings and blunders. Rather than standing above the fray, a prophet's fate was inextricably linked with that of his people. In saving his people, the prophet would also be saving himself, an intrinsic incentive to remember the concerns of those below when communing with those above.

Thus it was that Moses would die alongside his guilty Israelites. After they had committed still further sins in the desert, God declared that all of those wandering in the wilderness would die before entering the promised land. Only the next generation, free from the sins of its parents, would enjoy the fulfillment of God's promise. Despite his hard work and obedience to God, the prophet was forced to suffer the same punishment as his people. After a single longing glance from a hillside east of the Jordan River, Moses died before he could finally cross into the promised land.

A final recruitment criterion is evident in the relationship between God and his prophets. Though the prophets were close to their people, they were equally close to the divinity. They were God's right-hand men, handpicked to carry out his mission on earth. Each received unique blessings from God, they were given special powers to achieve their duties, and all were accorded a starring role in divine history—so long as they rose to the responsibility that came with proximity to power.

Abraham became the patriarch of not just a big family, but also the most blessed nation on earth; Moses acquired the ability to perform miracles; and Samuel anointed David to be king. But such great moments carried great duties. Abraham later endured one of God's most difficult tests of all when he was asked to sacrifice his own son, Isaac. Moses devoted his life to guiding a rebellious and ungrateful people through the wilderness. And Samuel had to dismiss the king he had personally enlisted.

To strengthen the prophets for such immense responsibilities, God required they accept a special nearness to him, and he did so not only with words but also through deeds. God divulged his divine plans to Abraham before their execution, and he revealed his name to Moses (the unvoweled YWHW, often spelled Yahweh and usually translated as "I am that I am"). On Mount Sinai, God even took visual form to engage Moses in direct dialogue. The prophets were invested with unique access, and for that they were required to shoulder responsibilities that lesser figures could not. The prophets alone had God's ear, and their unique status obligated them to represent all their people and to shoulder all of God's mission.

Lesson in Leading Up

The greater the gap between you and the superior you are seeking to lead, the more you need to be humble about your role, riveted on the welfare of those below, fully accepting of the responsibility you have accepted, and wholly cognizant of what is expected of you.

GOD ENCOURAGED HIS PROPHETS TO ARGUE WITH HIM

Although the God of the Hebrew Bible did not by nature feel impatience or suffer second thoughts, he often seems to be almost human in his exchanges with the prophets. With most mortals, God's voice thunders. With the prophets, though, he argues, even to the point of anger, but also listens, sometimes to the point of being persuaded. Rather than undermine his stature, such moments of biblical give-and-take solidify it—this is a deity who knows what it's like to suffer human frailties—at the same time that they help prophets make God's word more comprehensible to those on the ground.

By personifying what could otherwise not be made personal, the prophets were able to render God's message more persuasive, more memorable, more enduring. Once the followers understood the message, God would no longer need to tell them what to do. The prophets allowed God to lead more effectively through a method of communication not otherwise at his direct disposal.

So conceived, prophecy is the means through which God makes himself understood. He allows prophets to "argue" with him—and, more important, he often permits himself to be convinced by the urgings—in much the same way that parents allow their children to beat them in a running race. It is a way of making children feel capable, involved, almost *equal,* even though the parents' legs are obviously so much longer than their own. By involving the people intimately through his prophets, God drew them closer, thereby strengthening his covenant and improving the chances that his ultimate plans for humanity would one day be fulfilled.

Lesson in Leading Up

All institutions depend on a dynamic give-and-take among those at the top, the middle, and the bottom. The success of any hierarchy depends on communication and flexibility across the vertical divides.

EXECUTIVE PROPHECY

In serving as buffers, prophets convey intents downward and interests upward. They are not executive assistants, mechanically executing what the boss wants, nor are they grassroots advocates, simply voicing what the people want. Rather, they serve a thinking, translating, and mediating function, transforming what each wants into what all should achieve.

In holding that interstitial place, prophets make mistakes. Samuel will come to rue the day he anointed Saul as king of the Israelites, his sons prove a disgrace to his house, and his own people veer toward false idols. In the eyes of his Creator and himself, Samuel repeatedly came up short in executing his appointed mission.

Even when right, prophets are hardly assured of achievement, for their voices are not always recognized. When Abraham learns of God's plan for the destruction of Sodom and Gomorrah, he pleads for protection of the righteous who dwell within—and he prevails. Yet when Samuel learns of God's plan to dethrone Saul, he pleads for God to change his mind—and fails.

None of us is immune to the universal habit of forecasting future behavior from past experience, but the executive prophet resists the danger of adopting false expectations based on prior success or failure. Neither this triumph nor that disaster is taken to signify that future actions will always be triumphant or inevitably disastrous. Rather, executive prophets face each issue anew, judging each decree or plea on its own merits. They bring their experience to bear without being bound by it; they apply their intellect without being overconfident of it. They decide case by case whether an upward voice is now required or is still unwarranted.

To build upon but at the same time transcend their experience and intelligence, executive prophets draw on three simple principles: Understand the underlying mission, construct a creative means for attaining it, and stay the course. They must initially appreciate what the executive wants and what the people are capable of achieving. They then identify a common and transcendent ground, finding a fresh solution before others may even be cognizant of the problem. And finally, despite resistance and challenge, they courageously transform inventive insight into accepted reality.

Moses appreciated what God sought from the Israelites long before they recognized it themselves. At the same time, he understood that the Israelites were capable of rising to that mission even when their worship of false idols made God fear otherwise. And despite Moses' early reluctance to accept God's calling because of his limited communication ability, he becomes one of the great persuaders of all time, convincing a people to seek—at mortal risk to themselves—a more promising land and at the same time convincing their God that he should not abandon them when they had so egregiously strayed from the path set for them. Finally, Moses stayed steadfast when the hostilities around him would have undermined lesser mortals. For executing the calling of executive prophet, there can be no better example.

We might seem to have the option of sitting on the sidelines, but leading up itself is not an optional course. Through its agency, potential is released, unexpressed and sometimes inexpressible goals are achieved, and everyone—from those who wield the final power to those who seem to have no power at all—is served to the best of our human ability. While leading up is ultimately a matter of personal resolve, its consequences extend far beyond the borders of our personal lives.

CHAPTER 9

THE UPWARD LEADER'S CALLING

N ONE OF US is ever likely to face the extraordinary conditions confronted by Sandy Hill Pittman on Mount Everest, George McClellan on the peninsula, or Roméo Dallaire in Rwanda, or to suffer the calamitous events that befell Joseph Johnston, Beck Weathers, or Thomas Wyman. Few of us will reach the heights of public responsibility achieved by Charlene Barshefsky, Domingo Cavallo, or Peter Pace—or the pinnacles of private enterprise achieved by Robert Ayling, David Pottruck, or Eckhard Pfeiffer. Few, if any, will shape a nation's future as profoundly as did Robert E. Lee in 1863. All of us can only appreciate the accounts of what Abraham, Moses, and Samuel have given to others.

Yet we can all look to what they did—and in some cases did not do—to prepare ourselves for those times when we, too, are called to lead from below. Learning from successes and failures in the past is a potent recipe for securing triumphs and averting disasters in our own future.

Heroic moments and moments of great crisis make the best accounts, and the best accounts make the best teachers. But even when the scale of our endeavor is smaller, opportunities for leading up come to almost all of us. In the best organizations, leadership is companywide. As the great prophets of the Old Testament demonstrate, nobody's superiors, even God on high, are so superior that they can never benefit from guidance within the ranks.

But leading up is not a one-way street to the top. Upward leadership requires an ability to work in two directions at once, each with its hazards. Leading up isn't about rebellion or usurpation; it is about stepping into the breach when there is no one else to do it and about listening to such leadership when it emerges. Had the commander of the U.N. forces in Rwanda decisively—and convincingly—conveyed the signs of genocide, he might have acquired the means to stop it; had his superiors given more heed to his warnings of holocaust, it conceivably would not have come to pass. Had the mountaineers on Everest insisted that Scott Fischer not go up, he might have come down; had Fischer encouraged them to question him before he needed it, they might have been emboldened to do so when he did require it. We want—without the ironic twist—what movie mogul Samuel Goldwyn Jr. once said of his own operating style: "I don't want any yes-men around me," he declared. "I want them to tell me the truth, even if it costs them their jobs."

The fates of our superiors often depend on our actions, just as our own fates depend on the actions of those below us. While we must look for ways of leading up ourselves, we must also give our subordinates the means of leading up. Building that capacity in ourselves and others requires an appreciation for the measures that make the greatest difference.

Each of the sixteen people chronicled in this book was called to face a critical challenge upon which much depended. How they reacted is a measure not only of their own characters and of how well or poorly they were prepared to lead up by the people who were supposed to lead them, but also in many cases of the corporate cultures in which they functioned. A summary of the challenges and the practical implications of their individual responses appear on the following page.

Leaders	Institutions	Challenges	Implications
Joseph Johnston George McClellan Robert E. Lee	Confederate States of America United States of America Confederate States of America	Waging the Civil War	Keep your superiors well informed of what you have done, what you are doing, and what you plan to do.
David Pottruck	Charles Schwab & Co.	Moving brokerage onto the Internet	Persuade your boss of a new course with a path that is right, a rationale that is airtight, and a determination that is steadfast.
Roméo Dallaire	United Nations	Averting a national catastrophe	Step up to a moment when you can make the difference even if your superiors fail to see it and the risks are grave in seizing it.
Robert Ayling Eckerd Pfeiffer Thomas Wyman	British Airways Compaq Computer CBS	Retaining your board's confidence	Even if you're CEO, remember that your directors and investors are your bosses, and never surprise any of them.
Peter Pace	U.S. Marine Corps	Facing six bosses	Serve each superior as if he or she were your only boss, but let all know precisely what you are recommending to each.
Sandy Hill Pittman Beck Weathers	Mountain Madness Adventure Consultants	Ascending Mount Everest	Press your boss for elaboration of instructions, and step into the breach if the boss's leadership is wavering.
Charlene Barshefsky Domingo Cavallo	United States of America Republic of Argentina	Negotiating with China; converting national currency	Build the factual foundation that your superior needs to implement a controversial policy or initiative.
Abraham Moses Samuel	Old Testament	Interceding with the supreme being	Convey intents downward and interests upward, transforming what your superior and subordinates want into what all deserve.

THE DIFFERENCE THAT UPWARD
LEADERSHIP MAKES

When organizations fail to foster or refuse to accept upward leadership, the costs can be acute; when they receive upward leadership, the benefits can be great. The sharply contrasting styles of two naval commanders offer stark examples of each.

British Admiral Sir Clowdisley Shovell was sailing triumphantly home in 1707 from skirmishes against a French fleet in the Mediterranean. As he neared Great Britain, his ships became enveloped in a dense fog for several days, and he summoned his navigators to determine their location. The navigators concluded that the fleet was safely clear of the Brittany peninsula, but one of Sir Clowdisley's sailors approached him to report that he had independently tracked the fleet's location. The Royal Navy forbade navigation by inferiors, but the seaman was so alarmed by his calculations—they placed the fleet on a fatal path toward the Isles of Scilly, a string of 150 tiny islands off the southwest tip of England—that he felt compelled to step forward. Rather than heed the unsought counsel, the admiral hanged the sailor on the spot. Soon thereafter, the fleet's five warships smashed into the fog-enshrouded shoals, sending 2,000 men to a watery death.

Almost three centuries later, in equally hazardous waters off the British Isles, an American vessel faced peril of its own, but with dramatically different results. The captain of the USS *Daniel Boone,* a nuclear-powered submarine, was guiding his craft late one evening in 1979 toward a port on the coast of Scotland. Just before retiring to his quarters for the night, he ordered his sub to proceed without its running lights or yellow beacon, and he selected Thomas Flint, who had graduated from the U.S. Naval Academy just four years earlier, to pilot the vessel. Flint, serving for only his second time as "officer of the deck," was now fully responsible for a vessel thirty-three feet wide and more than a football field in length. With nuclear-tipped missiles and a full crew on board, Flint's premier obligation was for a safe and secure passage.

As Thomas Flint stood atop the submarine's conning tower that evening, the twinkling lights along the coastline gave him good reference points for his twelve-knot course toward a naval port adjacent to an air base at Prestwick. When a tiny flickering yellow light mysteriously came into view dead ahead, Flint queried his quartermaster about its origin. With navigational charts at his fingertips, the seasoned quartermaster concluded that it was a beacon at the Prestwick air base straight ahead. Flint kept a watchful eye for a while on the beacon until, almost imperceptibly, it seemed to be closing faster on him than the other lights at the air base. "It didn't feel right," he recalled. Ten minutes later he asked the officer below for reconfirmation of the beacon's identity. Yes, he was reassured, the light was indeed from the air base. Five minutes later Flint asked yet again, and now with irritation the quartermaster once more reaffirmed its source.

Moments later the light seemed to pop out of the darkness, only a half mile ahead. Then a "blacker than black" mass took form immediately in front of Flint, the yellow light squarely on top. With only seconds to act and no time to consult, he barked, "Left hard rudder, all ahead flank!" The submarine's engines roared, the vessel veered, and as it came abreast of the onrushing mass, Flint discerned a very familiar shape: another submarine. Now fearful of both hitting the shoals on the left and having his tail swiped by the onrushing sub, he ordered a hard right just seconds later, bringing the two subs back to parallel courses, only now some twenty-five yards apart instead of nose to nose.

So close were the two vessels that Flint could make out his counterpart's insignia on the other's conning tower. As the two submarines silently glided past each other, Flint's commander rushed on deck, turned to Flint, and said simply, "Tom, you saved the ship!"

The right decision in this instance had not been the obvious one. With shoals to the left, the prescribed tactic would have been to veer right. But since the oncoming sub was ever so slightly to the right, that decision would have proved fatal. Flint still does not understand precisely why he ordered the hard left, since the two subs were so closely aligned on their collision course. But his instinct served him well, and it served well the lives of more than 100 sailors and the careers of more than a few officers. And it was an instinct honed by training and a commander's willingness to be led from below. Unlike the commanders of the British navy nearly three centuries earlier, American naval commanders had set a premium on leadership in the ranks, and on this occasion that practice had served the navy well.

But even an institutional premium on upward leadership will lose its punch if not routinely practiced and reinforced. This was evident on February 9, 2001, when the nuclear submarine USS *Greenville* abruptly surfaced into a Japanese fishing boat, the *Ehime Maru*, sending nine passengers to the bottom of the sea just nine miles south of Honolulu's Pearl Harbor.

A U.S. Navy investigator reported that a visiting officer, Captain Robert L. Brandhuber, had sensed that the *Greenville*'s commander Scott D. Waddle was rushing preparations and cutting corners for a surfacing demonstration for sixteen civilians on board—but that Brandhuber said nothing to the commander about his concerns. Similarly, Lieutenant Commander Gerald K. Pfeifer, the second-ranking officer, who carried the most explicit obligation to challenge questionable procedures, had failed to voice his own doubts about their rapid pace, including an abbreviated periscope inspection of the horizon just before the surfacing. Pfeifer, the naval investigator said, "was thinking these things, but did not articulate them to the commanding officer." Another sailor on board knew that a sonar reading had revealed the presence of a surface ship near the *Greenville*, but he noted that the civilians on board made it difficult for him to convey the information to his commander. He also believed, evidently incorrectly, that the commander already knew of the sonar reading.

The naval investigator concluded that the crew members so respected their captain that they were reluctant to challenge him. Commander Waddle, said the investigator, "doesn't get a lot of corrective input from subordinates because he's very busy giving directions, and the ship has experienced a lot of success when he does." Had the institution more effectively stressed its principle of upward challenge, had the visiting officer and the commander's subordinates been emboldened to question his actions, five fishermen and four high school students on board the Japanese boat might be alive today.

A capacity for upward leadership has become so important that some executive search firms include it in their screening. In looking for the chief executive of a start-up enterprise, one search firm placed a premium on whether candidates were effective at upward persuasion—in this case with prospective investors. In another case, the search firm was seeking a chief financial officer for a national subsidiary of a multinational corporation. This time, the sine qua non was an ability to communicate upward with the parent's chief executive and chief financial officers.

A price can sometimes be placed on that capacity. The chairman of Samsung Group, Lee Kun Hee, decreed that Samsung should invest $13 billion to become a car producer, targeting 1.5 million vehicles by 2010. Automaking was already a crowded field, plagued by global overcapacity, but Lee was a powerful chieftain and a passionate auto buff, and none of his subordinates questioned his strategy. A year after the first cars rolled off the line in 1999, Samsung Motors was history. Many of Samsung's top managers had silently opposed the investment, and Lee later told them he was puzzled why none had openly expressed their reservations. By then, though, Lee had reached into his own pocket for $2 billion to placate angry creditors.

Sometimes the capacity to lead up can be nearly priceless. If your subordinates believe you'll always go on the line for them, they'll unswervingly do the same for you, as Peter Pace learned in Vietnam.

If they believe the opposite, they'll do the opposite, happier to see you falter than prosper, as other commanders learned the hard way in Vietnam when shrapnel seemed to come from behind the lines, not only the front.

A Bias for Upward Action

A common element in all of the experiences considered here is the presence or absence of a driving urge to make things happen on high, an unflinching willingness to take charge when not in command. A fortifying culture can nurture upward leadership, but in the end, it's up to the individual to act. Some people need reminders, others require none. David Pottruck stepped up on his own to persuade Charles Schwab of an online future, while Beck Weathers did not think to press Rob Hall for a contingency plan. Robert E. Lee revealed all to Jefferson Davis, while Joseph Johnston shared nothing. What made the difference was a profound personal bias for upward action.

As a case in point, consider a group of teachers in a large suburban high school. For more than a decade, they had worked for a tyrannical department chairman who micromanaged, dismissed ideas, and criticized everybody. Teaching languished, instructors quit, and students paid, and though the department's problems had become well-known within the school, the principal never intervened. Mustering all their courage to challenge a boss who had a record of forcing out critics, the teachers sent their chairman a letter detailing how he should mend his ways. To the surprise of most, the chairman wrote back, saying that he would have to change, and for the next two years he solicited weekly feedback from three teachers who had volunteered to provide upward coaching. In time, the superior changed in just the ways his subordinates had urged; he would not have if they had not so acted.

Individuals, in short, can and must make the difference. But organizations can make it infinitely easier for that to happen. Had the United Nations depended less on bureaucracy, it may have been more alert to its mission. Had the boards of British Airways, CBS, and Compaq Computer been less aloof, they might have enabled their chief executives to catch the wave before it toppled them. Leading up is the product of not only an individual bias for upward action but also a collective readiness to act.

Some Just Don't Get It

Like liverwurst and lederhosen, leading up just isn't for everyone. We've all known bosses who couldn't accept suggestions from below and who had no knack for downward leadership either. We've known colleagues and subordinates, too, who seemed utterly incapable of upward support. Can these paragons of antileadership transcend their own limitations? Sometimes the answer is simply no.

Charles, the founding owner of a hotel chain, had given all daily operating responsibilities to Robert, his chief executive. Under Robert's tutelage, the chain had a great year, and Robert expected to see a bonus of $1 million. Charles savored the good news but decided that Robert's performance was worth no more than $100,000. When the CEO learned that he was to receive only a tenth of what he thought he deserved, he went on strike, taking no calls, attending no meetings, making no decisions. Robert got the axe. Expert at leading down, Robert showed all the subtlety of a two-year-old when he was required to lead the boss toward his own vision of just compensation.

Mary, a rising analyst at a prominent information-services company, had hoped for guidance from Frank, her midlevel boss. But Frank's style proved a near perfect antimodel. He arrived late for meetings, even those he had called. When he scheduled a meeting for the entire office to hear a project report from Mary, he appeared half an hour late and then tapped on his laptop computer throughout what remained of her presentation. Later, when Mary asked Frank privately for reactions to her presentation, he offered a few cursory observations while simultaneously checking his voice mail, answering his e-mail, and placing phone calls. Mary saw him do the same with clients: When briefing them by telephone, he browsed his e-mail, rolled his eyes when client questions seemed beneath him, and occasionally raised a middle finger when client requests seemed burdensome.

In work guidance, Frank proved equally inept. The company sent Frank to open an office in London, and it asked him to continue overseeing Mary and the New York staff. When Mary completed her newest work assignment, she sent an e-mail to him in London, asking what he wanted her to do now. "Just keep researching whatever it was we agreed that you would be working on during this time," he replied. Unfortunately for Mary, no "whatever" had been previously agreed upon. "Whenever I think about Frank's antics," she said, "I can't help but think that I couldn't have invented a worse example of a manager if I tried!" Finally, in desperation, she approached her boss's boss, but he too offered no direction. Mary persisted, still believing if upper management were brought to it senses, it would get far more from its talented ranks, but several months later she threw in the towel, accepting a better-paying position at an arch rival.

What percentage of an average workforce has the potential to lead upward? Proportions will vary dramatically, depending on the existing corporate culture, but the experience of one banking executive suggests rough figures when starting cold. The manager had just taken charge of a major operation of a U.S. bank in 2000. The division required revitalization from its historic role as a passive asset manager into a far more aggressive role as a seller of asset-management services. The new executive believed that would only happen if everybody in his senior ranks stepped forward to produce it. Through speeches, messages, and forums, he pressed his top 100 people to excite the troops, devise new products, and strengthen the strategy. He discovered to his disappointment, however, that too few were ready for the task: One-third were reluctant to rise up, having long worked in a pecking order that had never valued such subordinate behavior in the past; another third was indifferent about doing so, waiting to see if the new guy at the top really meant what he said; and only a third was eager to do so, brimming with ideas for the new executive to consider. Granted, one in three might not sound like much, but in baseball it's an all-star average, and in business it can be a solid base to build on.

MOST CAN LEARN IT

Even if upward leadership now seems a distant concept in your organization, be heartened: Its absence is often more a matter of conceptual blinders than inherent incapacities. There's no "leadership pill" to get you where you want to go, no silver bullet, no magic ten-step program that will turn inherent followers into budding leaders, but upward leadership can be inspired if you're willing to take the time and do the often very hard work. This is a journey of many small steps, each one important.

Once established, a companywide culture of leading upward can serve as a kind of inertial guidance system, continually reminding managers that they are obliged to stand up without the need for any superiors to say so. For building that mind-set, five initiatives are in order:

1. **IDENTIFY MANAGERS FOR DEVELOPMENT.** Finding those with a capacity for upward leadership is an essential first step. Who has shown fearlessness when a leadership vacuum above threatened a product or program? Who seems willing to look in both directions for opportunities to lead and listen? Traditional leader-development programs have been reserved for a select few, but remember: Companywide leadership grows best when it grows at many points throughout the organization. If you look

widely when you identify the managers for development, then you are likely to be widely rewarded.

2. **COACH MANAGERS ONE-ON-ONE.** Begin by engaging those closest to you in a dialogue on upward leadership; then ask them to do the same with their associates. It is especially useful to discuss your own moments of upward success and setback, and then to ask others to synthesize lessons from their own past experiences. Providing them with private coaching and personal mentoring helps, too, and General Electric Company chief executive John F. Welch Jr. has done precisely that. GE had long used one-on-one mentoring of its next generation of top talent, but in 1999 Welch stood the concept on its head. He asked each of his 600 top executives to reach down in their ranks to find an Internet devotee who could teach them the ropes. "E-business knowledge is generally inversely proportional to both age and height in the organization," he explained. His reverse mentoring was intended to "change that equilibrium." Welch himself picked Pam Wickham, who ran GE's main website; chief financial officer Keith S. Sherin asked Nevin Zimmerman, the firm's e-commerce strategist; division head Lloyd G. Trotter selected Rachel Dorman, a developer of his unit's website. Dorman reported that the experience of looking up had emboldened her to better tell managers what they should be hearing from below. CFO Sherin said that his biweekly coaching from down under provided an invaluable sounding board for his prospective corporate Internet partnerships. Midlevel managers reported they had become more comfortable in feeding ideas upstairs and pressing their boss to change; top-level managers reported they had become more comfortable in eliciting insights from below.

3. **CREATE DEVELOPMENT PROGRAMS.** Introducing an upward component into existing or new management-development programs is also useful. In 1999, Ford Motor Company initiated

for some 2,000 managers an annual "new business leader" program built around an "up and out" thrust. The organizers formed teams to identify fresh ways of transforming the company's way of doing business. Ford executives coached them in the arts of upward persuasion, and the teams then proceeded to sell their ideas outside their own operations. Ford's vice president for human resources, David Murphy, explained the program's rationale: "We want people at all levels who will take risks, who are prepared to coach and to counsel, and who can make decisions." By program's end, participants were pumped. "I've got this idea that could transform the company," said Kris Rogers, who worked on Ford's receivables, "and no one is telling me that I can't try it out." Jason Harvey, a marketing manager, offered, "I always wondered, 'How do I bring this idea to the big boys?' " Now, "not only do I have an idea that can change the company, but I also have license to pursue it." David Murphy explained why these upward capacities had become so vital to the company: "We can't afford to wait for decisions to come down from the top." Otherwise, he said, the consumer "would be gone before those decisions even got made."

4. FOCUS MANAGERS ON UPWARD EXPERIENCE. Another avenue is to ask your managers to consider what others have achieved when their opportunity for upward leadership was either skirted or seized. By examining in detail what others have done, we can better appreciate what we should do ourselves. The more that past experience can be brought to life, the better it can inform present behavior. To appreciate what George McClellan, Joseph Johnston, and Robert E. Lee faced as they made their fateful decisions in 1862, you may want to take your managers for a day or two to the Virginia peninsula where those decisions helped shape our nation's history.

5. SET EXAMPLES FOR ALL. A final course is to begin behaving as though upward leadership seems natural. William Copacino, managing partner for Andersen Consulting's strategy division in America, had been told in 1997 by his immediate boss, Peter H. Fuchs, and the chief executive, George Shaheen, to grow his business by expanding his 2,000-person workforce by 30% per year to keep up with the rest of the company. Copacino studied the options, concluded that he could not hire the quality he required at such a torrid rate, and told his very demanding superiors that it simply could not be done. They heeded his warning. Just as important, an example of leadership had been set for all to see. Three illustrations from the world of health point to the same:

- A New York medical doctor told his staff nurses and physicians from the day they were hired that if he was doing anything wrong—or could be doing something better—they must tell him. He publicly commended all who did.

- When a drug company was acquired by a large U.S. pharmaceutical firm, it included a division whose products were unrelated to the new owner's core business. The parent took little interest in the division, allowing it to drift, even though the division's executives repeatedly asked for a vision of its future. The division began hemorrhaging talent and energy—until its president filled the void by concocting a strategy of his own.

- A hospital administrator had slashed a proposed $50 million renovation and expansion for one of its units back to $30 million, but the medical director for the unit believed the cut was unconscionable. She argued with the administrator to no avail, and even hired an outside group for an independent opinion. The consultants reached the same conclusion, and the medical director argued again for the full amount. When the hospital administrator angrily denounced still another reopening of the issue, the medical director asked to take the issue to the board, which the administrator grudgingly permitted. The board unanimously restored the original amount.

Leading up takes courage: the courage to be corrected, the courage to take over when others won't look your way, even the courage to buck the system and force your way to those who can set things right. The rewards aren't always great for those who take such steps, but the institutions they serve are almost always better for their gumption.

MANAGING AND LEADING

Sometimes we see managing and leading as exclusive spheres, each following its own logic, each with a separate purpose. But however different managing and leading might be conceptually, the truth is that the two are joined at the hip. Without successful managing up, businesses lack the structural sinew that holds day-to-day operations together; without successful leading up, they forfeit the courage and creativity that can come from anywhere in the company.

The prescriptions for managing up are many. Business school faculty John Gabarro and John Kotter have urged consistency and honesty for "managing your boss." Management expert Leonard Schlesinger advises: Stop whining about your boss, start thinking for your boss, get courageous when your boss is not, and know that "it doesn't take a wizard to build a better boss." A column in the *Wall Street Journal* recommends using job interviews to help spot "bad bosses before you get stuck working for them," and another column asserts that "competent bosses recognize" the "importance of managing up" and advocates telling your boss of your operation's achievements. AT&T has issued its own company guidelines for dealing with "problem bosses." Among the suggestions: Resolve as many business problems as you can before they ever reach the human problem above you. Writer Richard Stengel proposes the use of "strategic praise" but also warns that the "greater the status difference between you and your target, the more subtle your flattery should be." (Be wary, in short, of telling the CEO that he or she is a "genius" if you are a lowly technician.) Author Jeffrey J. Fox has said it is important "to make your boss look good," but it's even more so to make "your boss's boss look better." Above all, most say, any hint of manipulating your boss is sure to backfire.

Whatever your formula for managing up, building a method for leading up is essential as well. *Managing up* strengthens the organization; *leading up* can save it when the peril is greatest and the right course of action is most difficult to see from the lofty heights of the boardroom. For this, you will have to customize your way, but from Charlene Barshefsky and Robert E. Lee to Peter Pace and David Pottruck, we already have a rich lore of experience to help you take command when you're not in charge.

SOURCES

Introduction
Dao, James, and Nicholas D. Kristof. "His Early Promise Vanished, Bradley Plans to Quit Today," *New York Times*, March 9, 2000, pp. A1, 25.

Chapter 1: Informing Your Commander
Freeman, Douglas Southall. *Lee's Lieutenants: A Study in Command.* New York: Scribner, 1998.

———, ed. *Lee's Dispatches: Unpublished Letters of General Robert E. Lee to Jefferson Davis and the War Department of the Confederate States of America.* Baton Rouge: Louisiana State University Press, 1994.

Holzer, Harold. "The Image of Jefferson Davis as Commander in Chief," in *Jefferson Davis's Generals*, Gabor S. Boritt, ed. New York: Oxford University Press, 1999.

Sears, Stephen W. *Controversies and Commanders: Dispatches from the Army of the Potomac.* Boston: Houghton Mifflin, 1999.

———. *George B. McClellan: The Young Napoleon.* New York: Da Capo Press, 1999.

———. *To the Gates of Richmond: The Peninsula Campaign.* Boston: Houghton Mifflin, 1992.

Symonds, Craig L. "A Fatal Relationship: Davis and Johnston at War," in *Jefferson Davis's Generals*, Gabor S. Boritt, ed. New York: Oxford University Press, 1999.

———. *Joseph E. Johnston: A Civil War Biography.* New York: Norton, 1992.

Thomas, Emory M. "Ambivalent Visions of Victory: Davis, Lee, and Confederate Grand Strategy," in *Jefferson Davis's Generals*, Gabor S. Boritt, ed. New York: Oxford University Press, 1999.

Waugh, John C. *The Class of 1846: From West Point to Appomattox: Stonewall Jackson, George McClellan and Their Brothers.* New York: Ballantine, 1999.

Chapter 2: Convincing a Company to Turn Inside Out
Primary sources include the publications below and discussions with David Pottruck (September 2 and November 11, 2000, and March 15, 2001).

Barnett, Megan. "Schwab's MVP, the Person Who Has Done the Most to Bring Financial Services Online: David Pottruck," *Industry Standard*, April 24, 2000.

Buckman, Rebecca. "Schwab, Once a Predator, Is Now Prey," *Wall Street Journal,* December 8, 1999, pp. C1, 2.

Business Week. "The Top 25 Executives of the Year: Charles R. Schwab and David S. Pottruck: Schwab's E-Gambit," January 11, 1999.

Business Week. "The Top 25 Managers of the Year: David S. Pottruck and Charles R. Schwab, Charles Schwab Corp," January 8, 2001.

Byrnes, Nanette. "How Schwab Grabbed the Lion's Share," *Business Week,* June 28, 1999, p. 88.

Cascales, Maria J. "Charles Schwab Inc.: Creating an International Marketspace," Hong Kong: Center for Asian Business Cases, University of Hong Kong, 2000.

Ceron, Gaston F. "The Best Way to Trade Stocks," *Wall Street Journal,* November 27, 2000, pp. R6, 23.

Context Magazine. "Hearts and Souls: Schwab Co-CEO David Pottruck Says the Only Way to Succeed Is to Make Employees Passionate," June–July 2000.

Edmonston, Peter, and Charles Gasparino. "Merrill Lynch Linking with Charles Schwab? In Web Name Only," *Wall Street Journal,* November 29, 2000, p. C1.

Fraser, Andrew. "Online Investing: The Great Equalizer," *Wall Street Journal,* June 12, 2000, p. R6.

Gorham, John. "Charles Schwab, Version 4.0," *Forbes,* January 8, 2001.

Laderman, Jeffrey M. "Remaking Schwab," *Business Week,* May 25, 1998.

Lee, Louise. "Charles R. Schwab and David S. Pottruck: Schwab's E-Gambit," *Business Week,* September 27, 1999.

McGeehan, Patrick. "Competitors Don't Seem to Hurt Schwab," *New York Times,* December 30, 1999, pp. C1–2.

Monroe, Ann. "Charley's Web: Drawing Rivals into the Internet, Schwab Takes Its Biggest Risk," *Investment Dealers Digest,* June 21, 1999, pp. 20–25.

Nocera, Joe. "A Mug Only 20,000 Employees Could Love," *eCompany Now,* June 2000.

Pettit, Dave. "Making a Market: How Two Online Brokerage Firms Try to Stand Out from the Crowd," *Wall Street Journal,* June 14, 1999, p. R18.

Pottruck, David S., and Terry Pearce. *Clicks and Mortar: Passion Driven Growth in an Internet Driven World.* San Francisco: Jossey-Bass, 2000.

Schonfeld, Eric. "Schwab Puts It All Online," *Fortune,* December 7, 1998, pp. 94 ff.

Serwer, Andrew. "Online and Off, Schwab's the One," *Fortune,* May 10, 1999, pp. 181 ff.

Stepanek, Marcia. "How to Jump-Start Your E-Strategy," *BusinessWeek Online,* June 5, 2000.

Tempest, Nicole. "Charles Schwab Corporation (A) and (B)." Boston: Harvard Business School, 1999.

Useem, Jerry. "Internet Defense Strategy: Cannibalize Yourself," *Fortune*, September 6, 1999, pp. 121 ff.

Ward, Judy. "Everybody's Target," *Executive Edge Online*, April 2000.

Chapter 3: Begging Your Boss to Untie Your Hands

Primary sources include a discussion with and presentation by Roméo Dallaire on February 27, 2001, another discussion with Dallaire on March 27, 2001, the publications below, and information available at the websites of the Carnegie Commission on Preventing Deadly Conflict (www.ccpdc.org/pubs/rept97/toc.htm#commission), Human Rights Watch (www.hrw.org/reports/1999/Rwanda), International Criminal Tribunal for Rwanda (www.ictr.org), Organization of African Unity (www.oau-oua.org/Document/ipep/ipep.htm), Public Broadcasting System (www.pbs.org/wgbh/pages/frontline/shows/evil), United Nations (www.un.org/News/ossg/rwanda_p.htm), and United Nations Assistance Mission for Rwanda (www.un.org/Depts/DPKO/Missions/unamir_p.htm).

Carnegie Commission on Preventing Deadly Conflict. *Final Report.* New York: Carnegie Corporation of New York, 1997.

Gourevitch, Philip. *We Wish to Inform You That Tomorrow We Will Be Killed with Our Families.* New York: Picador/Farrar, Straus & Giroux, 1999.

Human Rights Watch. *Leave None to Tell the Story: Genocide in Rwanda.* New York: Human Rights Watch, 1999.

International Panel of Eminent Personalities to Investigate the 1994 Genocide in Rwanda and the Surrounding Events. *Rwanda: Preventable Genocide.* Addis Ababa, Ethiopia: Organization of African Unity, 2000.

Keane, Fergal. *Season of Blood: A Rwandan Journey.* London: Penguin Books, 1995.

Melvern, Linda. *A People Betrayed: The Role of the West in Rwanda's Genocide.* New York: Zed Books, 2000.

Off, Carol. *The Lion, the Fox and the Eagle: A Story of Generals and Justice in Rwanda and Yugoslavia.* Toronto: Random House Canada, 2000.

Prunier, Gerard. *The Rwanda Crisis: History of a Genocide.* New York: Columbia University Press, 1995.

United Nations. *Report on the Independent Inquiry into the Actions of the United Nations During the 1994 Genocide in Rwanda.* New York: United Nations, 1999.

Uvin, Peter. *Aiding Violence: The Development Enterprise in Rwanda.* West Hartford, Conn.: Kumarian Press, 1998.

Chapter 4: Retaining the Confidence of Your Directors and Investors

Primary sources include the publications below and a discussion with Robert Ayling on August 9, 2000.

Ashworth, Jon. "Writing Was on the Wall for Ayling," *Times* (London), March 11, 2000.

Barnes, Peter W. "CBS's Wyman Forced to Quit, Sources Assert," *Wall Street Journal*, September 11, 1986.

Barnes, Peter W., Laura Landro, and James B. Stewart. "Changing Picture: How the CBS Board Decided Chief Wyman Should Leave His Job," *Wall Street Journal*, September 12, 1986.

Boyer, Peter J. "CBS Says It Didn't Seek Bids," *New York Times*, September 8, 1986, p. D1.

———. *Who Killed CBS?* New York: Random House, 1988.

Burrows, Peter, with Ira Sager and Michael Moeller. "Can Compaq Catch Up?" *Business Week*, May 3, 1999, p. 162.

Business Week. "The 25 Top Managers of the Year," January 12, 1998.

Cole, Robert J. "Wyman Talks with Coke Cited," *New York Times*, September 12, 1986, p. D6

Done, Kevin. "Right Strategy, Wrong Man," *Financial Times*, March 12, 2000.

Doward, Jamie. "Some Executives Sold Their Shares in the Company Before Poor Earnings Report," *Observer*, April 25, 1999, p. 5.

Fabrikant, Geraldine. "Head of CBS Quits under Pressure; Paley in Key Role," *New York Times*, September 11, 1986, p. A1.

———. "Wyman's Support Waned Dramatically," *New York Times*, September 12, 1986, p. D6.

Francis, Bruce, and Tony Guida. "Interview of Pfeiffer," *CNNfn*, April 21, 1999.

Hamm, Steve. "Compaq's Rockin' Boss," *Business Week*, September 4, 2000, pp. 87–98.

Hamm, Steve, with Ira Sager and Peter Burrows. "Ben Rosen: The Lion in Winter," *Business Week*, July 26, 1999.

Hansell, Saul. "Compaq at a Crossroad: The Challenges for the Next Chief," *New York Times*, April 25, 1999, Section 3, p. 4.

Harris, Kathryn. "Tisch Makes Most of His Piece of the Action at CBS," *Los Angeles Times*, April 27, 1986, Business Section, p. 1.

Harrison, Michael. "Ethnic Tailfins Ditched by BA," *Independent*, July 12, 2000, p. 18.

Irish Times. "Confidence in BA Boss Finally Expired: Bob Ayling's Difficult Personality Contributed to His Departure," March 17, 2000, p. 64.

Jensen, Elizabeth. "CBS's Tisch Is Faulted by Insiders, Affiliates for Network's Struggle," *Wall Street Journal*, May 22, 1995, A1, 6.

Kaplan, Steven N. "Top Executives, Turnover, and Firm Performance in Germany," *Journal of Law, Economics, & Organization* 10 (1994): 142–159.

———. "Top Executive Rewards and Firm Performance: A Comparison of Japan and the U.S.," *Journal of Political Economy* (1994).

———. "Corporate Governance and Corporate Performance: A Comparison of Germany, Japan, and the U.S.," *Journal of Applied Corporate Finance* 9 (1997): 86–93.

Kirkpatrick, David. "Fast Times at Compaq," *Fortune*, April 1, 1996.

———. "Eckhard's Gone but the PC Rocks On," *Fortune*, May 24, 1999, pp. 153–158.

Landro, Laura, and Elizabeth Jensen. "A CBS Holder, Capital Group, Declines to Vote for Management-Backed Board." *Wall Street Journal*, May 25, 1995, p. B2.

Landro, Laura, Joanne Lipman, James B. Stewart, and Bob Davis. "Tisch Acts Fast to Exert Control at CBS, Backing Top Executives; Sauter Resigns," *Wall Street Journal*, September 12, 1986.

Lohr, Steve. "Compaq Computer Ousts Chief Executive," *New York Times*, April 19, 1999, p. A17.

McCartney, Scott, and Gary McWilliams. "Compaq's Rosen Wields Ax to Protect Legacy," *Wall Street Journal*, April 20, 1999, p. B1.

McWilliams, Gary. "Compaq's Stock Skids on Profit Warning," *Wall Street Journal*, April 13, 1999, p. A3.

———. "Ousted CEO of Compaq Offers Defense," *Wall Street Journal*, April 22, 1999, p. A3.

———. "Compaq Picks an Insider for Top Post," *Wall Street Journal*, July 23, 1999, p. A3.

McWilliams, Gary, and Joann S. Lublin. "Compaq Ousts Pfeiffer from CEO Post," *Wall Street Journal*, April 19, 1999, p. A3.

———. "Compaq Could Have Averted Missteps," *Wall Street Journal*, April 20, 1999, p. A3.

Menn, Joseph. "Compaq Ousts CEO," *Los Angeles Times*, April 19, 1999, p. C1.

Michaels, Daniel. "British Airways Sticking to Plan Dismissed CEO Had Chartered," *Wall Street Journal*, March 13, 2000, pp. A21, 24.

Parsley, David, and John Waples. "BA Offers Ayling's Job to American." *Sunday Times* (London), March 12, 2000.

Prokesch, Steven. "Competing on Customer Service: An Interview with British Airways' Sir Colin Marshall," *Harvard Business Review*, November–December 1995, pp. 100–112.

Ramstad, Evan. "Despite Pfeiffer's Accomplishments, Dell Computer Is Hot in Pursuit," *Wall Street Journal*, January 5, 1998, p. B4.

Silverman, Dwight. "Ex-Compaq Chief: Firing Was to Appease Wall Street," *Houston Chronicle*, April 20, 1999, p. A1.

———. "Schism in Management Blamed for Compaq Woes," *Houston Chronicle*, May 30, 1999, p. A1.

Silverman, Dwight, and Tricia Serju-Harris. "Compaq Chief Resigns Amid Stock and Profit Declines," *Houston Chronicle*, April 19, 1999, p. 1.

Skapinker, Michael. "The Last Ride of Bob Ayling," *Financial Times*, March 10, 2000, p. 11.

Slater, Robert. *This . . . Is CBS: A Chronicle of 60 Years*. Englewood Cliffs, N.J.: Prentice-Hall, 1988.

Smith, Sally Bedell. "Sharing the Throne at Black Rock," *New York Times,* September 14, 1986, Section 3, p. 1.

Sorkin, Andrew Ross. "British Airways Ousts Chief after Four Tumultuous Years," *New York Times,* March 11, 2000, pp. C1–2.

Taylor, Paul. "An Aggressive Bid for Internet Supremacy: 'The Big Pieces Are in Place,' " *Financial Times,* March 3, 1999, Survey Edition, p. 3.

Useem, Michael. *Investor Capitalism: How Money Managers Are Changing the Face of Corporate America.* New York: Basic Books/HarperCollins, 1996.

———. "Corporate Leadership in a Globalizing Equity Market," *Academy of Management Executive,* 12, 1998, pp. 43–59.

Vise, David A. "CBS Board Gathers as Rumors Fly; Speculation Centers on Power Struggle," *Washington Post,* September 1986, p. F1.

Wall Street Journal. "The Lesson at CBS," Editorial, September 15, 1986.

Walters, Joanna. "Headless BA in Shock at Ayling's Swift Demise," *Observer,* March 12, 2000.

Waples, John, and David Parsley. "Dropping the Pilot," *Sunday Times* (London), March 12, 2000.

Weiser, Charles R. "Championing the Customer," *Harvard Business Review,* November–December 1995, pp. 113–116.

Chapter 5: Keeping Your Head When You Have Several Superiors
Primary sources include the publications below and discussions with Peter Pace (April 9, 1999; March 15, May 30, and October 4, 2000); discussions with and observations of U.S. Marine commanders Charles Krulak (retired), Thomas Draude (retired), and Robert E. Lee on March 30, 2000; information available at the websites of the U.S. Department of Defense (www.defenselink.mil), U.S. Marine Corps (www.usmc.mil), and U.S. Marine Corps Forces, Atlantic (www.marforlant.usmc.mil). "The Commandant's Guidance" can be found at <www.usmc.mil/cmc.nsf/cmc>.

Carrison, Dan, and Rod Walsh. *Semper Fi: Business Leadership the Marine Corps Way.* New York: AMACOM, 1998.

Friedman, David H. *Corps Business: The 30 Management Principles of the U.S. Marines.* New York: Harper Business, 2000.

Jones, James L. *Commandant's Guidance.* Washington, D.C.: U.S. Marine Corps, July 1999.

Katzenbach, Jon R., and Jason A. Santamaria. "Firing Up the Front Line," *Harvard Business Review,* May–June, 1999, pp. 107–117.

Locher, James R. III. "Taking Stock of Goldwater-Nichols," *Joint Forces Quarterly,* Autumn 1996, pp. 10–16.

Townsend, Patrick L., with Joan E. Gebhardt. *Five-Star Leadership: The Art and Strategy of Creating Leaders at Every Level.* New York: John Wiley & Sons, 1997.

Chapter 6: Guiding Your Guide
Primary sources include the publications below and public presentations by Beck Weathers in 1997 and on May 14, 1998, and a discussion with Sandy Hill Pittman on May 29, 1998.

Anker, Conrad, and David Roberts. *The Lost Explorer: Finding Mallory on Mount Everest.* New York: Simon & Schuster, 1999.

Bennis, Warren, and Patricia Ward Biederman. *Organizing Genius: The Secrets of Creative Collaboration.* Reading, Mass.: Addison-Wesley, 1997.

Boukreev, Anatoli, and G. Weston Dewalt. *The Climb: Tragic Ambitions on Everest.* New York: St. Martin's Press, 1997.

Bromet, Jane. "The Days After: Going Home after Everest '96," *Climbing Magazine,* September 15, 1999, pp. 128 ff.

Coburn, Broughton. *Everest: Mountain without Mercy.* Washington, D.C.: National Geographic Society, 1997.

Curran, Jim. *K2: The Story of the Savage Mountain.* Seattle: Mountaineers Books, 1999.

Gabriel, Trip. "Scaling Corporate Heights without Going over a Cliff," *New York Times,* June 1, 1997, p. F 10.

Gammelgaard, Lene. *Climbing High: A Woman's Account of Surviving the Everest Tragedy.* Seattle: Seal Press, 1999.

Krakauer, Jon. *Into Thin Air: A Personal Account of the Mount Everest Disaster.* New York: Villard/Random House, 1997.

Pittman, Sandy Hill. "Peak Conditioning," *Vogue,* April 1994, pp. 234 ff.
———. "Cliff-Hanger," *Vogue,* August 1996, pp. 226 ff.

Potterfield, Peter. *In the Zone: Epic Survival Stories from the Mountaineering World.* Seattle: Mountaineers Books, 1996.

Salkeld, Audrey. "The Struggle for Everest: Mountaineering's First Great Problem," *Climbing Magazine,* September 1999, pp. 108–120.

Thomas, Robert McG. "Raymond Lambert, 82, Dies; Paved the Way on Mount Everest." *New York Times,* March 3, 1997, p. B10.

Useem, Andrea, and Michael Useem. "Himalayan Diary. A Trek from M.B.A. to Mountaintop: Lessons in Leadership Improve One's View," *Chronicle of Higher Education,* December 11, 1998, p. B10.

Weathers, Beck. *Left for Dead: My Journey Home from Everest.* New York: Villard/Random House, 2000.

Chapter 7: Designing a Future Your Boss Can't Quite Envision
Primary sources include the publications below and discussions with Charlene Barshefsky (April 7 and July 25, 2000, and March 12, 2001), and Domingo Cavallo (February 9, 2001); chief of staff for the U.S. trade representative, Nancy LeaMond (July 25, 2000), chief of public affairs, Brendan Daly (July 25, 2000), and the general counsel, Robert T. Novick (February 6, and March 5, 6, and 13, 2001). The agreement between the United States

and the People's Republic of China regarding WTO and market access, and related documents and websites, can be reached via <www.uschina.org/public/wto>. Further information is available from China's Ministry of Foreign Trade and Economic Cooperation at <www.moftec.gov.cn/moftec_en>, Office of the U.S. Trade Representative at <www.ustr.gov>, U.S. White House's China Trade Relations Working Group at <www.chinapntr.gov>, and the office of Domingo Cavallo at <www.cavallo.org.ar>.

Ashton, Chris. "Argentina Dries the Tears," *Australian Financial Review,* June 14, 1991, p. 32.

Baker, Stephen, and Elizabeth Weiner. "The Big Move to Free Markets," *Business Week,* June 15, 1992, p. 50.

Barham, John. "Cavallo: Argentina's Doctor No," *Australian Financial Review,* June 14, 1991, p. 33.

―――. "Argentina's Rebel with a Cause," *Financial Post,* January 7, 1992, p. 40.

Barshefsky, Charlene. "Trading with China Helps Connecticut, America," opinion page, *Hartford Courant,* May 5, 2000.

―――. "Hanging in the Balance," opinion page, *San Diego Union-Tribune,* May 17, 2000.

Beckerman, Paul. "Central-Bank 'Distress' and Hyperinflation in Argentina, 1989–1990," *Journal of Latin American Studies* 27, October 1995, pp. 663–682.

Bonasegna, Cristina. "Economy Gives Peronists Win in Argentina: Big Victory Endorses Menem's Austerity Plan," *Christian Science Monitor,* September 11, 1991.

Burgess, John. "Barshefsky: Ever Optimistic," *Washington Post,* December 3, 1999, p. E1.

Burkins, Glenn. "Clinton Gains Support of 42 Governors in Bid to Give China WTO Membership," *Wall Street Journal,* April 4, 2000, p. A2.

Cavallo, Domingo. *El Peso de la Verdad: Un Impulso a la Transparencia en la Argentina de los 90.* Buenos Aires: Planeta, 1997.

Cook, Peter. "Cavallo's Way," *Globe and Mail,* November 30, 1992, p. B2.

Cooper, Helene. "China's Effort to Join WTO at Key Point," *Wall Street Journal,* April 2, 1999.

―――. "Rubin Advised against China WTO Deal," *Wall Street Journal,* April 16, 1999, p. A2.

Cooper, Helene, and Bob Davis. "No Deal: Overruling Some Staff, Clinton Denies Zhu What He Came for—Lack of WTO Pact for China Opens Political Dangers for Both of the Leaders—Will Beijing Now Backpedal?" *Wall Street Journal,* April 9, 1999, p. A1.

―――. "Barshefsky Drove Hard Bargain, but Lost to Politics," *Wall Street Journal,* April 12, 1999.

Cooper, Helene, and David Rodgers. "China Trade Bill Passes Final Test: Senate," *Wall Street Journal,* September 20, 2000, pp. A2, 16.

Cooper, Helene, David Rodgers, and Michael M. Phillips. "White House Hints at Support for China Monitor," *Wall Street Journal*, April 13, 2000, p. A3.

Cooper, Helene, and Ian Johnson. "Clinton Maneuvers on China WTO Deal," *Wall Street Journal*, May 25, 2000, pp. A1, 10.

———. "Congress's Vote Primes U.S. Firms to Boost Investments in China," *Wall Street Journal*, April 12, 1999, pp. A2, 10.

De la Balze, Felipe A. M. *Remaking the Argentine Economy*. New York: Council on Foreign Relations, 1995.

Druckerman, Pamela. "Agentina's Cavallo Dusts Off His Legend," *Wall Street Journal*, November 17, 2000, p. A15.

Economist. "The Starting-Gun: Argentina," November 9, 1991, p. 43.

Economist. "Argentina's Economy: Nearly Time to Tango," April 18, 1992, p. 17.

Friedman, Thomas L., *The Lexus and the Olive Tree*. New York: Farrar, Straus & Giroux, 2000.

Fritz, Sara. "From Talks to Vote, Trade Official Guides China Deal," *St. Petersburg Times*, May 24, 2000.

Galuszka, Peter. "Global Wrap-up Argentina, *Business Week*, September 21, 1992, p. 49.

Gentile, Gary. "Film Execs Back Better China Ties," Associated Press, March 23, 2000.

Greenhouse, Steven. "Unions Deny Stand over Trade Policy Is Protectionism," *New York Times*, April 24, 2000, pp. A1, 6.

Greenhouse, Steven, and Richard W. Stevenson. "Unions March in Washington, Urging Congress to Defeat Trade Agreement with China," *New York Times*, April 13, 2000, p. A8.

Guillén, Mauro F. *The Limits of Convergence: Globalization and Organizational Change in Argentina, South Korea, and Spain*. Princeton, N.J.: Princeton University Press, 2001.

Hakim, Peter. "After These Elections, Don't Cry for Argentina," *Christian Science Monitor*, October 28, 1999, p. 21.

Heenan, David A., and Warren G. Bennis. *Co-Leaders: The Power of Great Partnerships*. New York: John Wiley & Sons, 1999.

Hillenbrand, Barry. "Barshefsky: 'It Is Political Legitimacy,' " *Time* (Asia), November 29, 1999.

Hunt, Albert R. "A Paper Tiger on Trade," *Wall Street Journal*, March 23, 2000.

———. "A Short-Term Trade Victory," *Wall Street Journal*, May 25, 2000, p. A27.

Kahn, Joseph. "China's Premier Twice Voices Displeasure over Not Getting into Club," *New York Times*, April 10, 1999, p. A5.

———. "Nobel Economists Back China's Joining Global Trade Group," *New York Times*, April 26, 2000, p. A8.

Kamm, Thomas. "Menem Cabinet Shuffled after Currency Dives," *Wall Street Journal,* January 30, 1991, p. A7.

———. "Argentine 'Miracle': Talk of Buenos Aires Is That Latest Revival in Economy Is for Real," *Wall Street Journal,* September 11, 1992, p. A1.

Kelly, Cristina Bonasegna. "Argentina Starts to Tango," *Christian Science Monitor,* January 6, 1992, p. 9.

Kiefer, Francine. "The Day the Red Ink Started to Vanish," *Christian Science Monitor,* January 17, 2001.

Knox, Paul. "Rising Star: Economy Minister Domingo Cavallo Fights Inflation by Tying Spending to U.S. Dollar Reserves," *Globe and Mail,* May 28, 1991, p. B5.

Lardy, Nicholas R. "Clinton Spurned a Great WTO Deal with China," *Wall Street Journal,* April 20, 1999, p. A22.

Lewis, Paul H. *The Crisis of Argentine Capitalism.* Chapel Hill: University of North Carolina Press, 1992.

Mann, Jim. " '50-50' Chance for China WTO Deal," *Los Angeles Times,* March 26, 1999, p. C3.

Michaels, Julia. "Argentines Raise Doubts about New Reform Plan," *Christian Science Monitor,* June 6, 1991.

Mitchell, Alison, and John M. Broder. "White House Tangles with China Now, with Congress Later," *New York Times,* April 20, 1999, p. A4.

Nash, Nathaniel C. "Turmoil, Then Hope in Argentina," *New York Times,* January 31, 1991, p. D1.

New York Times. "Domingo Cavallo's Achievement," editorial, August 10, 1996.

Phillips, Michael M. "Big Business Lobbies Hard as House China Vote Nears," *Wall Street Journal,* May 23, 2000, p. A28.

Roberts, Dexter, Paul Magnusson, and Mark L. Clifford. "Welcome to the Club," *Business Week* (International Edition), November 29, 1999, p. 34.

Robinson, Eugene. "Menem Appeals to Argentine Hearts," *Toronto Star,* May 7, 1989, p. H3.

Sanger, David E. "A China Trade Deal Is Now Up to Clinton," *New York Times,* April 7, 1999, pp. C1, 6.

———. "How U.S. and China Failed to Close Trade Deal," *New York Times,* April 10, 1999, pp. A1, 5.

———. "Rounding Out a Clear Clinton Legacy," *New York Times,* May 25, 2000, pp. A1, 10.

———. "New Realism Wins the Day: Threats Seemed Empty as China's Power Grew," *New York Times,* September 20, 2000, pp. A1, 16.

Schmitt, Eric. "Senate Votes to Lift Curbs on U.S. Trade with Beijing; Strong Bipartisan Support," *New York Times,* September 20, 2000, pp. A1, 16.

Schmitt, Eric, and Joseph Kahn. "House, in 237–197 Vote, Approves Normal Trade Rights for China," *New York Times,* May 25, 2000, pp. A1, 10.

Truell, Peter. "Inflation Imperils Argentine Democracy—as Economy

Skids, Leaders Lean Toward Military," *Wall Street Journal,* February 26, 1990, p. A6.

Vincent, Isabel. "Don't Cry for Argentina Economic Reform: The Country Is Battling Back from Decades of Syndicalist Nationalism, Left-Wing Terrorism and Right-Wing Oppression," *Globe and Mail,* December 27, 1991, p. B1.

———. "Turning Away from Peron's Path," *Globe and Mail,* January 13, 1992, p. A13.

Walsh, Elsa. "The Negotiator," *New Yorker,* March 18, 1996, pp. 86–97.

Warner, Susan. "A Home-Grown Example of China's Trade Partners," *Philadelphia Inquirer,* April 7, 2000, pp. C1, 8.

Weinstein, Michael M. "Limits of Economic Diplomacy: Modest Goals in Push to Bring China into Trade Group," *New York Times,* April 8, 1999, pp. C1, 2.

World Bank. *Argentina, the Convertibility Plan: Assessment and Potential Prospects.* Washington, D.C.: World Bank, 1996.

———. *Argentina, the Fiscal Dimension of the Convertibility Plan: A Background Report.* Washington, D.C.: World Bank, 1998.

St. Petersburg Times. "A Sound Deal," editorial, March 6, 2000, p. 12a.

Chapter 8: Persuading the Ultimate Authority

Muffs, Yochanan. *Love and Joy: Law, Language and Religion in Ancient Israel.* Cambridge, Mass.: Belknap Press of Harvard University Press, 1995.

Phillips, Richard D. *The Heart of an Executive: Lessons on Leadership from the Life of King David.* New York: Doubleday/Random House, 1999.

Chapter 9: The Upward Leader's Calling

Bellman, Geoffrey M. *Getting Things Done When You Are Not in Charge.* New York: Simon & Schuster, 1992.

Coleman, Kay. "Managing Your Boss," *The Right Match: A Magazine of Career Management.* Morristown, N.J.: AT&T, 1993.

Fisher, Roger, and Alan Sharp. *Getting It Done: How to Lead When You're Not in Charge.* New York: HarperBusiness, 1998.

Fox, Jeffrey J. *How to Become CEO: The Rules for Rising to the Top of Any Organization.* New York: Hyperion, 1999.

Gabarro, John J., and John P. Kotter. "Managing Your Boss," *Harvard Business Review,* May–June 1993, pp. 150–157.

Grant, Tom. "Ford Motor Company's New Business Leader Program," *Wharton Leadership Digest,* April 2000 (leadership.wharton.upenn.edu/digest/index.shtml).

Griffiths, Charles H., Jr. Testimony before U.S. Navy Court of Inquiry, Honolulu, Hawaii, March 5–7, 2001 (unofficial transcript at www.cnn.com/SPECIALS/2001/sub.collision/session5.html)

Hammonds, Keith H. "Grassroots Leadership—Ford Motor Company," *Fast Company,* April 2000, pp. 138 ff.

Heenan, David A., and Warren Bennis. "How to Be a Great No. 2," *Across the Board,* July–August, 1999, pp. 36–42.

Hymowitz, Carol. "Competent Bosses Recognize Importance of Managing Up," *Wall Street Journal,* February 20, 2001.

Kelley, Robert E. "In Praise of Followers," *Harvard Business Review,* November–December, 1988, pp. 1–8.

Kraar, Louis. "Behind Samsung's High-Stakes Push into Cars," *Fortune,* May 12, 1997.

———. "Lee Drops $2 Billion to Bail Out Samsung," *Fortune,* December 6, 1999, p. 64.

Mowday, Richard T. "The Exercise of Upward Influence in Organizations," *Administrative Science Quarterly* 23, 1978, pp. 137–156.

Muoio, Anna. "Boss Management: Unit of One," *Fast Company,* April 1999.

Murray, Matt. "GE Mentoring Program Turns Underlings into Teachers of the Web," *Wall Street Journal,* February 15, 2000, pp. B1, 16.

Myers, Steven Lee. "2 Officers Doubted Sub Commander's Order, Admiral Says," *New York Times,* March 7, 2001, p. A12.

———. "Sub's Crew May Have Hesitated to Question a Trusted Captain," *New York Times,* March 12, 2001, pp. A1, 10.

Porter, Lyman L., Robert W. Allen, and Harold L. Angle. "The Politics of Upward Influence in Organizations," *Research in Organizational Behavior* 3, 1981, pp. 109–149.

Schilit, Warren K., and Edwin A. Locke. "A Study of Upward Influence in Organizations," *Administrative Science Quarterly* 27, 1982, pp. 304–316.

Schlesinger, Len. "It Doesn't Take a Wizard to Build a Better Boss." *Handbook of the Revolution.* New York: Fast Company, 1997.

Sobel, Dava. *Longitude: The True Story of a Lone Genius Who Solved the Greatest Scientific Problem of His Time.* New York: Penguin, 1996.

Stengel, Richard. *You're Too Kind: A Brief History of Flattery.* New York: Simon & Schuster, 2000.

ACKNOWLEDGMENTS

I have sought to learn from those personally familiar with the events chronicled here, and many have provided invaluable firsthand accounts and primary documents. They are identified in the endnotes for each of the chapters, and their generous gift of time and information is greatly appreciated.

Five individuals provided editorial guidance throughout: Peter Cowen of Boston, John Mahaney and Ruth Mills of Random House, Howard Means of Washington, D.C., and Raphael Sagalyn of Sagalyn Literary Agency. From first blueprint to final copy, they have assisted virtually every aspect of this endeavor, and I am grateful for their excellent counsel throughout.

Colleagues and associates at the Wharton School of the University of Pennsylvania have been very helpful, including Elizabeth Bailey, Michael Baltes, Thomas Gerrity, Mauro Guillén, David Hess, John Joseph, Gerald McDermott, Robert Mittelstaedt, Mukul Pandya, and Harbir Singh. Others rendered special assistance in reaching the principals or documenting their actions, including Joanne Cuthbertson of Charles Schwab Corporation, Admiral Harold Gehman, Ricardo Insua and Andres Stella of Buenos Aires, Claudia Leo of the University of Michigan Press, and Allan Thompson of the *Toronto Star*.

Discussions with a number of family and friends have enriched my appreciation for the issues, including Julia Bell, Connie Timm, Terry Timm, Andrea Useem, Elizabeth Useem, Jerry Useem, John Useem, Ruth Useem, and Susan Useem. Andrea Useem also provided invaluable research and writing assistance for two accounts (chapters 3 and 8).

Several organizations and individuals have kindly consented to the use of their photographs. In the order of the photographs' appearance in the chapters, the sources are, beginning with chapter 1: Library of Congress, Prints & Photographs Division; Library of Congress, Prints & Photographs Division; Library of Congress, Prints & Photographs Division, Julian Vannerson, photographer; Corbis; Medford Historical Society Collection/Corbis; Library of Congress, Prints & Photographs Division, Alexander Gardner, photographer. Chapter 2: Charles Schwab & Co., Inc. Chapter 3: Roméo Dallaire and National Defence (Canada); United Nations Department of Public Information, Milton Grant, photographer; United Nations Department of Public Information, Milton Grant, photographer. Chapter 4: Robert Maass/Corbis; Robert Maass/Corbis; Agence France Presse/Corbis; Agence France Presse/Corbis; Reuters News Media Inc./Corbis. Chapter 5: Michael Useem; U.S. Department of Defense for all other photographs, except for the U.S. Navy for Admiral Ellis. Chapter 6: Scott Fischer and Woodfin Camp & Associates; Neil Beidleman and Woodfin Camp & Associates; Scott Fischer and Woodfin Camp & Associates; Michael Useem; Tom Kelly and Woodfin Camp & Associates. Chapter 7: School of Advanced International Studies, Johns Hopkins University; Agence France Presse; Agence France Presse/Corbis; Agence France Presse/Corbis; Reuters NewMedia Inc./Corbis; Michael Useem. Chapter 8: The Metropolitan Museum of Art, Purchase, 1871; Arte & Immagini srl/Corbis, Carlo Dolci, painter; Bettmann/Corbis.

INDEX

About the Author

MICHAEL USEEM is the William and Jacalyn Egan Professor of Management and Director of the Center for Leadership and Change Management at the Wharton School of the University of Pennsylvania. His university teaching includes M.B.A. and executive-M.B.A. courses on management and leadership, and he offers programs on leadership and change for managers in the United States, Asia, Europe, and Latin America. He also works on leadership development with many companies and organizations in the private, public, and nonprofit sectors. Recently, he published *The Leadership Moment: Nine True Stories of Triumph and Disaster and Their Lessons for Us All,* and, to experience such moments, he organizes groups of Wharton graduates, company managers, and other groups for treks up the slopes of Mount Everest, trips to Civil War battlefields, and other learning events for leadership development. He produces the monthly electronic *Wharton Leadership Digest* (http://leadership.wharton.upenn.edu/digest/index.shtml), and he can be reached at <useem@wharton.upenn.edu>.